Bob Reinalda & Ewa Kulesza
The Bologna Process—
Harmonizing Europe's Higher Education

Bob Reinalda
Ewa Kulesza

The Bologna Process—
Harmonizing Europe's Higher
Education

Including the Essential Original Texts

Foreword by Hans-Dieter Klingemann

2nd revised edition

Barbara Budrich Publishers,
Opladen & Farmington Hills 2006

A CIP catalogue record for this book is available from
Die Deutsche Bibliothek (The German Library)

© 2006 by Barbara Budrich Publishers, Opladen
www.barbara-budrich.net

paperback   ISBN 3-86649-042-9 –   978-3-86649-042-0
hardcover   **ISBN 3-86649-043-7 –**   **978-3-86649-043-7**

Das Werk einschließlich aller seiner Teile ist urheberrechtlich geschützt. Jede Verwertung außerhalb der engen Grenzen des Urheberrechtsgesetzes ist ohne Zustimmung des Verlages unzulässig und strafbar. Das gilt insbesondere für Vervielfältigungen, Übersetzungen, Mikroverfilmungen und die Einspeicherung und Verarbeitung in elektronischen Systemen.

Die Deutsche Bibliothek – CIP-Einheitsaufnahme
Ein Titeldatensatz für die Publikation ist bei Der Deutschen Bibliothek erhältlich.

Verlag Barbara Budrich 🅑 Barbara Budrich Publishers
Stauffenbergstr. 7. D-51379 Leverkusen Opladen, Germany

28347 Ridgebrook. Farmington Hills, MI 48334. USA
www.barbara-budrich.net

Copy-editor: Elizabeth Graham
Jacket illustration by disegno, Wuppertal, Germany – www.disenjo.de
Typeset by RS Beate Glaubitz, Opladen, Germany
Printed in Europe on acid-free paper by
paper & tinta, Warsaw, Poland

Contents

Part II: The Bologna Process and the European Union

Part III: The Intergovernmental Organizations

Contents   VII

Annexes

Acronyms

APEC	Asia Pacific Economic Cooperation
ASEAN	Association of South East Asian Nations
AUN	ASEAN University Network
BFUG	Bologna Follow-Up Group
BPC	Bologna Process Committee (ESIB)
BPG	Bologna Preparatory Group
CD-ESR	Steering Committee for Higher Education and Research (Council of Europe)
CEPES	UNESCO European Centre for Higher Education (Centre européen pour l'enseignement supérieure)
CEPSA	Central European Association of Political Science Associations
CERI	Centre for Educational Research and Innovation (OECD)
COMETT	Community Action Program in Education and Training for Technology
CoP2001	Committee on Prague 2001 (ESIB)
CRE	Confederation of European Rectors Conferences and Associations of European Universities
EAPAA	European Association of Public Administration Accreditation
ECA	European Consortium for Accreditation
ECNA	European Conference of National Political Science Associations
ECPR	European Consortium for Political Research
ECSC	European Coal and Steel Community
ECTS	European Credit Transfer System
EEC	European Economic Community
EFTA	European Free Trade Association
EHEA	European Higher Education Area
EI	Education International
ENIC Network	European Network of National Information Centres on Academic Mobility and Recognition (Council of Europe and UNESCO)
ENQA	2000: European Network for Quality Assurance in Higher Education 2004: European Association for Quality Assurance in Higher Education
EPAN	European Public Administration Network
EPSNET	European Political Science Network
ERA	European Research Area
ESIB	National Unions of Students in Europe
ETUCE	European Trade Union Committee for Education

EU	European Union
EUA	European University Association
EULAC	Follow-Up Committee of the European Union, Latin America and Caribbean Common Space for Higher Education
EURASHE	European Associations of Institutions in Higher Education
EURODOC	European Council of Doctoral Candidates and Young Researchers
EURYDICE	The information network on education in Europe
GATS	General Agreement on Trade in Services
GATT	General Agreement on Tariffs and Trade
IAPSS	International Association for Political Science Students
IAU	International Association of Universities
IBRD	International Bank for Reconstruction and Development (or: World Bank)
INES	International Indicators of Educational Systems project (OECD)
INQAAHE	International Network of Quality Assurance Agencies in Higher Education
ISCED	International Standard Classification of Education
NARIC	National Academic Recognition Information Centre (EU)
NEIC	National Equivalence Information Centre (Council of Europe)
NIB	National Information Body (UNESCO)
OECD	Organization for Economic Cooperation and Development
SEAMEO	South East Asian Ministers of Education Organization
TEEP	Transnational European Evaluation Project
TN-PA	Thematic Network in Public Administration
TNPS	Thematic Network in Political Science
UCTS	UMAP Credit Transfer Scheme
UMAP	University Mobility in Asia and the Pacific
UNESCO	United Nations Educational, Scientific and Cultural Organization
UNICE	Union of Industrial and Employers' Confederations of Europe
WTO	World Trade Organization

Foreword

By Hans-Dieter Klingemann

Successful academic teaching and research depends on communication and cooperation. Far too long have autocratic regimes prohibited the building of a truly worldwide community of scholars. Since the Second World War, European academia has profited from the growing process of European integration. In political science, for example, this process has lead to the formation of the European Consortium of Political Research (ECPR), the European Political Science Network (epsNet), and the European Conference of Chairs of National Associations of Political Science (ECNA) – to name just a few of the most important organisations to institutionalise communication and cooperation in the areas of teaching and research.

The general process of integration gained new momentum in 1988 as a result of European universities' proclaiming a Magna Charta Universitatum in Bologna. However, it reached a new level with the political decision to create a European area of higher education and research. This plan originated in a meeting between the ministers of Education of France, Germany, Italy, and the United Kingdom at the Sorbonne in May 1998. The resulting proposals promoted increased mobility between, and cooperation of, European universities. A year later, 29 countries convened in Bologna to continue the effort, and after further meetings in Prague, Berlin, and Bergen, today the "Bologna Process" involves nearly all European countries – both EU and non-EU members. This process is without parallel in modern European history and is highly significant for all actors involved.

Bob Reinalda and Ewa Kulesza are the first to comprehensively describe, analyse, and document the Bologna Process. In addition, they demonstrate that the European developments are taking place in a global context of increased academic communication and cooperation. This volume containing "everything you ever wanted to know about the Bologna Process" grew out of the activities of the European Political Science Network. Fittingly, it was supported by the European Commission's programme "Enhancing Political Science Teaching Quality and Mobility in Europe (EPISTEME)".

This book is a must for all who are actively involved in shaping the future of European academia, and for those who want to understand current trends in European education.

Berlin, May 2005   *Hans-Dieter Klingemann*

Part I:
The Bologna Process
and its Global Context

1. Everything You Ever Wanted to Know About the Bologna Process

a. European Academia in the 21st Century

Only a few people were aware of the dramatic restructure of European universities that was to follow upon the *Bologna Declaration* of 1999. A two-page document began to corrode existing structures and what is now known as the *Bologna Process* is laying the foundations of European academia in the 21st century. The declaration itself hardly has the form of an international resolution or convention, yet resulted in an intergovernmental arrangement to which, in early 2005, forty European countries are parties. Although the Bologna Process is an autonomous and almost pan-European intergovernmental arrangement, the European Union (EU) plays an important role in it. But the EU is not the only international organization engaged in the governance of changes taking place in higher education. And non-governmental organizations also play their roles. *This book tells everything about it and provides the main original texts.*

b. Objectives of the Book[1]

The purpose of the book is to offer a better understanding of the Bologna Process, by mapping what has taken place in higher education in various European and other international forums since the end of the 1990s. As far as we know, this has not yet been done. We do this:

1. *By revealing what is taking place in the intergovernmental arrangement that was created on the basis of the Bologna Declaration of 1999.* We follow the initiative to create the Bologna Process as well as its further evolution. We are interested in:

    a. the intergovernmental machinery created by the ministers of education,

---

1   The responsibility for the text and the choice of documents remains with us, but for their helpful and stimulating comments and information we would like to thank: Erkki Berndtson, Roger Duclaud-Williams, Gabriela Gregušová, Gérard Grunberg, Marian Janssen, Marijtje Janssen, Mathieu Segers and Rob Verhofstad.

    b. the definition of the policy field (ten action lines created in respective meetings), and

    c. the relationship between the nearly pan-European Bologna Process and the smaller European Union, which contributes to the Bologna Process with its own institutional machinery and its *acquis communautaire* in the field of higher education (even if education in fact is not an EU policy area);

2. *By placing the Bologna Process in a global context*. We do this:

    a. by introducing those intergovernmental organizations that are also active in the field of higher education issues, such as the Council of Europe, UNESCO and the Organization for Economic Cooperation and Development,

    b. by referring to the global development of trade in educational services, in particular the WTO General Agreement on Trade in Services (GATS),

    c. by beginning a comparison of European events with developments in other parts of the world. The North–South dimension is discussed by showing the change of strategy with regard to higher education in developing countries that took place in the World Bank between 1994 and 2002. And we have a closer look at developments in the Asian and Pacific region;

3. *By discussing the interaction between (inter)governmental and nongovernmental actors* in the field of higher education,

4. *By reproducing the most relevant original texts*. Nowadays, most of these texts can be found at the Internet. However, given the fact that quite a few actors have been engaged in the processes discussed we believe that for reasons of further study and assessment it is helpful to have them available in one book. Furthermore, websites are not permanent and sometimes change overnight. Older documents may be removed or transferred to other sections of a website. Sometimes only the latest version of a document is available.

The discussion of the Bologna Process still closely follows events as they are taking place. That is also true for our book. However, it will be necessary to start a more critical assessment of the Bologna process by examining the official rhetoric more critically. In the conclusion, we sum up aspects of both the Bologna Process and its wider context and raise some further questions. We hope that our book will contribute to answering those questions.

c. The Structure of the Book

The book has four parts. The first part introduces the Bologna Process and its global context; the second part concentrates on the Bologna Process and the European Union; the third part discusses intergovernmental organizations engaged in higher education issues; and the fourth part reviews non-governmental organizations engaged in the Bologna Process.

Part I: The Bologna Process and its Global Context
In the next chapter, we discuss the *two declarations of Bologna*: of 1988 and 1999. **Chapter 3** provides an overview of rapid changes that took place in higher education internationally during the 1990s. Those changes constitute the *global context* of the Bologna Process.

Part II: The Bologna Process and the European Union
The **fourth chapter** introduces *the start of the Bologna Process* and its predecessor, 'Sorbonne'. The **fifth chapter** provides an overview of the *ministerial follow-up meetings* in Prague (2001), Berlin (2003) and Bergen (2005). It contains statements as well as follow-up structures and activities. The **sixth chapter** discusses the *contributions to the Bologna Process of the European Union* (on the one hand state and ministers, on the other hand the European Commission). The activities are related to education as a traditionally restricted EU policy area. The chapter also discusses work by ENQA on quality assurance and by the NARIC network on academic recognition.

Part III: The Intergovernmental Organizations
The **seventh chapter** deals with *recognition of qualifications* and the *Council of Europe* and *UNESCO* conventions covering academic recognition. The **eighth chapter** discusses the guidelines for consumers that *UNESCO* and the *OECD* (Organization for Economic Cooperation and Development) are drafting on *quality provision in cross-border higher education*. The **ninth chapter** relates to *trade in higher education services* at the end of the 20th and the beginning of the 21st century. It discusses the *General Agreement on Trade in Services* (GATS). It explains which services in higher education are covered by the GATS, how the GATS operates and to what extent progress is being made. In addition, it raises the fierce controversies that arose on higher education and the GATS. The **tenth chapter** discusses the remarkable policy shift of the World Bank with regard to higher education in developing countries. It also describes changes taking place in higher education in Asia and the Pacific.

Part IV: The Non-Governmental Organizations
The **eleventh chapter** provides an overview of the major *non-governmental organizations* engaged in the Bologna Process. The **twelfth chapter** dis-

cusses, as an example of a discipline, the networks in the fields of *European political science and public administration* and their reactions to the Bologna Process.

Finally, there is a **conclusion** and a list of **websites**. The *annexes* contain the main **original documents** related to the Bologna Process and the policies of engaged international organizations. All documents were found on the Internet.

Second, updated edition

This new edition informs about the London Secretariat of the Bologna Process (p. 37) and replaced the *UNESCO/OECD Draft Guidelines for quality provision in cross-border higher education* by the final version, which was approved on 2 December 2005 by the OECD Council after an internal procedure at UNESCO (see Annex 16).

Bob Reinalda, Ewa Kulesza, February 2006

2. The Bologna Declarations of 1988 and 1999

This chapter introduces the declarations issued in Bologna (1988), at the Sorbonne (1998) and again in Bologna (1999), and defines the notions of the European Higher Education Area and the Bologna Process.

a. The Magna Charta Universitatum (1988)

The city of **Bologna** is the capital of the province of Bologna and the Emilia-Romagna region, north of Florence and at the northern foot of the Apennines in Italy. Its university, Università degli Studi di Bologna, is one of the oldest (perhaps *the* oldest) and most famous universities in Europe, dating from the 11th century. Today, Bologna is known for the Bologna Process, named after the *Bologna Declaration* of 1999. However, Bologna is also known for another declaration issued in 1988: the *Magna Charta Universitatum*.

In September 1988, rectors of European universities gathered in Bologna for the ninth centenary of the University of Bologna. They were aware that in four years' time the Internal Market of the European Union (the 'Europe 1992' Project) promised the 'definite abolition of boundaries between the countries of the European Community'. The rectors looked forward to more European cooperation and in their *Magna Charta Universitatum*, issued on 18 September, they expressed some fundamental principles and means regarding the role of universities in the changing European society.

The Magna Charta Universitatum is reproduced as Annex 1.

The *fundamental principles* about the roles of universities mentioned in the *Magna Charta* are:

1. The university is an autonomous institution;
2. Teaching and research in universities must be inseparable;
3. Freedom in research and training is the fundamental principle of university life; and
4. A university is the trustee of the European humanist tradition.

Among the *means* needed to implement the principles, number 4 declares: 'Universities – particularly in Europe – regard the mutual exchange of information and documentation, and frequent joint projects for the advancement of learning, as essential to the steady progress of knowledge. Therefore, as in the earliest years of their history, they encourage mobility among teachers and students; furthermore they consider a general policy of equivalent status, titles, examinations (without prejudice to national diplomas) and award of scholarships essential to the fulfilment of their mission in the conditions prevailing today'.

The *Magna Charta Universitatum* is mentioned here because of its fundamental principles about universities and its core idea about the cross-border exchange of knowledge, in particular through mobility of students and teachers.

b. The Bologna Declaration (1999)

In May 1998 the ministers of education of four major EU member states issued a declaration meant to enhance mobility between, and the cooperation of, European universities. This is the *Sorbonne Declaration*, named after the Sorbonne University in Paris, where they issued their declaration.

In June 1999 the ministers of education of 29 European countries convened in Bologna and issued a joint declaration called 'The European Higher Education Area'. By accepting the *Bologna Declaration* European countries, both EU and non-EU members, have committed themselves to achieving the creation of the *European Area of Higher Education* as a key way to promote citizens' mobility and employability and the continent's overall development. European higher education institutions have committed themselves by taking up a main role in constructing the European Area of Higher Education, also in the wake of the fundamental principles laid down in the Bologna *Magna Charta Universitatum* of 1988. What happened after these two declarations (Sorbonne and Bologna) is known as the *Bologna Process*, which also refers to its institutional form.

The Sorbonne Declaration of 1998 is reproduced as Annex 2.
The Bologna Declaration of 1999 is reproduced as Annex 3.

Two basic notions need to be clarified. One is *European Higher Education Area* (EHEA), the other is the *Bologna Process*.

The notion of a **European Higher Education Area** follows the idea of the European Economic Area, which extended the European Community's single market to the member states of the European Free Trade Association (EFTA). By analogy, the *Sorbonne* and *Bologna Declarations* widened the European Community's area for higher education to the other countries on the European continent. The *Sorbonne Declaration* speaks about an 'open European area for higher learning', which requires 'continuous efforts to remove barriers and to develop a framework for teaching and learning, which would enhance mobility and an even closer cooperation'. The efforts to remove barriers and to create a common framework are to be found in the ten action lines of the Bologna Process (see Table 2.1).

Table 2.1: The Ten Action Lines of the Bologna Process

Defined in Bologna: 1. Adoption of a system of easily readable and comparable degrees;   2. Adoption of a system essentially based on two cycles (undergraduate & graduate);   3. Establishment of a system of credits (such as ECTS);[2]   4. Promotion of mobility by overcoming obstacles;   5. Promotion of European cooperation in quality assurance;   6. Promotion of the European dimensions in higher education.   *Defined in Prague*:   7. Lifelong learning;   8. Involvement of students;   9. Promoting the attractiveness and competitiveness of the European Higher Education Area to other parts of the world.   *Defined in Berlin*:   10. Doctoral studies and the synergy between the European Higher Education Area and the European Research Area.

The major difference for the European Economic Area is that the European Higher Education Area is not based on an agreement between two international institutions (EU and EFTA). Instead, it is an autonomous intergovernmental arrangement, based on a common policy document (the *Bologna Declaration*) to which European countries (i.e. countries on the European continent) may become parties and in which the European Union also plays a role. The European Commission is an additional full member of the Bologna Process. The EU's main policies for the European Higher Education Area, however, are not defined by the European Commission but by the Council of Ministers and the European Council.

The notion **Bologna Process** refers to this intergovernmental arrangement of nearly all European countries, both EU and non-EU members, plus the European Commission, which meet more or less regularly to discuss the actions agreed upon. By now it has an institutional structure, composed of a Follow-Up Group, a Board and a Secretariat (see §5.c).

---

2   ECTS = European Credit Transfer System.

In chapter 4, the *Sorbonne* and *Bologna Declarations* will be discussed in more detail, but before doing so, it makes sense to get an impression of shifts in higher education related to the global market in education services. The shifts mentioned in the next chapter reveal the wider context of the Bologna Process.

3. 'Rapid Changes Taking Place in the Area of Higher Education': The Global Context

This chapter discusses governmental educational initiatives in the context of shifts in the global higher education market. It gives examples of new phenomena, such as distance learning or private universities, and reveals the ten leading 'exporters' of higher education services in the mid-1990s.

a. Changes Taking Place According to the WTO Council for Trade in Services

To better understand the Bologna Process, one has to know more about changes taking place in higher education, to which the Bologna Process was a policy response. One document is particularly helpful in this respect, because it provides an inventory of changes at the time. The document is called *Education Services* and is a 'background note' issued by the Secretariat of the World Trade Organization's **Council for Trade in Services** in September 1998.[3] Services can be traded just like goods and are of increasing importance in international trade. Since education is a service, it follows that this Council for Trade in Services, based on the 1994 GATS (*General Agreement on Trade in Services*), deals with education services. Its background note can be used as a reflection of changes taking place in the mid-1990s, even if it is mainly trade-oriented.

The WTO Council for Trade in Services notes that 'rapid changes are taking place in the area of Higher Education' and mentions two kinds of indications:

1. The revision by UNESCO in 1997 of its *International Standard Classification of Education* (ISCED) adopted in 1976. ISCED modified its categories related to higher (tertiary) education by recognising 'non-university types of study' and incorporating two types of higher education: 'advanced theoretical professional' and 'practical/occupational'. The

---

3 WTO Council for Trade in Services, *Education Services. Background Note by the Secretariat.* S/C/W/49, 23 September 1998. Available at: www.wto.org/english/tratop_e/serv_e/education_e/education_e.htm.

same goes for the *United Nations Central Product Classification* (UN CPC).[4] In defining their commitments with regard to education and using the UN CPC, WTO member states have introduced additional distinctions with regard to higher education, such as private/public, compulsory/non-compulsory and international/national education.

2. Changes in international and domestic market structures have promoted the appearance of activities closely related to education services, such as educational testing services, student exchange program services and 'study abroad' facilitation services. These are not instructional activities as such, but *activities designed to support educational processes*.

b. Governmental Initiatives and Differences between Countries

The WTO Council relates the changes in higher education to the *economic importance of the sector*. It refers to the crucial role of education in fostering economic growth, and personal and social development, as well as reducing inequality. It also sees a direct relationship between level of education and vulnerability to unemployment. The *link between education and employment* has resulted in numerous *governmental initiatives aimed at promoting human capital development*. This is the case in both South-East and East Asia and the European Union. South-East Asian countries began to include education in their development plans and to make generous budgetary provisions for higher education. EU programs related to vocational training undertaken in the 1980s and its 1994 program based on the idea of lifelong training are mentioned.

Almost all developed countries increased education expenditure, with an overall increase of almost 150 per cent between 1980 and 1994, from 487 US dollars per inhabitant in 1980 to 1,211 US dollars in 1994, while the share of spending remained constant at about 5 per cent.

The WTO Council notes that with regard to education as a *public consumption item*, provided most often free of charge, or at prices not reflecting the costs of producing it, expenditure per student tends to be higher for richer than poorer countries. With regard to education as a *private consumption item*, with a price determined freely by the providing institutions, it is noted that there are significant variations among OECD[5] countries (ranging from 2 to over 22 per cent of total expenditure on education) and that private sector expenditure is particularly significant at the tertiary level of education in such countries as Japan, Korea and the United States.

---

4   See for these classifications Annex 17.
5   See §8.b for the Organization for Economic Cooperation and Development, which represents the world's most advanced industrial economies.

c. Shifts in the Structure of the International Education Market

Various shifts with regard to higher education seem to change the structure of the education market. Basic education provided by the government falls within the domain of services, which in GATS terms, are supplied neither on a commercial basis nor in competition. Other forms of education however, are in the private domain. A shift seems to have taken place from the public to the private domain, but given the diverse character of institutional arrangements, it is difficult to distinguish clearly between public and private domains. Examples of shifts that are changing the structure of the education market are:

1. the increase of *adult learning* in different types of higher education, which involves new, often privately-funded education services;
2. the emergence of *'non-university' institutions and programs*, the networking of institutions and programs, and 'franchise' arrangements as a response to new consumer needs and interests in higher education institutions;
3. the proliferation of *distance learning* based on modern information and communication technologies;
4. the creation of innovative *arrangements between public and private entities*, such as universities and large firms ('virtual universities');
5. the provision of *financial support by governments as a lump sum* for universities to spend as they see it; consequences of this shift are more competition and institutional reforms to cut costs and raise revenues; the effort to attract more fee-paying students, including foreign ones, is one of the results;
6. *entrepreneurship of universities*, balancing academic quality with business management in order to attract new funding, as a result of the general movement away from public financing toward greater market responsiveness; and finally
7. the establishment of *private universities* in countries where they did not exist before.

In more general terms the WTO Council for Trade in Services argues that international trade in services in higher education has experienced important growth. Manifestations of this growth are:

- increasing numbers of students going abroad for study;
- exchanges and linkages between faculties and researchers;
- increased international marketing of curricula and academic programs;
- establishment of 'branch campuses' abroad; and
- development of international mechanisms for educational cooperation between academic institutions.

d. Some Indications of the Size of the International Education Market (mid-1990s)

The leading *exporter* of education services – for instance in the form of foreign students – is the United States, followed by France, Germany and the United Kingdom. However, the US faces increasing competition from other countries, such as Australia and New Zealand, in particular for Asian students. In 1994, 70,000 foreign students were enrolled in Australian higher education. They contributed about 2 billion Australian dollars to the economy.

In 1996, US exports of education services are estimated at 7 billion US dollars, whereas its import of education services – US students studying abroad – totals 1 billion US dollars. US exports in this sector make higher education the country's fifth largest service sector export. In 1996/1997 the number of foreign students in US colleges and universities total led nearly 460,000, most of them from Asia. Between 1989 and 1993 foreign student enrolment in US higher education grew at rates ranging from 3 to 6 per cent per annum.

Based on the 1997 UNESCO *Statistical Yearbook* the following table presents the ten leading exporters of higher education services in the mid-1990s. The United States comes first, followed by three large exporters (France, Germany and the United Kingdom) and six smaller ones.

Table 3.1: The Ten Leading Exporters of Higher Education Services in the Mid-1990s

Ranking	Host Countries	Total Number of Foreign Students	Year
1.	United States	453,787	1995/1996
2.	France	170,574	1993/1994
3.	Germany	146,126	1993/1994
4.	United Kingdom	128,550	1993/1994
5.	Russian Federation	73,172	1994/1995
6.	Japan	50,801	1993/1994
7.	Australia	42,415	1993
8.	Canada	35,451	1993/1994
9.	Belgium	35,236	1993/1994
10.	Switzerland	25,307	1993/1994

Source: WTO Council for Trade in Services, *Education Services. Background Note by the Secretariat.* S/C/W/49, 23 September 1998, Table 3, p. 20.

The five *major countries sending large numbers of students* to the US in the year mentioned in the table are: China (72,300), Japan (45,500), South Korea (36,200), India (31,700) and Canada (23,000). The five countries sending large numbers of students to France are: Morocco (20,300), Algeria (19,500),

Tunisia (6,000), Germany (6,000) and Cameroon (4,700). The five countries sending large numbers to Germany are: Turkey (21,000), Iran (10,600), Greece, (8,000) Austria (6,700) and China (5,800). The five countries sending large numbers of students to the United Kingdom are: Malaysia (12,000), Hong Kong (10,000), Germany (9,400), Ireland (9,000) and Greece (8,700).[6] Seen from the perspective of a global market, there is difference between the US, which is strongly oriented towards Asia, and the three European countries, which are more oriented towards their former colonies or specific trade partners.

The message of the WTO document is fourfold:

1. There are more and more new international activities to support higher national educational processes.
2. Governments are engaged by investing in higher education, in particular because of a link between education, and economic growth and employment.
3. Considerable differences in the ways of financing higher education exist between countries.
4. Increasing international competition takes place at world level, where the US is the market leader of higher education services and other countries are trying to get a larger market share.

In this WTO document the *European Union* is hardly, or not at all, mentioned as an actor trying to get its market share. This may be regarded as an indication of EU weakness in the international education market, notwithstanding the fact that some major EU member states are mentioned as relatively large players, even if they do little to exploit the promising Asian market.

It can be asked whether the international situation of the mid-1990s constituted a *window of opportunity* for countries feeling the need to enhance their international position and to simultaneously find solutions for domestic problems with their education systems. Countries wanting a larger market share needed internationally oriented universities. And if Europe wanted an equal share in the global market, it had to develop a common approach. Against the background of this international window of opportunity, the Bologna Process seemed to offer a way to enhance the international character of European universities and to change domestic higher education structures.

---

6   WTO Council for Trade in Services, *Education Services. Background Note by the Secretariat*. S/C/W/49, 23 September 1998, Table 4, p. 20.

Part II:
The Bologna Process and the European Union

4. The Start of the Bologna Process

This chapter goes into the ministerial initiative which brought about the Sorbonne Declaration of 1998 and its follow-up structure. It then discusses the Bologna Declaration and its follow-up structure for the period between 'Bologna' and 'Prague' two years later.

a. Paris, Sorbonne 25 May 1998: The Sorbonne Declaration

The 1998 *Sorbonne Declaration* resulted from an invitation from the French minister for education, Claude Allègre, to his British, German and Italian colleagues, Tessa Blackstone, Jürgen Rüttgers and Luigi Berlinguer. Experiencing problems in their education systems, they looked for international means to reform higher education in their own countries. In a forum meeting held at the Sorbonne in Paris, on the occasion of the 800th anniversary of the Sorbonne University, the ministers of the four major EU member states agreed the text of a joint declaration on 'harmonisation of the architecture of the European higher education system' (see *Annex 3*).

The *Declaration* of the four ministers stresses that European students seldom have the benefit of a study period outside their national boundaries, whereas Europe is 'heading for a period of major change in education and working conditions, to a diversification of courses of professional careers, with education and training throughout life becoming a clear obligation'. There is a necessity to 'remove barriers and to develop a framework for teaching and learning, which would enhance mobility and an ever closer co-operation'.

The *action lines* mentioned in the declaration are: the recognition of two main cycles (undergraduate and graduate); the use of credits and semesters; international recognition of the first cycle; a graduate cycle with a shorter master's degree and a longer doctoral degree; and staff and student mobility. Students would be encouraged to spend at least one semester in universities outside their own country.

The 1997 European convention on the recognition of higher education qualifications in the academic field within Europe is mentioned as a position to build on (for this convention developed by the Council of Europe and, UNESCO see §7.b).

The call by the four ministers to create, and join, a *European Area of Higher Education* was directed – it should be noted – at both member states of the EU and other European countries,[7] whereas all European universities were invited to 'consolidate Europe's standing in the world through continuously improved and updated education for its citizens'.

Follow-up Structure and Activities

The declaration attracted favourable attention from quite a few countries, both within and outside the EU. This shows that the proposed solutions for national education problems were appreciated, but it must also be recognised that the four initiators sent their directors-general of higher education around Europe to collect support for their initiative. Other stakeholders in the project have been university rectors and presidents, who, according to the *Sorbonne Declaration*, 'have engaged in widespread thinking along these lines'.

The Italian minister for education and the rector of the University of Bologna hosted a follow-up forum in Bologna. The preparations for this new forum were discussed at an informal meeting of EU Ministers of Education and at a meeting of the Directors-General and representatives of the universities.

Under the Austrian EU Presidency, a **Steering Committee** was set up to prepare for the Bologna Forum. It consisted of the Directors-General of Higher Education of the EU Troika (at the time, Austria, Germany and Finland) and Italy. It was agreed that the country holding the EU Presidency would chair the Steering Committee and that France and the United Kingdom would also be represented.

Financially supported by the European Commission, the Confederation of European Union Rectors' Conferences and the Association of European Universities (CRE) prepared a report on *Trends in Learning Structures in Higher Education* (7 June 1999).[8] The report conrains information on, and analyses of, trends in higher education structures in the member states of the EU and the European Economic Area. The studies for this report by Guy Haug and Jette Kirstein helped the Steering Committee to draft the declaration to be discussed in Bologna, because it presented an outline of divergence and convergence within these learning structures.

---

7   Allègre, who has knew the American university system well, wanted to change the entire
    French education system as well as the academic research system in order to give them a
    new impetus in the changing global context. He met with strong resistance fron, amongst
    others, trade unions and teachers. Looking for an international way to bypass this opposi-
    tion, he opted for a pan-European solution, also given the fact that education was not
    considered a policy field for common EU action (see §6.a).
8   The report can be found at www.bologna-bergen2005.no.

b. Bologna 18-19 June 1999: The Bologna Declaration

At the end of the two-day Bologna Forum, on 19 June 1999, the ministers of education of 29 European states (15 EU members and 14 non-EU) adopted a joint declaration, which became widely known as the *Bologna Declaration* (see *Annex 3*, which also contains the list of signatories).

It is stated that a 'Europe of Knowledge is now widely recognised as an irreplaceable factor for social and human growth and as an indispensable component to consolidate and enrich the European citizenship'. The declaration contains 3 *main goals* (international competitiveness, mobility and employability) and 6 instrumental objectives or *action lines*:

1. adoption of a system of easily readable and comparable degrees;
2. adoption of a system essentially based on two cycles (undergraduate end graduate);
3. establishment of a system of credits (such as ECTS);
4. promotion of mobility by overcoming obstacles;
5. promotion of European cooperation in quality assurance; and
6. promotion of the European dimensions in higher education.

The declaration was supported by an 'explanation' prepared by the Confederation of European Union Rectors' Conferences and the Association of European Universities. They argued that the declaration reflects a search for a common European answer to common European problems. 'The process originates from the recognition that in spite of their valuable differences, European higher education systems are facing common internal and external challenges related to the growth and diversification of higher education, the employability of graduates, the shortages of skills in key areas, the expansion of private and transnational education, etc.' They also argued that the declaration is not just a political statement, but a binding commitment to an action program. Furthermore they referred to the global competitiveness of European higher education and the new avenues it was opening up by becoming more attractive to students from other world regions.

The explanation by European rectors and universities is reproduced as Annex 4.

Follow-up Structure and Activities

The 29 signatory states agreed to attain the objectives set out in the *Bologna Declaration* through intergovernmental cooperation, in collaboration with higher education institutions. They agreed to meet again in Prague in May 2001 in order to assess the progress achieved and to agree on further steps.

The organization of the Bologna Process was decided by the EU ministers, who met in September 1999 in Tampere, Finland. They decided to establish two groups to prepare the Prague meeting:

1. a **Consultative Group** of all signatory states plus representatives from the European Commission and the Confederation of European Union Rectors' Conferences and the Association of European Universities; and
2. a restricted **Steering Group** (also called Follow-Up Group) consisting of the member states holding the EU Presidency in the two years from Bologna to Prague (Finland, Portugal, France, Sweden) and the Czech Republic, plus representatives from the European Commission and the Confederation of European Union Rectors' Conferences and the Association of European Universities.

The *Consultative Group* met in November 1999 in Helsinki, under the Finnish EU presidency, and drafted a program of events and themes. They planned three international seminars to discuss the topics of credit accumulation and transfer systems, Bachelor-level degrees and transnational education. In 2000, the Consultative Group accepted three more players as observers, one intergovernmental organization and two non-governmental ones: the Council of Europe, a student platform called ESIB and the European Association of Institutions in Higher Education (EURASHE), which represents the professional institutions.

In January 2000 the *Steering Group* met in Lisbon, under the Portuguese EU Presidency. It decided that, apart from the non-governmental contributions and the outcomes of the three seminars, a specific report should be prepared for the meeting in Prague. It commissioned Professor Pedro Lourtie as general rapporteur. It also decided that, unlike the Bologna Forum, the meeting of the academic institutions should be held in advance of the ministers' conference.

The Creation of the European University Association (EUA)

The two university organizations, the *Confederation of European Union Rectors' Conferences* and *Association of European Universities* (CRE), offered to organize this academic meeting jointly. They regarded the combination of intergovernmental cooperation and an input by non-governmental European organizations with competencies in higher education as a unique opportunity for higher education institutions 'to shape their own European future and to play a crucial role in the development and implementation of the Bologna process'. This motivation resulted in another report, *Trends II* (19 May 2001), which surveyed the other signatory countries of the *Bologna Declaration*.[9] The agreed academic meeting took place on 29–30 March 2001 in Salamanca, Spain, and became known as the *Salamanca Convention of European Higher Education Institutions*. During the convention the two or-

---

9   The report can be found at www.bologna-bergen2005.no.

ganizations actually merged and continued as *European University Association* (EUA; see §11.a for more information on the EUA).

During the Swedish EU Presidency students united in *ESIB, the National Unions of Students in Europe*, organized a convention in Göteborg, Sweden from 22–25 March 2001. They issued the *Student Göteborg Declaration*, which discusses the *Bologna Declaration*, in particular the social implications, the higher education area and the role of students (for more on ESIB, see §11.c).

The results of all actions, including the documents issued by the Salamanca Convention and the Student Göteborg Convention, can be found in the official 'Lourtie Report', *Furthering the Bologna Process*, which was presented as a contribution to the meeting of ministers in Prague.

The 'Contents' and 'Executive Summary' of the Lourtie Report are reproduced as Annex 5.[10]

---

10 The full report can be found at www.bologna-bergen2005.no.

5. The Bologna Process From Prague (2001) to Berlin (2003) and Bergen (2005)

This chapter follows the Bologna Process during, and between, the ministerial meetings in Prague (2001), Berlin (2003) and Bergen (2005). It reveals what is said in the official communiqués and explains the governance structures created by the European ministers of education.

a. Prague 19 May 2001: The Prague Communiqué

In Prague the number of signatory countries rose from 29 to 32, as three more countries, Croatia, Cyprus and Turkey, were accepted as new members of the Bologna Process. Liechtenstein followed as number 33.

In their *Prague Communiqué* the ministers of education reaffirmed the objective of establishing the *European Higher Education Area*, as mentioned in the *Bologna Declaration*, by 2010. They welcomed the contributions by the EUA and ESIB and took note of the 'constructive assistance' of the European Commission. The *Prague Communiqué* issued after the meeting contains elaborations on the six earlier action lines. *Three new action lines* were added as important elements of the European Higher Education Area:

7. lifelong learning;
8. involvement of students; and
9. promoting the attractiveness and competitiveness of the European Higher Education Area to other parts of the world.

It was decided that the ministers would meet again in the second half of 2003 in Berlin, in order to review progress made, and set directions and priorities for the next stages of the process towards the European Higher Education Area. The ministers encouraged the Follow-Up Group to arrange seminars to explore various areas such as cooperation concerning accreditation and quality assurance; recognition issues and the use of credits in the Bologna Process; the development of joint degrees; the social dimension with specific attention to obstacles to mobility; the enlargement of the process; and lifelong learning and student involvement.

The Prague Communiqué is reproduced as Annex 6.

Follow-up Structure and Activities

The ministers also discussed the further organization of the Bologna Process. They wanted some changes in the follow-up structure created in Bologna and decided that there should be two groups:

1. The **Follow-Up Group** (BFUG: Bologna Follow-Up Group) composed of all signatory states, new participants and the European Commission. The Follow-Up Group will be chaired by the EU Presidency at the time.
2. The **Preparatory Group** (BPG: Bologna Preparatory Group) composed of representatives of the countries hosting the previous ministerial meeting and the next ministerial meeting, two EU member states and two non-EU member states (these four to be elected by the Follow-Up Group), the EU Presidency at the time and the European Commission. The Preparatory Group will be chaired by the representative of the country hosting the next ministerial meeting (in this case Germany).

The former Steering Group was abolished, as the steering task had become entirely the responsibility of the Follow-Up Group. The term used for the European Commission, which now has a more formal status than before, is 'special status of an additional full member' in the Bologna Process.

The non-governmental organizations (EUA, EURASHE and ESIB) and the Council of Europe 'should be consulted in the follow-up work'.

During the period between Prague and Berlin the *Bologna Follow-Up Group* met six times. It constantly monitored the Bologna Process and discussed issues of the enlargement of the process as well as possible directions for further development. It appointed Professor Pavel Zgaga as general rapporteur to the Berlin meeting.

The Follow-Up Group organized ten around two themes: seminars issues relating to degree structures and qualifications; and the social dimension of higher education. Six further cluster of themes discussed were:

1. cooperation concerning accreditation and quality assurance;
2. recognition issues and the use of credits;
3. development of joint degrees;
4. degrees and qualification structures;
5. social dimension of the Bologna Process, with special attention to the obstacles of mobility; and
6. lifelong learning in higher education.

During the period between Prague and Berlin the *Bologna Preparatory Group* met nine times. It assumed a key role in collecting and managing the necessary information and set up the official website with all relevant information: www.bologna-berlin2003.de (still available). It was responsible for arranging the Berlin meeting. The Preparatory Group was also given a mandate to get in contact with other stakeholders, such as employers and trade unions, and organizations with special expertise, such as accreditation, not directly represented in the Bologna Process. It held occasional hearings with representatives of these bodies.

The Bologna Process itself an intergovernmental process of European states that are signatories to the *Bologna Declaration*. Membership of the *European Union* is not a requirement. What occurred in this period, however, can best be described as a *growing convergence with EU processes* aimed at strengthening European cooperation in higher education. The decisions taken by the European Council meetings and the EU Education Councils between 2000 and 2001, according to Zgaga, altered the *Bologna Declaration* from 'a voluntary action to a set of commitments' in the framework of EU decisions on higher education (see chapter 6 for the EU contribution).

The *Council of Europe* also became an important contributor to the Bologna Process. It served as a bridge between those countries party to the Bologna Process and the remaining European countries, in particular Southern-Eastern Europe and the Russian Federation. Furthermore the Council of Europe contributed to the field of recognition issues (see chapter 7).

Once again the *non-governmental organizations* contributed to the process. The European University Association was responsible for the *Trends III* report, titled *Progress towards the Higher Education Area*.[11] It analyses and compares developments from the point of view of the major actors in the process: governments, national rectors' conferences, higher education institutions and students.

In May 2003 the EUA organized a convention in Graz, Austria, on strengthening the role of institutions. In June 2003 EURASHE, which represents professional higher education institutions, organized a conference in Hungary and confirmed that institutions of professional higher education do belong to the emerging European Higher Education Area.

In November 2001 ESIB organized a conference in Brussels and issued a *Brussels Student Declaration*, which stresses that, apart from educational, structural and institutional changes, access to higher education on an equitable basis is crucial to the European Higher Education Area.

The outcomes of the events and recommendations from the seminars, plus information on the steering of the Bologna Process can be found in the *Zgaga Report*.

In the introduction to his report Zgaga argues that the Bologna process enters 'a demanding phase in which answers to particular problems detected in the last follow-up period should be found, and detailed strategies and 'tuned' structural as well as social tools should be developed. Berlin is a crucial landmark in this process'.

The 'Contents' and 'Executive Summary' of the Zgaga Report are reproduced as Annex 7.[12]

---

11 Also available at www.bologna-berlin2003.de and www.bologna-bergen2005.no.
12 The full report plus attached other reports (summary of *Trends III* and contributions by European Commission, EUA, ERASHE and Council of Europe) can be found at www.bologna-bergen2005.no.

b. Berlin 18–19 September 2003: The Berlin Communiqué

At the ministerial meeting in Berlin, 33 signatory states were present. They accepted 7 new members, which made a total of 40 signatories. The new member states are: Albania, Andorra, Bosnia and Herzegovina, Holy See, Russia, Serbia and Montenegro, and the Former Yugoslav Republic of Macedonia.

Non-members in the Bologna Process are six Council of Europe members (Armenia, Azerbaijan, Georgia, Moldova, San Marino and Ukraine) and Belarus.

The resulting communiqué released was entitled *Realising the European Higher Education Area*. In its preamble, the ministers:

– underlined the importance of the *social dimension* of the Bologna Process. 'The need to increase competitiveness must be balanced with the objective of improving the social characteristics of the European Higher Education Area, aiming at strengthening social cohesion and reducing social and gender inequalities both at national and at European level';
– reaffirmed their position that higher education is '*a public good and a public responsibility*' (italics added, BR/EK);
– took into consideration the conclusions of the *European Councils* of the EU in Lisbon (2000) and Barcelona (2002), which, apart from its purpose of making Europe the most competitive and dynamic knowledge-based economy in the world, called for further action and closer cooperation in the context of the Bologna Process;
– acknowledged the support of the *European Commission* and the *Council of Europe* for the implementation of the Bologna Process;
– agreed that efforts shall be undertaken in order to secure closer links overall between the higher education and *research systems* in their countries;
– recognised the contributions by the non-governmental organizations; and
– welcomed EULAC, the Follow-Up Committee of the European Union, Latin America and Caribbean Common Space for Higher Education as a guest.

The Berlin Communiqué is reproduced as Annex 8.

With regard to the 9 *action lines* originating from Bologna and Prague, the ministers defined three intermediate priorities for the next two years and set specific goals for each of them. The *three priorities* are:

1. *quality assurance* (including the need to develop mutually shared criteria and methodologies);
2. *the two-cycle degree system* (including the development of an overarching framework of qualifications for the European Higher Education Area); and

3. *recognition of degrees and periods of studies* (all signatory countries should ratify the Lisbon Recognition Convention and by 2005 every student graduating should receive the Diploma Supplement).

The ministers also decided to go beyond the existing two main cycles of higher education (undergraduate and graduate), and proposed to include the doctoral level as the *third cycle* in the Bologna Process. Assuming that the emerging *European Higher Education Area* (EHEA) will benefit from synergies with the *European Research Area* (ERA), thus strengthening the basis of the Europe of Knowledge, they stressed the need to promote closer links between the two areas and the importance of research as an integral part of higher education across Europe. This resulted in a *tenth action line*:

10. Doctoral Studies and the Synergy between EHEA and ERA.

The ministers decided to hold the next conference in the city of Bergen, Norway in May 2005.

Follow-Up Structure and Activities

The ministers entrusted the implementation of their decisions to a structure based on a Follow-Up Group, a Board and a Secretariat. This means that the structure was somewhat changed and enlarged. The three bodies are:

1. The **Follow-Up Group** (still BFUG) is composed of all signatory states and the European Commission. The Council of Europe and UNESCO/ CEPES as well as the non-governmental organizations EUA, EURASHE and ESIB are consultative members. The Follow-Up Group will be chaired by the EU Presidency, with the host country of the next ministerial meeting as vice-chair (i.e. Norway). The group will meet at least twice a year. The Follow-Up Group is entrusted with the implementation of all issues covered in the *Berlin Communiqué*, the overall steering of the Bologna Process and the preparation of the next ministerial meeting. It must also further define the responsibilities of the Board and the tasks of the Secretariat and take care of a stocktaking process (see below). The Follow-Up Group may convene ad hoc working groups.

2. The **Board** is composed of the chair, the vice-chair, the preceding and the following EU Presidencies, three participating countries elected by the Follow-Up Group for one year and the European Commission. The Council of Europe and the non-governmental organizations EUA, EURASHE and ESIB are consultative members (hence UNESCO/CEPES is excluded from this body). The Board is chaired by the EU Presidency and has to oversee the work between the meetings of the Follow-Up Group. The Board may also convene ad hoc working groups.

3. The **Secretariat** will be provided by the country hosting the next ministerial meeting. It supports the overall follow-up work.

With a view to the goals set for 2010, the ministers expected that taking stock of progress achieved in the Bologna Process will be helpful. They charged the Follow-Up Group with organizing a *stocktaking process* before the meeting in 2005 and undertaking to prepare detailed reports on the progress and implementation of the three priorities set for the next two years (quality assurance, two-cycle system and recognition of degrees and periods of studies).

At its first meeting after the Berlin meeting the *Follow-Up Group* defined the responsibilities of the Board and the tasks of the Secretariat. It decided to substitute the major report by a general rapporteur by a shorter report, to be prepared by the Secretariat and presented by the Follow-Up Group. All reports requested by the ministers should be submitted through the Follow-Up Group and under its responsibility. A *Trends IV* report by the EUA is regarded as a useful supplement to the reports coming from the Follow-Up Group.

With regard to the *Board*, the Follow-Up Group decided that the Board should coordinate and monitor the implementation of the work program, support the Follow-Up Group in its activities, and provide efficiency to the management of the Bologna Process. Among the Board's responsibilities are the organization of events, assistance to new members as they seek to meet the Bologna objectives, and the coordination of the preparation of the stocktaking. In addition, the Board should organize working groups composed of Follow-Up Group members and/or experts on special issues chosen by the Follow-Up Group, and oversee the preparation of the next ministerial meeting (19–20 May 2005). The Follow-Up Group may delegate tasks to the Board, but formal decisions are the responsibility of the Follow-Up Group itself.

The *Secretariat* was set up by the Norwegian Ministry of Education and Research and is operational from December 2003. Its website is www.bologna-bergen2005.no. It has a staff of three. The tasks include administrative and operational responsibility for the next ministerial conference, secretarial functions and, under specific mandate from the Follow-Up Group or Board, execution of special tasks concerning the implementation of the work program.

One of the documents prepared for Bergen is *Requirements and Procedures for Joining the Bologna Process* (6 July 2004). It clarifies the criteria for admission of new members in Bergen, but also consolidates both principles and action lines of the Bologna Process into a single document. It contrains sections on principles and objectives, and reports from potential new members and procedures for applying.

The Requirements and Procedures for Joining the Bologna Process are reproduced as Annex 9.

Applicant states in Bergen are (as of February 2005) Armenia, Azerbaijan, Georgia, Moldova and Ukraine.

c. Bergen 19–20 May 2005: The Bergen Communiqué

At the ministerial meeting in Bergen, Norway, in May 2005, the five applicants (Armenia, Azerbaijan, Georgia, Moldova and Ukraine) were welcomed as new participants in the Bologna Process. This means that from Bergen on, 45 countries participate and are members of the Follow-Up Group (see *Annex 3* for all participants). Both Kazakhstan and Kosovo had also applied: the former by the deadline, the latter afterwards. Their applications were in accordance with the prescribed procedure but were not accepted because Kazakhstan and Kosovo are not signatories to the European Cultural Convention adopted by the Council of Europe in 1954 (see for this convention §7.a).

The communiqué released by the ministers of education in Bergen was entitled *The European Higher Education Area – Achieving the Goals*. The ministers confirmed their commitment to coordinating their policies through the Bologna Process to establish the European Higher Education Area by 2010. They underlined the central role of higher education institutions, and staff and students as 'partners' in the Bologna Process. With regard to the stocktaking process – a way of monitoring the implementation of their earlier decisions – the ministers noted 'significant progress' and discussed the three priorities (degree system, quality assurance and recognition of degrees and study periods) in more detail. Although there was 'substantial progress' in these areas, it will also be important to ensure that progress is 'consistent across all participating countries'. The ministers therefore saw a 'need for greater sharing of expertise to build capacity at both institutional and governmental level'.

Under the heading 'Further challenges and priorities', the ministers underlined the importance of research in underpinning 'higher education for the economic and cultural development of our societies and for social cohesion'. They also renewed their commitments to the social dimension (making quality higher education equally accessible to all) and to mobility (they urged institutions and students to make full use of mobility programs, advocating full recognition of study periods abroad within such programs). Finally, they maintained that the European Higher Education Area must be open and attractive to other parts of the world. They asked the Follow-Up Group to elaborate and agree on a strategy for the external dimension. Two final sections discussed taking stock of progress in time for the ministerial meeting in London in 2007, and preparations for 2010. The major aspects of this communiqué will be discussed below.

The Bergen Communiqué is reproduced as Annex 10a.

The meeting in Bergen had two goals: 1. taking stock of the progress made since the meeting in Berlin in September 2003, and 2. setting directions for the further development of the European Higher Education Area. This time it was not a general rapporteur, but the Bologna Follow-Up Group that had written the general report: *"From Berlin to Bergen"*, which may be regarded as an indication of institutionalisation. The report's structure remained roughly the same. It reviewed all the activities that were undertaken, and included the recommendations to the ministers by the Follow-Up Group.

The 'Index' and 'Executive Summary' of the General Report "From Berlin to Bergen" are reproduced as Annex 10b.

Two reports were written by Working Groups appointed by the Follow-Up Group. One is the *Bologna Process Stocktaking Report*, the other *A Framework for Qualifications of the European Higher Education Area*. Three other reports were written by non-governmental organizations. The European University Association contributed its *Trends IV: European Universities Implementing Bologna*, written by Sybille Reichert and Christian Tauch. The European Association for Quality Assurance in Higher Education (ENQA) presented its *Standards and Guidelines for Quality Assurance in the European Higher Education Area* and the students' organization ESIB published its survey *Bologna with student eyes*. The stocktaking report and the reports by NGOs had been funded with support from the European Commission in the framework of the Socrates Program. Finally, five statements were sent in: from the European Commission, the Council of Europe, the EUA, EURASHE and ESIB.[13]

During the ministerial meeting in Bergen, four working groups met and discussed: 1. doctoral studies and the synergy between higher education and research; 2. lifelong learning; 3. quality assurance and recognition in a global perspective; and 4. institutional autonomy and governance. These working groups took place in parallel with the ministers' meeting. The draft communiqué was discussed during a plenary session.

Stocktaking: Procedure, Results and Follow-up Activities

In March 2004, the Bologna Follow-Up Group established a Working Group to conduct the stocktaking or evaluation exercise. The major sources of information were the national reports, requested by the ministerial meeting in Berlin, and information from EURYDICE, the information network on education in Europe.[14] The Working Group asked EURYDICE to extend the report it had prepared for the Berlin meeting, *Focus on the Structure of*

---

13 All documents can be found at www.bologna-bergen2005.no.
14 Its website is www.eurydice.org.

Higher Education in Europe, beyond the 31 countries covered to all countries participating in the Bologna Process. All 40 countries sent in their national reports and provided EURYDICE with the information. The ESIB survey, which covers only 32 countries, was also used.

The Working Group wanted to give a 'big picture' overview of progress on the three priority action lines and developed a scoreboard for each country, based on 10 criteria and 5 colour codes. The ten criteria are: *(for quality assurance)* 1. Stage of development of the quality assurance system; 2. Key elements of evaluation systems; 3. Level of participation of students; 4. Level of international participation, cooperation and networking; *(for two-cycle degree system)* 5. Stage of implementation of the two-cycle system; 6. Level of student enrolment in the two-cycle system; 7. Access from first cycle to second cycle; *(for recognition of degrees and periods of study)* 8. Stage of implementation of Diploma Supplement; 9. Ratification of Lisbon Recognition Convention; and 10. Stage of implementation of ECTS. The colour codes are: green (excellent performance), light green (very good performance), yellow (good performance), orange (some progress has been made) and red (little progress has been made yet).

Based on its analysis of the scoreboards for each country and average scores for the forty countries, the Working Group concluded that 'the collective and voluntary inter-governmental process is a success' (p. 5).[15] Almost all participating countries have embarked upon the reform process along the lines articulated by the Bologna Declaration. The great majority of countries fall within the categories of excellent and very good performance. 'In that respect, Ministers can be confident that the European Higher Education Area (EHEA) is beginning to take shape,' according to the Working Group (p. 26). The highest average scores were established for ratification of the Lisbon Recognition Convention, the implementation of ECTS and the implementation of the two-cycle degree system. The lowest rates of progress were established for participation of students in quality assurance processes, level of student enrolment in the two-cycle degree system and international participation in quality assurance. Given these and other weaknesses, the Working Group argued that additional mechanisms should be put in place to further strengthen the progress on the action lines. It made five specific recommendations.

The Bologna Follow-Up Group agreed with the Working Group's analysis and advised the ministers about the need for more compliance in various issues. In the *Bergen Communiqué*, the ministers indicated various actions to be taken. For instance, the Follow-Up Group was asked to report on the implementation and further development of the *'overarching framework'* for qualifications in the European Higher Education Area, comprising three cy-

---

15 The report by the Working Group on stocktaking can be found on www.bologna-bergen2005.no.

cles (including, within national contexts, the possibility of intermediate qualifications), generic descriptors for each cycle based on learning outcomes and
competences, and credit ranges in the first and second cycles. The European
Commission was asked to consult all parties to the Bologna Process on the
aspects of lifelong learning. And finally ENQA, whose proposed standards
and guidelines for quality assurance had been adopted,[16] was asked to further
develop the practicalities of implementation in cooperation with EUA,
EURASHE and ESIB.

The ministers charged the Follow-Up Group with continuing and widening the stocktaking or evaluation process and reporting in time for the next
ministerial meeting in London in 2007. In particular, they shall look for progress in: a. implementation of the standards and guidelines for quality assurance as proposed in the ENQA report; b. implementation of the national
frameworks for qualifications; c. the awarding and recognition of joint degrees, including at the doctorate level; and d. creating opportunities for
flexible learning paths in higher education, including procedures for the recognition of prior learning. They expect that the implementation of the three
intermediate priorities will be largely completed by 2007. They also charged
the Follow-Up Group with presenting comparable data on the mobility of
staff and students as well as on the social and economic situation of students
in participating countries.

The Governance of the Bologna Process

In Bergen the ministers endorsed the follow-up structure set up in Berlin. It
included three new consultative members: the European Association for
Quality Assurance in Higher Education (ENQA), the trade union Education
International (EI) Pan-European Structure and the Union of Industrial and
Employers' Confederations of Europe (UNICE). This raises the number of
consultative members of the Follow-Up Group to eight, six NGOs (EUA,
EURASHE, ESIB, ENQA, EI and UNICE) and two intergovernmental organizations (Council of Europe and UNESCO-CEPES). The European
Commission is now mentioned as 'a voting member' of the Follow-Up
Group. In their communiqué, the ministers referred both to 'preparing for
2010' and to the situation beyond 2010. In this last respect they argued: 'As
the Bologna Process leads to the establishment of the EHEA, we have to consider the appropriate arrangements needed to support the continuing
development beyond 2010'. They asked the Follow-Up Group to explore
these issues.

A special issue with regard to governance, mentioned in the *Bergen
Communiqué*, is *institutional autonomy*. While moving closer to 2010, the

---

16   The ENQA report can be found on www.bologna-bergen2005.no.

ministers undertake to ensure that higher education institutions enjoy the necessary autonomy to implement the agreed reforms and recognise the need for sustainable funding of institutions. This is an issue raised by EUA. The *Trends IV* report concluded that the latest findings regarding attitudes to reform in universities contrasted sharply with the view expressed by institutional leaders in the *Trends III* report. According to *Trends IV*, general acceptance of the need for reforms seems to be widespread in universities. Efforts to internalise the reform process and to incorporate Bologna issues have been made. Continuous reform and innovation are a reality. But if reforms are to be successful, there needs to be a much greater awareness throughout society that this current period represents a major cultural shift, which is transforming long-accepted notions of higher education and that implementing the reforms in a sustainable way needs time and support. Governments, according to the conclusion of *Trends IV*, 'must be sensitive to the fact that the goals will not be achieved simply by changing legislation. Institutions need more functional autonomy as a fundamental condition for successful reform and accept that this implies strengthening governance structures, institutional leadership and internal management. The question of the funding of reform has to be addressed and with it the broader issues of investment in higher education as a means of the demands of Europe's developing knowledge societies' (p. 5). It remains to be seen whether these EUA expectations will fit with the promise by the ministers to ensure that higher education institutions enjoy the necessary autonomy to implement the agreed reforms.

In its statement for the ministerial meeting in Bergen, issued on 11 May 2005,[17] the European Commission argued that Europe needs a new kind of partnership between the state and the university, 'balancing autonomy, responsibility and self-governance on the one side with strategic guidance from governments; a stable and medium-term funding framework (which should incorporate a creative mix of public and private funding); and real accountability towards society'. Simultaneously equitable access for all qualified students must be ensured, independently of the funding mix chosen. 'Sufficient investment in, and sound management of higher education are core determinants of the future of each region and country in Europe and of the future of Europe in the world' (p. 5). In order to stimulate the debate on this issue the Commission published the Communication *Mobilising the brainpower of Europe: enabling universities to make their full contribution to the Lisbon Strategy* in April 2005.

The governance of the Bologna Process itself was also discussed in the background document that the Follow-Up Group prepared for the Bergen ministerial meeting, *The European Higher Education Area Beyond 2010*. The Follow-Up Group argued that the Bologna Process started off as 'inter-

---

17 See www.bologna-bergen2005.no.

governmental cooperation' relying on the participation of the academic community and of the student representatives. This means that the process is based 'on cooperation and trust between the partners'. It also mentioned that the European Commission, which has increasingly contributed to organising and supporting various action lines and seminars through its programs, the Council of Europe and UNESCO-CEPES have been associated in the shaping and implementing of the process. It characterised the Bologna Process as 'a voluntary cooperation between different national systems overseen by the Bologna Follow-up Group and associating the various partners'. It also referred to the fact that no legally binding provision exists, except for the Lisbon Recognition Convention. This means that the whole arrangement is based on 'mutual trust' (p. 2). Given that the European Area for Higher Education should be considered as a common framework for the time after 2010, ministers, according to the Follow-Up Group, should consider a continuing follow-up mechanism that may meet the challenges of a dynamic higher education sector. In Bergen the ministers followed this conclusion.

In its background document, the Follow-Up Group also discussed the Bologna Process in the context of the European Union and beyond. It argues that, from an EU perspective, the Bologna Process fits into the broader agenda defined by the Lisbon agenda and that the European Commission has played a supportive and complementary role in areas such as quality assurance, recognition of degrees and study periods, the establishment of a European qualifications framework and the promotion of student and staff mobility. However, the Bologna Process has 'its own identity', as can be seen from the perception of the process outside Europe. This means, according to the Follow-Up Group, that the Bologna Process should be 'able and willing to share its findings and experiences with those countries in geographical proximity that are willing to engage in quality assurance, qualification frameworks and descriptors, or curricula for a changed degree structure'. In order to make European higher education attractive to other parts of the world it is important to support universities that encourage quality within Europe and the perception of that quality outside Europe. This external dimension of the Bologna Process, as put forward by the Follow-Up Group, was not elaborated by the ministers in Bergen, but instead they asked the Follow-Up Group to elaborate a strategy for the external dimension.

The Follow-Up Group's background document, The European Higher Education Area Beyond 2010, is reproduced as Annex 10c.

In its statement for the Bergen ministerial meeting, issued on 11 May 2005, the European Commission spoke about an *alarming situation* with regard to various issues and about the need of profound reforms. The Commission mentioned figures for the 25 member states of the EU, but regarded them as representative for the 45 participating countries in the Bologna Process. 'While Europe is certainly a highly educated society, only 21% of the EU working-age population has achieved tertiary education, significantly lower than in the US (38%), Canada (43%) or Japan (36%), as well as South Korea (26%).' Tertiary enrolments have been stronger and grown faster in other parts of the world, mainly because families and individuals contribute much more, whereas most of Europe sees higher education as a 'public good'. 'In the EU, about 52% of the age group is enrolled in higher education. The EU is slightly ahead of Japan (49%) but lags behind Canada (59%) and far behind the US (81%) and South Korea (82%).' The EU also remains behind in research performance. 'While the EU educates more graduates in science and technology and produces more PhDs overall, nothing like as many go into research as they would in the US or Japan, we have about 5.5 researchers per 1,000 employees, marginally less than Canada or South Korea, but way below the US (9.0) or Japan (9.7). Two recent surveys emphasising research found that there are only a handful of European universities in the top 50 in the world. The rapid growth of Asian universities, both public and private, is now also challenging Europe – and the US – in terms of doctoral candidates in science and engineering' (p. 3). Although the Commission views this situation as alarming, its fears are not expressed in the *Bergen Communiqué*.

d. London, May 2007

From 1 July 2005 the United Kingdom has taken over responsibility for the Secretariat of the Bologna Follow-Up Group and its Board. It provides information and news about developments in the Bologna Process and about how the work programme will be taken forward until the next Ministerial Meeting in London in May 2007. Information can be found on the website www.dfes.gov.uk/bologna/.

6. The European Union and Higher Education

This chapter starts with a discussion of the place of the European Union in the field of education. While the EU's role has been limited, the Bologna Process has enlarged it. The chapter continues with general contributions to the Bologna Process by the EU and more specific contributions in the fields of quality assurance and recognition of academic qualifications.

a. Education as an EU Policy Area

Within West-European integration, education policies have always been restricted. There is no common European policy on (higher) education. Competence for the content of education and for the organization of studies has remained at national level.

Education was excluded from the Treaty of Rome for the European Economic Community (EEC) (1957), because this was seen as national in scope, notwithstanding the importance of education for social and economic welfare. Nonetheless, the early treaties contained some statements on vocational training and diplomas, which were to become the basis for later incremental decision-making. These statements refer to retraining former employees of the coal and steel industry (ECSC, 1951), common efforts with respect to occupational and continuation training, and to occupational retraining (EEC Treaty, 1957, Articles 118 and 125), as well as mutual recognition of diplomas and certificates (Article 57), and common training for nuclear specialists (Euratom Treaty, 1957). Recognition of diplomas and vocational training was regarded as important in the context of the free movement of labour. At the time, however, this was not a high priority of the European Economic Community. Hence, implementation of these articles remained restricted. The same goes for the Council Decision 63/266/EEC of 2 April 1963, laying down general principles for implementing a common vocational training policy.[18]

---

18 The signing of the Rome treaties encouraged plans for a 'European University', but it was not until 1972 that European Community member states signed a convention establishing the European University Institute. This was opened in Florence (Italy) in 1976. The first of-

Articles 57, 118 and 125 from the 1957 Treaty of Rome are reproduced as Annex 11.

It was not until 1974 that a first meeting of ministers of education gathered. In 1976 the Council of Ministers of Education came up with a resolution concerning a program of action on education. But once again the framework for cooperation remained weak. It took until the *Single European Act* of 1986 before the need for a European dimension in education was emphasized. In May 1988 a Council resolution invited the Community and the member states to integrate the European dimension into the school curriculum, teaching material and teacher training. In November 1991 the European Commission issued a *Memorandum on Higher Education in the European Community* (COM(1991)349). The *Treaty of the European Union*, known as the *Maastricht Treaty* (1992), became even more explicit. Article 126 stated that the Community should contribute to the development of quality education 'by encouraging cooperation between the Member States and, if necessary, by supporting and supplementing their action, while fully respecting the responsibility of the Member-States for the content of teaching and the organisation of education systems and their cultural and linguistic diversity'. Community actions should be aimed at :

- developing the European dimension in education;
- encouraging the mobility of students and teachers by encouraging inter alia, the academic recognition of diplomas and periods of study;
- promoting cooperation between educational establishments;
- developing exchanges of information and experience on issues common to the education systems of the member states;
- encouraging the development of youth exchanges and of exchanges of socio-educational instructors; and
- encouraging the development of distance learning.

Furthermore the Community and the member states were required to foster cooperation with third countries and the competent international organizations in the field of education, in particular the Council of Europe.

This legal framework, however, was problematic in the sense that member states were reluctant to accept European intervention in their domestic education systems. According to Article 126, the responsibility of member states for the content and the organization of education systems and their cultural and linguistic diversity had to be 'fully' respected. The 1993 Commission's *Green*

---

ficial mention of a European University was in article 9.2 of the 1957 Euratom Treaty. see J.-M. Palayret (ed.), *A University for Europe. Prehistory of the European University Institute in Florence (1948–1976)*, s.l.: Presidency of the Council of Ministers, Department of Information and Publishing, 1996, p. 48.

Paper on the European Dimension of Education (COM(93)457 Final) shows that the Commission was fully aware of this national sensitivity.[19]

The Erasmus and Socrates Programs

Nonetheless, during the second half of the 1980s the European Commission had started various projects in the field of vocational training, under such names as COMETT (Community Action Program in Education and Training for Technology, 1986) and FORCE (a program for the development of continuing vocational training, 1990). A series of initiatives in the form of subsidized action programs proved to be less controversial than the goals formulated in the Single European Act and, later, the Treaty of Maastricht. The *European Community Action Scheme for the Mobility of University Students*, to be known as Erasmus (originally 1987–1994), belongs to the same non-controversial strategy. In 1995 the *Socrates Program* was designed to encourage innovation and improve the quality of education through closer cooperation between educational institutions in the EU and European Economic Area. It combines a number of new and older initiatives, among them the Erasmus program for mobility of university students.

Given these activities the question was raised whether the Community was really competent in the field of higher education. The European Court of Justice confirmed the Community's position by arguing that higher education was to be regarded as part of the preparation for work on the labour market.[20] Not all member states appreciated the Community's stronger position, since they preferred a stronger grip on their domestic labour markets. Under the

---

19 EU information on education can be found at http://europe.eu.int/pol/educ/index_en.htm. EU documents can be found at http://europe.eu.int/documents/index_en.htm. Green papers are discussion papers on a specific policy area published by the Commission, whereas white papers are documents containing proposals for Community action.

20 The judgement by the European Court of Justice of 13 February 1985 (Case 293/83 of *Françoise Gravier* versus City of Liège) argued that, 'although educational organization and policy are not as such included in the spheres which the Treaty has entrusted to the Community institutions, access to and participation in courses of instruction and apprenticeship, in particular vocational training, are not unconnected with Community law. It appears from the measures and programs adopted in that area by the Council that the common vocational training policy referred to in Article 128 of the Treaty is gradually being established. It constitutes, however, an indispensable element of the activities of the Community, whose objectives include inter alia the free movement of persons, the mobility of labour and the improvement of the living standards of workers. It follows that the conditions of access to vocational training fall within the scope of the Treaty,' according to the summary. A recent judgement by the Court of 15 March 2005 (Case C-209/03 of the Queen (on the application of *Dany Bidar*) versus London Borough of Ealing and the Secretary of State for Education and Skills) is in line with the earlier judgement by arguing that assistance covering maintenance costs of students falls within the scope of application of the EC treaty for the purposes of the prohibition of discrimination on grounds of nationality. See, for judgements, http://curia.eu.int/jurisp/html/text.htm.

condition of high unemployment, they retained barriers against the free movement of labour in the European Community rather than weaken their domestic autonomy. Governments were also aware that the Commission's activities in the field of vocational training – through subsidizing and evaluating sub-national projects – had given it a stronger voice in policy formulation in this field. Hence, governments regarded the Commission's engagement in the fields of vocational training and higher education as a threat.

The 1992 Maastricht Treaty therefore tried to circumvent interference by the European Commission in domestic education systems by introducing the principle of *subsidiarity*. This principle stresses that decisions should be taken at the lowest level consistent with effective action within a political system. Within the EU, in practice, it provided a way of limiting the EU's competence. The *Treaty of Amsterdam* (1997) did not change this (Article 126 became Article 149). The treaty contains a commitment to promote lifelong learning for all EU citizens. Hence, the EU's role in education policy remains that of a complementary one, with particular emphasis on quality education, adding a European dimension and encouraging lifelong learning.

Articles 47 and 149–150 from the consolidated version of the Treaty establishing the European Community are reproduced as Annex 12.

b. EU Contributions to the Bologna Process

The first commitments of the European Commission to the emerging Bologna Process created by the ministers of education were financial contributions to the general rapporteur to the Prague meeting and the two *Trends* reports undertaken by the organizations of universities.

For the Prague meeting (2001), where the Commission received the special allocation of an additional full member in the Bologna Process, the Commission contributed a note entitled *From Prague to Berlin, The EU Contribution*. In this note, the Commission strates that most of the nine action lines of the Bologna Process 'coincide with Commission policies, supported through the Socrates program over the years'. The note then presents short descriptions of ten concrete measures, with which the Commission 'may give new support to the objectives of the Bologna process and realise its own policies'. This is one measure for each action line plus one 'overall support to the Bologna process through Monitoring/Reports/Seminars'. This means that in 2002, the Commission supported the *Trends III* report, an official Prague/Berlin rapporteur and a limited number of official Bologna seminars that would fit the policies of the program.

The support for the Bologna Process and the realization of the Commission's own policies are possible because the Bologna action lines 'coincide with EU policy in higher education, well-known to the broad – and not only academic! – European public through programs such as Socrates/Erasmus, Tempus, Cards, etc.', according to the general rapporteur to the Berlin meeting (Zgaga Report, p. 18).

Lisbon, Nice and Barcelona

More important, perhaps, is that this support to the Bologna Process and this EU action in the field also fit into the policies of the heads of states and governments, who discussed education in the European Council meetings in Lisbon in March 2000, in Nice in December 2000 and in Barcelona in March 2002. The European Council in *Lisbon* set an ambitious and strategic goal for the EU for the next decade and in that respect stressed the importance of 'establishing a European Area of Research and Innovation' as well as 'education and training for living and working in the knowledge society'.

The European Council in *Nice* in December 2000 discussed 'mobility of students and teachers' and 'research and innovation' in the context of its new incentive for an economic and social Europe under the heading 'Europe based on innovation and knowledge'. With regard to research and innovation the European Council appreciated initiatives to improve the transparency of research results and the attractiveness of scientific careers. With regard to mobility of students and teachers, the European Council approved a resolution by the Council concerning an action plan for mobility. The interesting issue in this resolution is that it is based on the awareness that a Europe of knowledge is also an economic necessity[21] and on the conviction that increasing the mobility of young people, schoolchildren, students, researchers, all those being educated and their teachers in Europe is 'thus a major political goal and that it requires simultaneous commitment and effort by the European Community and the Member States'. The resolution welcomes a mobility action plan which was submitted to the ministers of education at the Sorbonne on 30 September 2000. The major objectives of that plan are to define and democratise mobility in Europe, to promote appropriate forms of funding and to increase mobility and improve the conditions for it.[22]

These aims were confirmed in a more profiled way by the European Council in Barcelona two years later, this time setting the objective of 'making these educative and training systems a world quality reference by 2010'. The EU Ministers of Education translated this ambition into 'a series of

---

21 'that in an internationalised economy increasingly founded on knowledge, openness to foreign cultures and the ability to educate oneself and work in a multilingual environment are essential to the competitiveness of the European economy'.

22 Resolution of the Council and of the Representatives of the Governments of the Member States meeting within the Council of 14 December 2000 concerning an action plan for mobility. See http://europe.eu.int/index_en.htm for the Conclusions of the Presidency, European Council, Nice, 7–9 December 2000.

shared objectives for the different education and training systems in Europe' and plan to evaluate the progress in reaching these shared objectives against 'Reference Levels of European Average Performance' or 'European Benchmarks'. It can be noted that these statements correspond to the visions expressed in the *Bologna Declaration* and the *Prague Communiqué* (see the Zgaga Report, p. 18, footnote 6), or as expressed by the Commission in its note *From Berlin to Bergen, The EU Contribution* (17 February 2004): 'From an EU perspective, the Bologna process fits into a broader agenda defined in Lisbon in March 2000' (p. 1).

The Role of the Universities in the Europe of Knowledge

In 2002 and 2003, the EU Directorate General of Education and Culture released successive *Progress Reports* on what the Commission was doing. These activities 'relate to all action lines of the Bologna process as well as to the monitoring and reporting activities and to concrete Bologna follow-up events'. In most cases, the Commission was implementing measures in direct partnership with the higher education sector of the EU member and associate countries but also other countries (*Zgaga Report*, p, 18). Furthermore, in December 2002 the Commission launched the so-called *Copenhagen Process*, based on the Bologna Process, in order to enhance European cooperation in vocational education and training.

In February 2003 the Commission published its report *The role of the universities in the Europe of knowledge* (COM(2003)58 final), in which it explained that the EU needed a healthy and flourishing university world and that Europe needed excellence in its universities, 'to optimise the processes which underpin the knowledge society and meet the target, set out by the European Council in Lisbon' (p. 2). And in November 2003 the Commission presented a draft for an interim report on the implementation of the shared objectives to be submitted jointly by the Commission and EU ministers of education to the European Council in spring 2004. There are five *new challenges facing European universities*, according to the 2003 report:

1. an increased demand for higher education;
2. the internationalization of education and research;
3. the need to develop effective and close cooperation between universities and industry;
4. the proliferation of places where knowledge is produced; and
5. the reorganization of knowledge.

The growth of the knowledge economy requires universities to become more closely involved in community life. 'Alongside and as a natural result of the exercise of its fundamental missions to produce and transmit knowledge, the university today functions particularly as a major source of expertise in numerous areas. It can and must increasingly become a forum of reflection on knowledge, as well as of debate and dialogue between scientists and people' (p. 9).

In conclusion, two things may be noted with regard to EU education policies. *First*, the European Council added a new element to EU education policies by discussing education as a contribution to the setting up of a European knowledge society. *Second*, the Bologna Process as an education project has been included in the work of the Commission, and has, in fact, streamlined and enlarged the Commission's activities in the field of education.

c. ENQA and Quality Assurance

On 24 September 1998 the Council of Ministers of Education adopted a *Recommendation on European cooperation in quality assurance in higher education* (98/561 EC).[23] The broad objectives of this proposed cooperation include:

1. encouraging and developing the exchange of information and experience, in particular on methodological developments and examples of good practice;
2. fulfilling the requests for expertise and advice from the authorities concerned in the member states;
3. supporting higher education institutions, which wish to cooperate in the field of quality assurance on a transnational basis; and
4. promoting contacts with international experts.

The *Annex* contains indicative features of quality assurance.

The indicative features of quality assurance are reproduced as Annex 13.

A European pilot project of 1994–1995 had demonstrated the value of sharing and developing experience in quality assurance. The Council resolution led to the establishment of the **European Network for Quality Assurance in Higher Education (ENQA)** on 29 March 2000 in Brussels. The European Commission convened the meeting, which was attended by public authorities responsible for higher education and 50 representatives of European quality assurance organizations. The European Commission supports ENQA through the Socrates program. Membership of ENQA was open to quality assurance agencies, public authorities responsible for higher education and European associations of higher education institutions of the European Union as well as representation from Central and East European countries. Cooperation through ENQA is pursued by developing links between quality assurance and

---

23   Also to be found at www.enqa.net.

other existing EU activities, particularly in the framework of the Socrates and Leonardo da Vinci programs, and by examining opportunities for joint efforts in the field of recognition of qualifications for professional purposes.

The network has a *Steering Group*, elected for three years, and a *General Assembly*. In September 2003 a reform process was launched for the transformation of the network to an association with membership criteria and a code of principles. In November 2004, ENQA was changed from a network into an association. ENQA now stands for **European Association for Quality Assurance in Higher Education**. Its aim is to disseminate information, experiences, good practices and new developments in the field of quality assessment and quality assurance in higher education between interested parties: public authorities, higher institutions and quality assurance agencies. Now, membership is open to quality assurance agencies in the signatory states of the Bologna Process. In February 2005, 40 agencies and associations had joined.

d. ENQA and the Bologna Process

The Steering Group of ENQA closely followed the European debate on the process which followed upon the *Bologna Declaration* of June 1999, which also calls for the promotion of European cooperation in quality assurance. According to the Steering Group, the *Bologna Declaration* parallels closely the Council recommendation of 1998. This recommendation underlined the need for EU member states to face the task of organizing their higher education system in ways that respect existing academic standards, training objectives and quality standards, as well as the need for transparent educational systems required for transnational mobility.

In its position paper to the Prague meeting of the Bologna Process in 2001, ENQA saw itself as well into the process of making its network 'a viable framework for providing answers and solutions to issues such as those raised by the Bologna Declaration'.[24] It was fully aware that new developments challenge the purely national context for quality assurance which can be found in European countries. The need for change to a large extent is related to internationalization and is visible in such changes as a growing international market for higher education, transnational education and a need for recognition of degrees due to graduate mobility. 'The Bologna declaration can be viewed as a European response to these developments'.

---

24 ENQA, *Follow-Up on the Bologna Declaration: a European quality assurance system* (2001). Available at www.bologna-berlin2003.de.

Accreditation

That European higher education institutions perceived themselves as confronted by new challenges that demand new solutions, preferably at a European level was demonstrated by a project launched in 2000 by the Association of European Universities. This project aimed at exploring the context and feasibility of accreditation as a European solution to the challenges of internationalization and the framework of the *Bologna Declaration*. It recommended setting up a European platform of higher education institutions, also involving students, quality assurance and accreditation agencies, professional organizations and recognition centres, as well as national and regional education authorities. ENQA became associated with this project, but also argued that a pan-European solution may not be the only or most effective answer.

Examples of more limited and possibly regional organisations could be relevant as well, as is demonstrated by the cooperation of Nordic quality assurance agencies and the common efforts of the Dutch and Flemish ministers of education, which later resulted in a *Netherlands–Flemish Accreditation Organization*. In November 2003 a *European Consortium for Accreditation in Higher Education* (ECA) was established. In 2005, it had 13 member organizations from eight countries (in Western Europe). ECA's aim is to achieve mutual recognition of accreditation decisions among the participants by the end of 2007. The members believe that mutual recognition will contribute to the recognition of qualifications and the mobility of students in Europe and will make life easier for institutions and programs operating across borders. The members of ECA have agreed on a joint *Code of Good Practice* with 17 standards.[25]

Another issue for discussion according to the Steering Group of ENQA should be the extent to which a European platform could function as a meta-accreditation agency in the same way as the US Council for Higher Education Accreditation functions as an accreditor of US agencies.

Quality Assurance

In May 2001, the ministers of education meeting in Prague invited ENQA to collaborate in establishing a common framework of reference for quality assurance, which would work directly towards the establishment of the European quality assurance framework by 2010. The *Prague Communiqué* gave ENQA a major de facto mandate to cooperate with higher education institutions and national agencies, as well as with bodies from countries not member of ENQA, to collaborate in establishing a common framework of

---

25 To be found at www.bologna-bergen2005.no and at www.ecaconsortium.net.

reference and to disseminate best practice. This resulted in cooperation with associations such as ESIB, EUA and EURASHE in the context of a survey of methodologies applied by member agencies. The survey concluded that there was increasing convergence in evaluation methods and procedures even if national agencies still varied in many respects.

ENQA also set up a major *Transnational European Evaluation Project* (TEEP) and began cooperation with the ENIC and NARIC networks. TEEP is a pilot project established to assess the viability of European transnational quality evaluation in three disciplines (history, physics and veterinary science). Closer contacts with the NARIC and ENIC networks (discussed below and in the next chapter) were set up in order to improve linkage between the recognition of degrees and the quality assurance of corresponding programs.

In September 2003, ENQA prepared a *statement* for the ministers of education meeting in Berlin, in which it proposed to open membership to all signatory states to the Bologna Process, to develop in close cooperation with the relevant stakeholders a European Register of Quality Assurance Agencies and a code of principles for ENQA agency members, focusing on their internal quality mechanisms.[26]

The *Berlin Communiqué* was regarded as a recommendation by the ministers to contribute even more directly to the European quality assurance process. The main task for ENQA prior to the 2005 Bergen meeting would be the identification of relevant quality assurance procedures and criteria. There should be an active coordination between ENQA and higher education institutions on identification of quality. ENQA established two working groups, one on an adequate peer review system for agencies and another one on an agreed set of standards, procedures and guidelines. The work done by these two working groups were presented to the *Bologna Follow-Up Group* in September and October 2004.

In 2004 ENQA drafted a report for the ministers on European quality assurance. In December 2004 an outline of the report was presented to the *Board* of the Bologna Process, whereas members of ENQA were invited to comment on the final draft in early 2005. Eventually ENQA will report, through the Bologna Follow-Up Group, to the next ministerial meeting in Bergen in May 2005.

In the meantime, to a certain extent pre-enpting ENQA results, the *European Commission* reached the conclusion that within the EU the implementation of the Council recommendation of 1998 demonstrates remarkable progress in establishing quality assurance systems and promoting cooperation, but that these positive developments are insufficient. 'More far reaching measures are needed in order to make European higher education perform better and become a more transparent and trustworthy brand for our own citizens and for students and scholars from other continents', according to the Commission in

---

26 Idem.

an explanatory memorandum, in which the Commission proposes to the Council of Ministers and to the European Parliament to adopt a new recommendation, which would build on the recommendation of 1998 and contribute to the aim of mutual recognition of quality assurance systems and assessments across Europe. This is the *Proposal for a Recommendation of the Council and of the European Parliament on further European cooperation in quality assurance in higher education (Presented by the Commission)* (COM(2004)642 final) of 12 October 2004.

The proposed recommendation on further European cooperation in quality assurance is reproduced as Annex 14.

There are five steps to achieve mutual recognition, according to this proposal:

1. the introduction of internal quality assurance mechanisms in higher education institutions;
2. the application of a common set of standards, procedures and guidelines (being developed by ENQA);
3. the creation of a European register of quality assurance and accreditation agencies;
4. the introduction of university autonomy in the choice of an agency; and
5. member state competence to accept assessments and their consequences.

e. The NARIC Network and Academic Recognition

One more EU body has to be mentioned in this context. This is the **NARIC Network of National Academic Recognition Information Centres**. It was created in 1984 at the Commission's initiative to help in regulating title recognition. Most NARICs (*National Academic Recognition Information Centres*) do not take policy decisions but offer on request authoritative information and advice about foreign education systems and qualifications. The main users of this service are higher education institutions, study advisers and students. Now the NARIC Network aims at improving academic recognition of diplomas and periods of study in the EU member states and the European Economic Area countries.

With regard to academic recognition there have been three major activities. The *first* one is recognition of qualifications, including prior learning and professional experience, allowing entry or re-entry into higher education. NARIC's work in this respect became closely related to the implementation of the joint *Council of Europe and UNESCO Convention of 1997* on the recognition of qualifications concerning higher education in the European region (to be discussed in the next chapter). In this field the NARIC Network cooperates closely with the ENIC Network of the Council of Europe and

UNESCO. They meet together and have a common website: www.enic-naric.net.

The *second* activity is related to the recognition of short study periods in relation with student mobility. The instrument attached to this activity is the *European Credit Transfer System* (ECTS). These transferable credits were introduced in 1989 in the context of the Erasmus program. It is a student-centred system based on the study workload required to achieve the objectives of a program, objectives preferably specified in terms of the learning outcomes and competences to be acquired. The system facilitated the recognition of periods of study abroad and thus enhanced the quality and volume of student mobility in Europe. According to the Bologna Process, ECTS is developing into an accumulation system to be implemented at various levels. A kindred system was set up in 1993 in Asia and the Pacific as the *UMAP Credit Transfer Scheme* (UCTS) by UMAP (University Mobility in Asia and the Pacific).[27]

The *third* activity refers to recognition of full degrees. The instrument attached to this is the *Diploma Supplement*. The idea of a Diploma Supplement was initiated by UNESCO and revised by a joint European Commission, Council of Europe and UNESCO working party that tested it and refined it. The Diploma Supplement is a document attached to a higher education diploma aimed at improving international transparency and at facilitating the academic and professional recognition of qualifications. It is designed to provide a description of the nature, level, context and status of the studies that were pursued and successfully completed by the individual student named on the original qualification to which this supplement is appended.

---

27 See www.enic-naric.net/instruments.asp?display=other_regions&topic=tools. It is a volun-
    tary association of government and non-government representatives of the higher education
    (university) sector in the Asia-Pacific region. It aims to achieve enhanced international un-
    derstanding through increased mobility of university students and staff. See. also §10.d.

Part III:
The Intergovernmental Organizations

7. The Council of Europe and UNESCO on Recognition of Qualifications

This chapter starts with the regional conventions covering academic recognition which were adopted by the Council of Europe and UNESCO. The most important one is the Lisbon Recognition Convention of 1997. This convention created a Committee, which issues recommendations and codes of good practice. The Council of Europe has an observer position in the Bologna Process and performs a bridge function between 'Bologna' and 'non-Bologna' countries.

a. The Council of Europe and UNESCO Conventions Covering Academic Recognition

The **Council of Europe** was created in 1949 as a regional organization aiming to achieve a greater unity between its member states. In 1954 it adopted a *European Cultural Convention*, designed to foster the study of the languages, history and civilisation of European states, and of the civilisation which is common to them all.

Since the early 1950s the Council of Europe and the **United Nations Educational, Scientific and Cultural Organization** (UNESCO), adopted seven *conventions covering academic recognition* in Europe. The last one in 1997 was a joint one. These conventions set standards and deal with equivalence of diplomas and periods of university study and with the recognition of qualifications. In chronological order these conventions are:

1. *European Convention on the Equivalence of Diplomas leading to Admission to Universities* (Council of Europe, No. 15, Paris, 11 December 1953; plus a Protocol, No. 49, Strasbourg, 3 June 1964);
2. *European Convention on the Equivalence of Periods of University Study* (Council of Europe, No. 21, Paris, 15 December 1956);
3. *European Convention on the Academic Recognition of University Qualifications* (Council of Europe, No. 32, Paris, 14 December 1959);
4. *International Convention on the Recognition of Studies, Diplomas and Degrees in Higher Education in the Arab and European States bordering on the Mediterranean* (UNESCO, Nice, 17 December 1976);

5. *Convention on the Recognition of Studies, Diplomas and Degrees concerning Higher Education in the States belonging to the European Region* (UNESCO, Paris, 21 December 1979);
6. *European Convention on the General Equivalence of Periods of University Study* (Council of Europe, No. 138, Rome, 6 November 1990); and
7. *Convention on the Recognition of Qualifications concerning Higher Education in the European Region* (joint Council of Europe and UNESCO convention; Council of Europe, No. 165, Lisbon, 11 April 1997; also known as the 'Lisbon Recognition Convention', see below).

Europe has not been the only region to adopt such conventions. Under the auspices of UNESCO, four more regional conventions came into being, if we exclude the convention of Arab and European states bordering the Mediterranean of 1976 mentioned above. These four were adopted between 1974 and 1983 and deal with the recognition of studies, diplomas and degrees in higher education. The four are:

1. *Regional Convention on the Recognition of Studies, Diplomas and Degrees in Higher Education in Latin America and the Caribbean* (Mexico City, 19 July 1974);
2. *Convention on the Recognition of Studies, Diplomas and Degrees in Higher Education in the Arab States* (Paris, 22 December 1978);
3. *Regional Convention on the Recognition of Studies, Certificates, Diplomas, Degrees and other Academic Qualifications in Higher Education in the African States* (Arusha, Tanzania, 5 December 1981); and
4. *Regional Convention on the Recognition of Studies, Diplomas and Degrees in Higher Education in Asia and the Pacific* (Bangkok, 16 December 1983).

In order to bring consistency to the various documents and refer to new developments in higher education UNESCO adopted a *Recommendation on the Recognition of Studies in Higher Education* on 13 November 1993. Two more regional documents should be mentioned because they provide policies and practices with regard to recognition between European countries and the United States, respectively the Russian Federation. These are the *Guidelines for the Mutual Recognition of Qualification between Europe and the U.S.A.* (1994) and the *Mutual Recognition of Qualifications: and the Russian Federation and the Other European Countries* (2000).[28]

---

28 Available at www.enic-naric.net/instruments.asp. Council of Europe conventions can be found at http://conventions.coe.int; UNESCO ones at http://erc.unesco.org.

b. The 1997 Lisbon Convention on the Recognition of Qualifications

The reasons for elaborating a joint Council of Europe and UNESCO convention in the early 1990s, which resulted in the 1997 Lisbon Recognition Convention, were the developments in higher education in Europe since the 1960s. The predominant change was the diversification of higher education. In the early 1990s, students in higher education could attend both traditional universities and non-university institutions and in universities they could also follow non-traditional programs of shorter duration with a stronger emphasis on professional education. Other changes were the rapid increase in the number of private institutions and of academic mobility.

Since their conventions had not been updated the Council of Europe and UNESCO decided to produce a new convention to ultimately replace then and to avoid a duplication of effort. Support from UNESCO also sprang from the belief that it would benefit all members of both organizations. It would also help to avoid a 'two track' Europe and to link the European region to other regions of the world.

The *Convention on the Recognition of Qualifications concerning Higher Education in the European Region,* or *Lisbon Recognition Convention,* was adopted in April 1997. It entered into force on 1 February 1999. In February 2005 the Council of Europe had 40 ratifications and the UNESCO as well (it should be noted that the UNESCO European Region also has some non-European members, such as Canada, Israel and the US). Thirty-six of the 40 countries that have ratified the Lisbon Convention are members, or applicants to be member, of the Bologna Process.

The major components of the convention are that holders of qualifications issued in one country shall have adequate access to an assessment of these qualifications in another country, and without any discrimination. The responsibility to demonstrate that an application does not fulfil the relevant requirements – and this is significant – lies with the body undertaking the assessment and not with the applicant.

Furthermore, each country shall recognize qualifications as similar to the corresponding qualifications in its own system, unless it can show that there are substantial differences between its own qualifications and the qualifications for which recognition is sought. Recognition of a higher education qualification issued in another country shall have a broad application, in particular access to further education studies on the same conditions as candidates from the country in which recognition is sought, and/or the use of an academic title, subject to the laws and regulations of the country in which recognition is sought.

Finally, all countries shall develop procedures to assess whether refugees and displaced persons fulfil the relevant requirements for access to higher education. They shall also appoint a national information centre and encourage their higher education institutions to issue the *Diploma Supplement*, jointly developed by the European Commission, the Council of Europe and UNESCO (discussed in the previous chapter).

c. The Committee of the Lisbon Recognition Convention and its Recommendations

To oversee, promote and facilitate the implementation of the convention, two bodies are mentioned: the Committee of the Convention, and the ENIC Network. The **Committee of the Convention on the Recognition of Qualifications concerning Higher Education in the European Region**, also known as **Committee of the Lisbon Recognition Convention**, is described in article X.2. It is composed of one representative of each party to the convention, but not the European Community. It shall promote the application of the convention and oversee its implementation. To this end it may adopt, by majority, recommendations, declarations, protocols and models of good practice to guide the competent authorities in their implementation of the convention and in their consideration of applications for the recognition of higher education qualifications. The Committee has its own *Secretariat*.

The Committee of the Lisbon Recognition Convention has produced various documents. The first one dates from 1999, when a *Recommendation on International Access Qualifications* was adopted. In June 2001 the Committee of the Lisbon Recognition Convention adopted a *Code of Good Practice in the Provision of Transnational Education*. This refers to higher education study programs and other educational services by means of transnational arrangements. Simultaneously the Committee adopted a *Recommendation on Procedures and Criteria for the Assessment of Foreign Qualifications and Periods of Study*. And in June 2004 the Committee adopted a *Recommendation on the Recognition of Joint Degrees* in order to facilitate the recognition of joint degrees by removing legal obstacles and introducing legal provisions that would facilitate such recognition. Considerations and principles are explained in an appendix to the recommendation.

The Code of Good Practice in the Provision of Transnational Education is reproduced as Annex 15.

d. The ENIC Network of the Council of Europe and UNESCO

Before making its decisions the Committee of the Lisbon Recognition Convention shall seek the opinion of the ENIC Network, to which all parties shall appoint a member from their national information centre. In June 1994 the Council of Europe and UNESCO had decided to replace their previous separate networks of national information centres on academic mobility and recognition[29] and to establish the joint ENIC Network. **ENIC Network** stands for **European Network of National Information Centres on Academic Mobility and Recognition**. In the context of the Lisbon Recognition Convention the ENIC Network does not only advise, but also upholds and assists the practical implementation of the convention by the competent national authorities.

ENIC has a secretariat provided by the Council of Europe and UNESCO and cooperates closely with the NARIC Network of the EU (discussed in the previous chapter), both with regard to their common website and their joint meetings.

At their annual meeting in Vilnius in June 1999 the **ENIC and NARIC Networks** declared their willingness and ability to contribute to the Bologna Process. They started to discuss their contributions and established a *Working Party on Recognition Issues in the Bologna Process*, which in January 2001 produced a final report. It clarifies the main results and outlines considerations for the recognition agenda. Since with the Lisbon Convention the international legal framework is largely in place, the focus should now be on the enforcement of existing legislation and the elaboration, codification and promotion of Europe-wide standards for recognition. Apart from codes of good practice the report underlines the importance of instruments for transparency, such as the Diploma Supplement.

The report clarifies that recognition of the labour market will grow significantly in importance. This shift, according to the report, entails a switch of focus for most recognition agencies to a relatively new target group with specific needs. The report also refers to the concept of lifelong learning, which requires different methods and procedures of assessment.

The progress in the work of the ENIC and NARIC Networks can be found in their *Vaduz Statement on the European Higher Education Area* of May 2003 and their *Strasbourg Statement on Recognition Issues in the European Higher Education Area* of June 2004. The two networks regard their contribution to the Bologna Process, according to the Vaduz Statement, as helping to build bridges between education systems and qualifications and as forums for the further development of recognition policies in Europe and beyond. Both statements contain information about progress with regard to specific issues. In 2004 the two networks adopted a Charter for national information centres which will better enable the two networks to play a key role in the implementation of the Bologna Process in their respective countries. The Charter will also guide the two networks in fulfilling the same role in the European region.

---

29 The UNESCO network of *National Information Bodies* (NIBs) and the Council of Europe network of *National Equivalence Information Centres* (NEICs).

e. Other Council of Europe Contributions to the Bologna Process

Apart from its joint activities with UNESCO in the field of recognition, the Council of Europe has made other contributions to the Bologna Process. It regards itself as a firmly established and important contributor through its observer status in the formal structures of the Bologna Process (Follow-Up Group), its mediating role between member countries and European countries that are not (yet) party to it, and as a forum for debate between governmental and non-governmental representatives. The Council of Europe's mediating role between 'Bologna' and 'non-Bologna' countries was realised by approaching its member states all over Europe, helping disseminate information on the Bologna Process, and providing advice on higher education reform. It organized various conferences and seminars in order to discuss higher education reform in countries such as Serbia and Russia. Debate between governmental and non-governmental actors was made possible because both the European University Association and ESIB have observer status at the Council of Europe and attend the meetings of the relevant *Steering Committee for Higher Education and Research* (CD-ESR). At the 2001 and 2002 plenary sessions of the Steering Committee, its round table debate focused on the Bologna Process. As a result, its work program and activities have been structured around three pillars:

1. the *European Higher Education Area*, which includes recognition of qualifications;
2. *public responsibility for higher education*, which includes the definition of the responsibility of public authorities for aspects of higher education such as framework, and provision and finance, as well as trade in higher education as a supplement to higher education provision within national systems; and
3. *higher education governance*.

Two more issues will gain importance, according to the Steering Committee. These are the role of law in higher education (new generations of law for higher education) and research policy.

The Council of Europe organized various official Bologna seminars, such as one on recognition issues in the Bologna Process (Lisbon, April 2002) and another one on public responsibility for higher education and research (Strasbourg, September 2004).

8. UNESCO and OECD Guidelines on Quality Provision in Cross-Border Higher Education

Apart from its cooperation with the Council of Europe on recognition issues, UNESCO has developed a joint project with the Organization for Economic Cooperation and Development. This chapter provides information on both organizations' activities in the field of higher education and on their common project for guidelines on quality provision in cross-border higher education. The OECD disagrees with the Bologna Process's ambition to enhance convergence of programs and qualifications.

a. UNESCO and Higher Education in a Globalized Society

UNESCO was founded in 1945 and one year later became a specialized organization of the United Nations. It promotes collaboration among nations through education, science, culture and communication in order to promote respect for justice, the rule of law, human rights and fundamental freedoms. Most states in the world are UNESCO members.

In 1998 UNESCO organized world conferences on higher education. A *World Declaration on Higher Education in the 21st Century* was issued in the same year. In 2002 a Forum on Higher Education, Research and Knowledge as well as a Global Forum on International Quality Assurance, Accreditation and the Recognition of Qualification in Higher Education were launched as follow-up activities. In 2003 UNESCO's position on higher education in the context of globalization was expressed in its document *Higher Education in a Globalized Society*.[30]

UNESCO's position is that education in a globalized society shall assure equity of access and respect cultural diversity as well as national sovereignty. UNESCO is also committed to assuring the quality of global provision of higher education in an increasingly diverse higher education arena and raising the awareness of stakeholders, especially students, on emerging issues. This position aims to establish the conditions under which the globalization of higher education benefits all.

---

30 UNESCO documents can be found at http://portal.unesco.org/education/.

The **Global Forum on International Quality Assurance, Accreditation and the Recognition of Qualifications** was set up in Paris on 17–18 October 2002. It serves to promote international cooperation in higher education by providing a platform for dialogue between different stakeholders and building bridges between intergovernmental organizations. The first Forum meeting proposed an action plan focussing on UNESCO's *standard-setting capacities* (such as monitoring and updating the regional conventions discussed in chapter 7) and on *capacity-building and information functions* (such as research and analytical studies on the impact of new higher education developments in different regions, training workshops and elaboration of tools to inform stakeholders on recent developments in higher education). The second Forum meeting in June 2004 also took into account the increasing dimensions of access in the globalized world.

Preserving the quality of higher education, promoting equal access to higher education, and protecting as well as empowering learners for informed decision making are central to the work of the Global Forum. They are regarded as key challenges for higher education in a more globalized world. One of the major activities undertaken by UNESCO, together with the OECD, has been the development of guidelines on quality provision in cross-border higher education (see below).

b. The OECD and Consumer Protection in Cross-Border Higher Education

Like UNESCO, the Organization for Economic Cooperation and Development (OECD) is based in Paris. It has 30 of the world's advanced industrial economies committed to the principles of the market economy and pluralist democracy as its members. It promotes economic growth, employment and improved standards of living. This intergovernmental organization does not produce regulations, such as international conventions, but creates recommendations and 'good practices', supported by frequently collected statistics and evaluations, leaving it to its member states to enact these general guidelines in day-to-day policy-making. The EU's 'open method of coordination' is rather similar to this OECD method, given its establishment of indicators and benchmarks and its periodic monitoring, evaluation and peer review.

The OECD's engagement in the development of indicators for educational performance dates back to the early 1960s. In 1964 an OECD European ministers of education conference recommended thar the OECD develop a model handbook for effective educational investment planning. A 'Green Book' helped with gathering educational statistics in the OECD. It was followed by the *International Indicators of Educational Systems* project (INES), annual publications of educational statistics and a Program for International Student Assessment. The *International Standard Classification of*

Education (ISCED), developed by UNESCO, was revised and further developed by the OECD, which established a **Centre for Educational Research and Innovation** (CERI).

During the 1980s, strong pressure was put on the OECD to conduct more statistical work on educational indicators, both on inputs and outcomes (costs and sources of finance, learning achievements, employment trends, curriculum standards and the like). This resulted in the annual publication of *Education at a Glance* (since 1992). This by now authoritative publication provides comparative data about the performance of education systems in OECD member states against 36 indicators. During the whole development *outcome measures* (effectiveness) have become more important than *input measures*. This must be understood against the background of global competition, and the international education market, which has become stronger since the 1980s and 1990s.

The development of educational indicators and the regular collection of statistical data enable OECD member states (as well as non-member states given the fact that the results are published) to observe and adapt to trends in education. States are also free to ignore major trends. However, states that are not monitoring the general trends risk becoming uncompetitwe in the international market. In case of discrepancies in the data, the OECD will discuss these at both expert and ministerial level. If required, the ministers will issue a decision which describes the preferred strategy. Once again, the member states are not obliged to comply with this strategy. In the end the OECD statistics will inform them about the successes, or non-successes, of the various options.

Trade in Educational Services and Consumer Protection

OECD ministers of education requested the OECD to examine the implications of internationalization of demand for competences and supply of higher education and training services. With regard to higher education, they recommended concentration on two issues: trade in educational services, and key trends and issues in international e-learning activities. The Internationalization of Tertiary Education project carries out various activities. One is convening all stakeholders through **OECD Forums on Trade in Educational Services**. The first Forum was held in Washington DC in May 2002, the second in November 2003 in Trondheim, Norway. Other activities are analyzing the size of cross-border higher education activities in the OECD area, improving international statistics and indicators, analyzing trends in international quality assurance, accreditation and recognition of qualifications, and analyzing trends and good practices in e-learning. The final activity to be mentioned is developing guidelines on quality provision in cross-border higher education.

In 2003 at the second Forum on Trade in Educational Services the OECD discussed enhancing *consumer protection* in the field of higher education against the background of the increased internationalization of higher education systems. In addition to the traditional form of cross-border education, i.e. students travelling abroad to study, new developments in cross-border education increased. Examples are the emergence of e-learning, for-profit providers, joint campuses and transnational consortia. These new developments challenge existing national quality assurance and accreditation frameworks and agencies, whereas increasing student and staff mobility has put the issue of mutual recognition of academic and professional qualifications higher on the agenda. One of the risks for learners is that they may become victims of rogue providers, so-called 'degree mills', offering low-quality educational experiences and qualifications of limited validity. The existence of such degree mills may also have repercussions for the reputation of well-established national higher education systems.

The OECD concluded that existing initiatives on international quality assurance, accreditation and recognition of qualifications had to be strengthened and implemented. Its decision to develop guidelines, in close collaboration with UNESCO, was based on the assumption that countries prefer to have national control of quality assurance and accreditation in their own higher education system. Consequently, the guidelines are not legally binding. Member states are expected to implement the guidelines as appropriate in their national context.

c. The UNESCO/OECD Guidelines on Quality Provision in Cross-Border Higher Education

In October 2003 both UNESCO and the OECD Centre for Educational Research and Innovation were allowed by their constituencies to work on the development of common guidelines on quality provision. A first drafting meeting took place in April 2004. All member states of the two organizations were invited. Stakeholders, such as higher education institutions, student associations, quality assurance and accreditation agencies, teachers' associations and professional bodies, were invited as observers. A draft of the guidelines was discussed during a second meeting in October 2004 and a third one in January 2005. The draft was open for comments by the OECD and UNESCO member states as well as public comment. Following its General Conference in October 2005 UNESCO issued the Guidelines under the responsibility of the Secretariat. The OECD Council approved the final version on 2 December 2005.

The four main policy objectives of these guidelines are:[31]

---

31 The Guidelines can be found at www.oecd.org under the section on education, or at the
    UNESCO website http://portal.unesco.org/education/.

1. protection of students and learners from the risk of misinformation, low-quality education and qualifications of limited validity;
2. readable and transparent qualifications, to increase their international validity and portability; reliable and user-friendly information sources should facilitate this;
3. transparent, coherent, fair and reliable recognition procedures, which impose as little burden as possible to mobile professionals;
4. intensified international cooperation berween national quality and accreditation agencies, in order to increase mutual understanding.

The *Guidelines for Quality Provision in Cross-Border Higher Education* recommends actions to six stakeholders: 7 guidelines for governments, 9 guidelines for higher education institutions and providers delivering cross-border higher education, 3 guidelines for student bodies, 7 guidelines for quality assurance and accreditation bodies, 6 guidelines for academic recognition bodies and 4 guidelines for professional bodies.

A draft proposal for a *Dissemination, implementation and review process of the UNESCO/OECD Guidelines on quality provision in cross-border higher education* followed the suggestion that UNESCO and the OECD survey the implementation of the guidelines in the various countries and report their assessment of the results to the UNESCO Executive Board and the OECD Council. It distinguished between dissemination, actual implementation and review of the guidelines. It was suggested that states appoint one or more national coordinators to manage these activities and that UNESCO and the OECD set up a small *Inter-Secretariat Steering Committee* for this purpose. In December 2005 the OECD issued a recommendation focusing mainly on implementation, although there is a small instruction on surveying. The recommendation instructs 'the relevant OECD bodies, if and when possible in co-operation with the relevant UNESCO bodies, to survey developments by appropriate stakeholders in countries regarding implementation of the Recommendation and to assess the Guidelines in light of developments in cross-border higher education, and reports to the Council as appropriate'.

The UNESCO/OECD Guidelines are reproduced as Annex 16.

d. The OECD on the Bologna Process

The OECD discussed the Bologna Process in its document *Enhancing consumer protection in cross-border higher education: key issues related to quality assurance, accreditation and recognition of qualifications* of November 2003 (p. 17). It argues that contemporary higher education systems are affected by two conflicting trends. On the one hand there is an increasing *diversification* in institutions, programs, qualifications, delivery modes, and teaching and learning settings. On the other hand there is a process of *convergence and standardization* going on in the same aspects of educational systems. The issue of recognition acknowledges the diversity of programmes and qualifications, but is trying to arrive at some common understanding of the academic and professional functions and qualifications.

Work aims to go further than common understanding and increased conformity in programs and qualifications. The Bologna Process, according to the OECD, is a good example of this because of its ambition to arrive at comparable and compatible degree structures in the participating countries. Professional recognition arrangements, in particular in the regulated professions, may contribute to increased uniformity in curricula, learning outcomes and qualifications. The OECD points to an increased understanding among international experts and policy-makers that it is of limited value to try to achieve *convergence in the formal input and process characteristics of programs*. The way programs are organized, the delivery mode, the specific teaching and learning setting, even the exact amount of time and workload invested in them, are increasingly diverging, but this divergence does not intrinsically affect the comparability of outcomes. The OECD believes that is of much more use to try to improve the comparability *of learning outcomes*, especially if these are described as competencies that are relevant for academic and professional practice. Descriptions in terms of the learning outcomes and competencies 'may help to determine their commonality, and, hence, contribute to their recognition across countries' (p. 17). Accordingly, recognition agencies, credential evaluators and employers will need to reexamine their assessment criteria and procedures for comparing programs and qualifications in order to accommodate learning outcomes and competencies and not focus only on input and process characteristics.

9. The World Trade Organization and Trade in Services (GATS)

This chapter deals with trade in services. It shows the exports and imports of the higher educational services of eight countries in 1997 and 2000. It discusses the WTO GATS regime. It explains which services in higher education are covered by the GATS, explains how the GATS operates and shows the extent to which WTO member states have engaged in liberalizing this sector. And it presents controversies between protagonists and antagonists of the GATS as well as between the US and the EU.

a. Trade in Higher Education Services: A Rough Estimate (1997–2000)

In 2002, the Organization for Economic Cooperation and Development estimated the size of the international market in higher education services at the end of the 20th century. In 1999 approximately 1.47 million students were studying abroad in OECD countries. The overall market value of this consumption abroad equals around 30 billion US dollars, corresponding roughly to 3 per cent of total trade in services in OECD countries.[32]

Table 9.1 shows the value of exports and imports of higher education services[33] in eight countries in million US dollars and as a percentage of total exports/imports in services in 1997 and 2000, measured as the receipts or payments of foreign students studying abroad (which means that not all educational services are included: see below).[34]

In 2000 the *largest exporter* of these higher education services of the eight countries is the US, followed by the UK and Australia. Growth in exports between 1997 and 2000 is shown by the US, Canada and Venezuela;

---

32 K. Larsen, J.P. Martin and R. Morris, *Trade in Education Services: Trends and Emerging Issues*, Working Paper, May 2002, revised version, p. 10. Available at www.oecd.org, Forum on Trade in Educational Services section.

33 One form of *export* of education services is receiving foreign students; *imports* then refer to nationals studying abroad.

34 Larsen et al., pp. 7-8.

decreases in exports between 1997 and 2000 are shown by the UK, Australia and New Zealand.

In 2000 the *largest importer* of these higher education services is the US, followed by Italy, Canada and Australia. Growth in imports between 1997 and 2000 is shown by the US and Canada; decreases in imports between 1997 and 2000 are shown by the UK, Australia and Venezuela.

Table 9.1: Exports and Imports of Higher Educational Services of Eight Countries in 1997 and 2000

	1997				2000			
	EXPORTS		IMPORTS		EXPORTS		IMPORTS	
Country	US$ million	% total services	US$ million	% total services	US$ million	% total services	US$ million	% total services
United States	8,346	3.5 %	1,396	0.9 %	10,280	3.5 %	2,150	1.0 %
United Kingdom	4,080	4.3 %	182	0.2 %	3,758	3.2 %	150	0.2 %
Australia	2,190	11.8 %	410	2.2 %	2,155	11.8 %	356	2.0 %
Italy	N.A.		N.A.		1,170	2.1 %	849	1.5 %
Canada	595	1.9 %	532	1.4 %	796	2.1 %	602	1.4 %
New Zealand	280	6.6 %	N.A.		199	4.7 %	N.A.	
Poland	16	0.2 %	41	0.7 %	N.A.		N.A.	
Venezuela	4	0.3 %	165	3.0 %	60	4.9 %	113	2.7 %

N.A. = Not available.
Source: K. Larsen, J.P. Martin and R. Morris, *Trade in Education Services: Trends and Emerging Issues*, Working Paper, May 2002, revised version, Tables 1 and 2, pp. 7–8.

Although the United States remains the largest exporter of higher educational services, it must also be noted that the homeland security policies following the 11 September 2001 events are undermining the openness of the American education system to foreign students. Many foreign students, in particular those coming from countries with Islamic populations, have to wait for months in trying to seek visa or to reach their universities in the US. Many of them are seeking for alternative countries. Harvard and other American universities have been complaining about the fact that they are receiving fewer foreign students.

b. The General Agreement on Trade in Services (GATS) of 1994

The increasing importance in education services has caused its incorporation in international trade agreements, both at the regional and the global level. At the global level, the *General Agreement on Tariffs and Trade* (GATT) concluded its successful Uruguay Round in 1994 with its transformation of GATT into the *World Trade Organization* (WTO) and with a special agreement on trade in services, named **General Agreement on Trade in Services (GATS)**.

Which Are the Services in Higher Education Discussed in GATS?

There are four modes in the WTO classification of supplying goods and services across borders: cross-border supply, consumption abroad, commercial presence and presence of natural persons. Focussing on trade in higher education services these four modes provide the following overview:[35]

Mode 1: Cross-border supply. In this case only the service itself crosses the border. It is expected that cross-border supply of educational services will grow rapidly through the use of new information technologies for distance learning, based on cable and satellite transmissions, audio and video conferences, education software, CD-Roms and the Internet. Other examples are virtual education institutions and corporate training through ICT delivery. Initiatives in this area have been launched by private universities and companies.

Mode 2: Consumption abroad. In this case it is the service consumer moving to another country to obtain the service in question. The clearest example is a student travelling abroad to study. As indicated above, international flows of students represent large amounts of money and at present they constitute the largest share of the global market for education services.

Mode 3: Commercial presence. This refers to the commercial establishment of facilities abroad by education providers, such as local branch universities and partnerships with domestic education institutions. Other forms are language training companies and private training companies.

Mode 4: Presence of natural persons. This refers to natural persons travelling to another country on a temporary basis to provide an educational service. Examples are professors, researchers and teachers.

How Does the GATS Operate?

The overall aim of the GATS, according to the preamble, is the expansion of trade in services under conditions of transparency and progressive liberalization as well as promotion of economic growth and development world-wide. It recognizes the needs and rights of governments to regulate in order to meet national policy objectives. It also aims at an increasing participation of developing countries in trade in services, which may be encouraged by reinforcing their domestic services capacity, efficiency and competitiveness.

All WTO member states are bound by the GATS rules. All service sectors are covered by the GATS, with the exception of much of air transport and 'services supplied in the exercise of governmental authority' (Article I.3(b)), by which is meant services 'supplied neither on a commercial basis, nor in competition with one or more service suppliers' (Article I.3(c)).

---

35   Idem, pp. 4–5. Also P. Sauvé, *Trade, Education and the GATS: What's In, What's Out, What's All the Fuss About?*, paper, May 2002, pp. 7–8 (same website).

The GATS consists of *three core components*:

1. a framework of rules that lays out obligations governing trade in services, such as transparency, most-favoured-nation (MFN) treatment, market access and national treatment;
2. annexes on specific services sectors; and
3. schedules of commitments detailing the liberalization commitments by each WTO member state.

For any given service in which a WTO member state chooses to make a *'commitment'*, it can set limitations sector by sector and mode by mode with regard to market access and national treatment commitments (MFN and transparency are general obligations). Article XVI consists of six different types of limitations on market access which must be 'scheduled' if WTO member states wish to maintain them. Article XVII also permits member states to schedule and maintain limitations on non-discrimination. Furthermore a member state can make 'horizontal' restrictions, which refer to all sectors.

Member states may choose the sectors and modes of services they wish to include in their schedules as well as the limitations on market access and national treatment they wish to maintain through so-called 'negotiation rounds'. Negotiations take place in the WTO **Council of Trade in Services** (already mentioned in chapter 3) with a review of progress in the negotiations scheduled.

Commitments and Limitations

In 2002, 42 member states had made *commitments* for at least one education sub sector. There are five sub sectors: 1. primary education; 2. secondary education; 3. higher education; 4. adult education, and 5. other. This makes education, together with the energy and audio-visual sectors, one of the sectors where WTO member states have been least inclined to schedule liberalization commitments. 25 of these 42 member states have included commitments for at least 4 of the 5 education sectors: 30 on primary education, 35 on secondary education, 32 on higher education, 32 on adult education and 20 on 'other'. Among OECD countries 5 member states have made no commitments and two thirds of the OECD countries have made commitments in 4 out of 5 education sectors.

The definition of Education Services in the WTO context is reproduced as Annex 17.

The overall picture with regard to limitations is that WTO member states have chosen to impose considerably more *limitations* on trade in educational services in modes 3 and 4 (commercial presence and presence of natural persons) than in modes 1 and 2 (cross-border supply and consumption abroad). Furthermore member states have in general put slightly more limitations on trade in primary and secondary education than on higher and adult education. Primary and secondary education is regarded as basic schooling in most OECD countries.[36]

c. Negotiations and Controversies on Higher Education and the GATS

The growing importance of trade in services in higher and adult education and anticipated market opportunities have moved some governments to put proposals for further liberalization of trade in these services. Negotiations under the GATS resumed formally in January 2000, according to Article XIX, which provides for successive rounds of negotiations beginning not later than 2000 and periodically thereafter with a view to achieving a progressively higher level of liberalization. Member states are expected to negotiate and continue the process of progressive liberalization by broadening and deepening their liberalization commitments. This means that this GATS round of negotiations is supposed to be completed in January 2005.

In October 1998, the US sent the first communication on education services to the Council for Trade in Services indicating possible areas for future discussion and work.[37] In December 2000, the US sent another communication on higher education, adult education and training, proposing a discussion of various aspects of an open regime in the education and training sector. It includes a list of obstacles in the sector and proposes that WTO member states make commitments, based on the list of obstacles, and that they inscribe in their schedules 'no limitations' on market access and national treatment. In June 2001, New Zealand sent in a communication in favour of further liberalization of trade in education services. Australia sent a negotiating proposal in October 2001, followed by Japan in March 2002. Both are in favour of further liberalization, but Japan also stresses the need to establish measures to maintain and improve the quality of the services through protection of consumers from low quality and ensuring the international equivalence of qualifications. There was no EU proposal and the number of proposals received is rather restricted. This may be an indication that governments, even those in favour of more trade liberalization, prefer to retain their right to determine their own domestic educational policies.

In addition to its communications to the Council for Trade in Services, the US opened a general campaign within the WTO itself in favour of the liber-

---

36 Larsen et al., pp. 11–12.
37 The communications can be found at www.wto.org/english/tratop_e/serv_e/education_e/ education_e.htm.

alization of trade in services, led by US trade representative Robert Zoellick. When he addressed the European Commission, he revealed that the US regarded the European market as rather closed and encouraged it to become more open, the Commission was taken by surprise and did not have an immediate answer.

Switzerland was the only country to send in another Communication. It did so on 18 March 2006.

The NGOs' Joint Declaration against the GATS (2001)

The negotiations and US pressure for further liberalization elicited strong feelings in the educational field. A fierce public debate showed that education is a politically sensitive sector for multilateral trade negotiations. On 28 September 2001, the Association of Universities and Colleges of Canada, the American Council on Education, the European University Association and the Council for Higher Education Accreditation issued a *Joint Declaration on Higher Education and the General Agreement on Trade in Services*. They argued that they are committed to reducing obstacles to international trade in higher education using conventions and agreements outside a trade policy regime, but that their respective countries should not make commitments in higher education services, or in the related categories of adult education and other education services in the context of the GATS. 'Where such commitments have already been made in 1995, no further ones should be forthcoming'. European students, through the ESIB, expressed their doubts about the so-called commodification of education. The two major concerns about liberalization of trade in services, according to Larsen et al., are

1. that the co-existence of public and private services calls into question the status of public services excluded from the scope of the GATS; and
2. that the GATS threatens governments' sovereign rights to regulate and pursue social policy objectives.[38]

Pierre Sauvé of the OECD Trade Secretariat argues that the critical assessments originate in the context of a backlash against globalization and the commercialization that it brings to some activities previously insulated from the market. He believes that much of the public policy debate is rooted in a number of fallacies about the GATS design and operation. Instead of disputing the economic case for open markets, the GATS debate generally focussed on 'the respective roles that the market and the state (as both regulator and direct purveyor of services such as education and health) should be assuming, as well on the threat to national regulatory sovereignty allegedly posed by

---

38   Larsen et al., p. 13.

trade and investment rule-making'.[39] This conclusion is in line with the one by Larsen et al. quoted above.

Attitudes started to change somewhat, as was shown by the vice-chancellor of the university of Ghent in Belgium. As a board member of the European University Association, he tried to explain the resistance to the GATS developments but, in the same speech, while urging caution, he also spoke in favour of the liberalization of trade in services, from a personal perspective. He prefers to describe education in terms of the stakeholder model, 'a delicate set of balances between a number of parties, namely our students, their parents, our staff, government, the working world, and society at large'. This stakeholder model should be used in defining the position of the education world with regard to the GATS. In his eyes, the GATS proves the presence of yet another stakeholder in this complicated model, namely the international community. 'It would be unwise and unhealthy to ignore this new stakeholder, but it would be equally unwise to allow this new stakeholder to define the other balances'.[40]

No EU Commitments in Education

The European Commission discussed trade in services. In February 2003, European Trade Commissioner Pascal Lamy announced that the EU is much in favour of the internationalization of trade in services, but also proposed no commitments in education and health services. This means that the Commission will not further commit these sectors to the free market rules of the GATS.

When the WTO ministerial conference took place in Cancún, Mexico in September 2003, the GATS was not a key agenda item. The meeting in Cancún was foreseen as a decisive half-way point in the Doha Development Agenda, which was agreed at the ministerial conference in Doha, Qatar in November 2001. The Doha Development Agenda proposes both further market liberalization and additional rule-making, underpinned by commitments to take measures necessary to integrate developing countries into the world trading system. The Cancún meeting, however, failed to agree on any of the issues as a result of coalitions formed by development countries. It took until July 2004 before WTO members agreed on a scheme for further negotiations, also for trade in services. Now member states are requested to make more commitments and to improve their offers before 1 May 2005. Negotiations in the light of reciprocity will refine the offers until the next WTO ministerial conference in Hong Kong in December 2005.

---

39 Sauvé, p.14; see the same page for his refutation of the fallacies.
40 A. Oosterlinck, *Trade in Educational Services: A European Union Perspective*, paper, May 2002, p. 8 (at the OECD website).

In a speech in December 2003, US Trade Representative Robert Zoellick had identified education and training as one of the four key priorities of the US in the GATS negotiations. He argued that the biggest barriers to trade in education and training services are rules that prevent for-profit companies from operating training programs or providing for-profit education in some countries. But when, in January 2005, the new European Trade Commissioner, Peter Mandelson, submitted requests for improved market access for services, he declared that the EU does not seek commitments that would dismantle or undermine public services. Only the US receives a request on higher education services, but this is limited to privately-funded education services.

10. The World Bank and Higher Education in Developing Countries

This chapter discusses the World Bank, a specialized organization of the United Nations that originated from the 1944 Bretton Woods Conference. It is concerned with long-term project and economic development finance. During the 1990s the World Bank went through a learning process and adapted its main policies towards higher education in developing countries.

a. The World Bank's 1994 Position: Lessons of Experience

Since 1963, the *International Bank for Reconstruction and Development* (IBRD), better known as the *World Bank*, has been active in supporting the growth and diversification of tertiary education systems in developing countries and in promoting essential policy reforms to make the sector more efficient and relevant. During the early 1990s the World Bank began a study on higher education in developing countries in order to draw lessons from recent experience. In 1994, the World Bank published its report *Higher Education: The Lessons of Experience,*[41] in which it examined the main dimensions of the higher education crisis in developing countries. Facing shrinking budgets, higher education was in crisis throughout the world, but the crisis was most acute in the developing world, where fiscal adjustments had been harsher than in the developed world. And, given their relatively low enrolment ratios, it had been more difficult for developing countries to contain pressures for enrolment expansion. This resulted in a dramatic compression of per-student expenditures since the late 1970s. In Sub-Saharan Africa, for instance, these expenditures decreased from an average of 6,300 US dollars in 1980 to 1,500 US dollars in 1988. Simultaneously, higher education in most developing countries had been the fastest growing segment of the education system during the past twenty years, with female enrolment rates growing faster than male enrolment rates. Whereas various developed countries responded to the funding crisis of higher education by introducing innovative policies aimed at increasing the efficiency of higher education and

---

41 To be found at the website www1.worldbank.org/education/tertiary/publications.asp.

stimulating greater private funding, most developing countries were unable to begin such educational reform.

In its *Lessons of Experience* the World Bank followed developments in the developed world and discerned four key directions for higher education reform in developing countries:

1. encouraging greater differentiation of institutions, including the development of private institutions;
2. providing incentives for public institutions to diversify sources of lending, including cost-sharing with students, and linking government funding closely to performance;
3. redefining the role of government in higher education; and
4. introducing policies explicitly designed to give priority to quality and equity objectives.

Reflecting on its own experiences, the World Bank concluded that some of its past investments had been based on a narrow manpower rationale. Those projects were mainly directed toward individual institutions and did not focus sufficiently on sectoral policy issues. World Bank projects had proved most successful where they helped shape a coherent sub-sectoral development program, supported the implementation of policy reforms and investments, and supported the development of a national scientific training and research infrastructure as well as industrial capacity.

Although higher education investments are important for economic growth, the World Bank also stressed that there is evidence that higher education investments have lower social rates of return than investments in primary and secondary education, and that investments in basic education can also have more direct impact on poverty reduction. These insights are reflected in World Bank's higher education policies for developing countries: 'primary and secondary education will continue to be the highest priority subsectors in the Bank's education lending to countries that have not yet achieved universal literacy and adequate access, equity, and quality at the primary and secondary levels. In these countries, our involvement in higher education will continue to be mainly to make its financing more equitable and cost-effective, so that primary and secondary education can receive increased attention at the margin' (p. 12).

Reform of higher education by strategies for mobilizing greater private financing through cost-sharing and the promotion of private institutions, will help developing countries to free up some of the incremental public resources needed to improve quality and access at the primary and secondary levels, according to the World Bank. Its lending policy for higher education focussed on support for countries' efforts to adopt policy reforms that will allow the subsector to operate more efficiently and at lower public cost. The World Bank's lending for higher education thus remained restricted to those countries prepared to adopt a higher education policy framework 'that stresses a differentiated institutional structure and diversified resource base, with greater emphasis on private providers and private funding' (p. 13).

b. The World Bank/UNESCO Task Force on Higher Education and Society (2000)

Learning processes by international institutions in the sense of questioning original implicit theories underlying its programs and projects are rare but, in the field of higher education during the 1990s, the World Bank provides such an example. World Bank contributed to the UNESCO Conference on Higher Education in the 21st century in 1998, and acknowledged that some exiting changes had taken place in higher education, such as a trend toward mass higher education and a growing governmental interest in establishing policy mechanisms to ensure quality and accountability in higher education. The World Bank representatives argued that concerted international action was needed in order to find solutions that are consistent throughout the world.[42] The learning process resulted in a World Bank report, issued in 2002, with a vision completely different from the 1994 report discussed above.

The World Bank and UNESCO set up a **Task Force on Higher Education and Society**. It brought together education experts from 13 countries to explore the future of higher education in the developing world. The background of this Task Force was the understanding the World Bank had gained that the world economy is changing as knowledge supplants physical capital as the source of present and future wealth. Information technology, biotechnology and other innovations are leading to remarkable changes in the way people live and work. And as knowledge becomes more important, so does higher education. 'Countries need to educate more of their young people to a higher standard; a degree is now a basic qualification for many skilled jobs. The quality of knowledge generated within higher education institutions, and its accessibility to the wider economy, is becoming increasingly critical to national competitiveness', according to the Task Force.[43]

The new understanding poses a challenging to the developing world, where many governments and international donors have assigned higher education a relatively low priority since the 1980s. The Task Force now speaks about a narrow and misleading economic analysis, because economists have tended to measure only increases in earnings, rather than the contribution that highly educated people make as economic and social entrepreneurs, and

---

42 E. El-Khawas, R. DePietro-Jurand and L. Holm-Nielsen, *Quality Assurance in Higher Education: Recent Progress; Challenges Ahead*, Working Paper, World Bank, October 1998, available at the World Bank website.

43 At its website www.tfhe.net/report/downloads/summary_of_findings.htm.

leaders and representatives of their countries on the world stage. This economic analysis has contributed to the view that public investment in universities and colleges brings meagre returns compared to investment in primary and secondary schools, and that higher education magnifies income inequality. The Task Force stressed that urgent action to expand the quantity and improve the quality of higher education in developing countries should be a top development priority. Developing countries need higher education to provide increasing numbers of students, especially those from disadvantaged backgrounds, with specialized skills.

This new vision is reflected in the report that the World Bank published in February 2000 for the Task Force on Higher Education and Society under the title *Higher Education in Developing Countries: Peril and Promise*. The report asks three questions:

1. What is the role of higher education in supporting and enhancing the process of economic and social development?;
2. What are the major obstacles that higher education faces in developing countries?; and
3. How can these obstacles best be overcome?

The answer to the first question is that higher education supports development by promoting income growth, encouraging enlightened leadership, expanding choices and increasing relevant skills. These benefits are not automatic but are linked to the character of higher education systems and institutions and the broader social, economic and political systems within which they are situated. Major obstacles are the absence of vision, a lack of political and financial commitment, conditions of initial disadvantage and the disruptions of globalization. According to the Task Force, higher education must overcome formidable impediments if it is to realize its potential contribution to society. Some of these are determined by external forces of considerable power and must be taken as given (for instance, demographic change, fiscal stringency and the knowledge revolution), others can be removed or mitigated (for instance, ineffective management of higher education). The problems facing higher education are not insurmountable because existing resources can be used more efficiently. Countries that continue to neglect higher education will tend to become increasingly marginalized in the world economy, whereas progress is most likely in countries that develop a clear vision of what higher education can contribute to public interest, according to the task force. 'Piecemeal fixes must be avoided in favour of a holistic approach, focusing on the complementary and mutually reinforcing nature of a range of possible solutions' (p. 92).

The recommendations of the Task Force fall into two main categories: increasing resources and improving the efficiency with which resources are used. It is argued that governments need to develop a new role as supervisors

of higher education, rather than directors. They should concentrate on establishing the parameters within which success can be achieved, while allowing
specific solutions to emerge from the creativity of higher education professionals. The areas where immediate practical action is needed are (pp. 11–12):

1. **Funding**. The Task Force suggests a mixed funding model to maximize
   the financial input of the private sector, philanthropic individuals and institutions, and students. It also calls for more consistent and productive
   public funding mechanisms.
2. **Resources**. The Task Force makes practical suggestions for the more effective use of physical and human capital, including an urgent plea for
   access to the new technologies needed to connect developing countries to
   the global intellectual mainstream.
3. **Governance**. The Task Force proposes a set of principles of good governance and discusses tools that promote their implementation. Better
   management will lead to the more effective deployment of limited resources.
4. **Curriculum development**. This must take place in two contrasting areas,
   on the one hand science and technology, and on the other general education. The Task Force believes that, in the knowledge economy highly
   trained specialists and broadly educated generalists will be at a premium,
   and that they continue to learn as their environment develops.

c. The World Bank on Constructing Knowledge Societies (2002)

In 2002, the World Bank published a report *Constructing Knowledge Societies: New Challenges for Tertiary Education*. It replaces the 1994 report
Lessons of Experience and offers an operational framework based on the
Peril and Promise report of the independent World Bank and UNESCO Task
Force on Higher Education and Society published in 2000. The World Bank
indeed recognized the need to embrace a more balanced, holistic approach to
investments and to encourage improvements in the entire lifelong education
system, irrespective of a country's income level. The report emphasizes that
tertiary education can no longer be viewed as a discrete subsector of education. 'Rather, it must be seen as but one critical element that buttresses a
holistic system of education – a system which must become more flexible,
diverse, efficient, and responsive to the knowledge economy' (p. xi).

The new trends emphasized by the World Bank are the emerging role of
knowledge as a major driver of economic development; the appearance of
new providers of tertiary education; the transformation of modes of delivery
as a result of the information and communication revolution; the rise of market forces in tertiary education and the increase in requests from World Bank

clients for financial support for tertiary education reform. The main messages of the new World Bank policies are:

1. Social and economic progress is achieved principally through the advancement and application of knowledge.
2. Tertiary education is necessary for the effective creation, dissemination, and application of knowledge and for building technical and professional capacity.
3. Developing and transition countries are at risk of being further marginalized in a highly competitive world economy because their tertiary education systems are not adequately prepared to capitalize on the creation and use of knowledge.
4. The state has a responsibility to put in place an enabling framework that encourages tertiary education institutions to be more innovative and more responsive to the needs of a globally competitive knowledge economy and to the changing labour market requirements for advanced human capital.
5. The World Bank can assist its client countries by drawing on international experience and mobilizing the resources needed to improve the effectiveness of their tertiary education systems (p. 6).

Although the World Bank met with sympathy for its new policy orientation, there have been criticisms, in particular regarding the value of non-OECD countries' catching up a with knowledge society dominated by the needs of highly developed countries, rather than providing knowledge that is helpful to local needs of developing countries. Another criticism refers to the general problem of 'brain drain', which will be the result of increased student mobility from developing countries to the developed world. And a final problem is the amount of money available, given the fact that only four per cent of the World Bank's budget is destined for education.[44]

d. Quality Assurance and Accreditation in East Asia and the Pacific

A state-of-the-art report on quality assurance and accreditation in higher education in East Asia and the Pacific was given by Marjorie Peace Lenn in a working paper issued in August 2004.[45] She regards quality as an evolving,

---

44 A critical analysis of the World Bank's educational policies in the 20th century can be found in S.P. Heyneman, 'The history and problems of education policy at the World Bank 1960–2000', *International Journal of Educational Development*, 23/3, May 2003, pp. 315–37.
45 Working Paper Series No. 2004-6, available at www1.worldbank.org/education/tertiary/publications.asp. The paper contains descriptions of the national quality assurance bodies in 13 countries in the region.

rather than a steady, concept. Prior to the mass education movement in Europe in the 1990s, external quality review existed essentially in the United States (for all institutions of post-secondary and higher education) and in the United Kingdom (for the polytechnic but not the university sector). According to Peace Lenn, in the last dozen years, the number of countries which have embraced quality assurance as a mode of evaluating the quality of its higher education sector has increased to approximately 60 in every region of the world (p. 4). She describes the purposes of quality assurance as: defining higher education, assisting in reform efforts, providing a basis for future planning, providing a structure for educational improvement, maximizing communication across education and assisting users to make better decisions.

The three primary modes of quality assurance globally are: 1. *assessment* (an evaluation which results in a grade); 2. *audit* (a check on what an institution explicitly or implicitly claims about itself); and 3. *accreditation* (an evaluation of whether an institution qualifies for a certain status and is the primary choice of governments for national systems of quality assurance). Of these three modes the third mode, accreditation, is the most widely used regionally and globally, and the most beneficial for purposes of development and capacity-building. In East Asia and the Pacific, accreditation takes place in 11 countries (Cambodia, China, Hong Kong, India, Indonesia, Japan, South Korea, Malaysia, Mongolia, the Philippines and Vietnam) and Thailand is seeking to join.

In 1991 the **International Network of Quality Assurance Agencies in Higher Education** (INQAAHE) was established as a gauge for the growth of quality assurance in higher education globally. This network started with 20 member countries in 1991 and reached 60 member countries in 2003. Of the 15 major national quality assurance bodies operating in 13 countries in East Asia and the Pacific (25 per cent of all bodies), 12 were founded since 1991 and 11 of them since 1994. The 13 countries include Australia, China, Hong Kong, India, Indonesia, Japan (two institutions), Korea, Malaysia, Mongolia, New Zealand, the Philippines (two institutions), Thailand, and Vietnam, whereas Cambodia has the potential for establishing a national accreditation council.

Of the 15 national quality assurance bodies in the 13 Asian and Pacific countries:

- 12 were founded by governments and three by universities (one Japanese institution, New Zealand and one Philippine institution);
- all but China, Mongolia and Vietnam claim some level of independence or autonomy from government (although the extent of independence can be discussed for one Japanese institution, Korea, one Philippine institution and Thailand);
- government officials sit on, or chair, the national bodies in 7 cases (Australia, China, Korea, Mongolia, one Philippine institution, Thailand and Vietnam); and

- only 3 of the 15 bodies have international members or reviewers (Hong Kong, one Japanese institution, and New Zealand) (pp. 15–16).

The INQAAHE network's offices move every few years, but are expected to become more permanent in the near future. On 18 January 2003, the **Asia Pacific Quality Network** was formed by a vote of the members meeting at a regional conference in Hong Kong. Six areas of priority were identified and project committees assigned:

1. compilation of quality indicators;
2. gathering and dissemination of information on quality assurance agencies in the region;
3. compilations of information on national qualifications frameworks;
4. facilitation of regional training and development workshops;
5. quality assurance of distance education; and
6. staff exchange and secondment among quality assurance agencies.

Another regional network to be mentioned is related to the *Association of South East Asian Nations* (ASEAN). In 1995, the ten member states of ASEAN,[46] which as a trade bloc is in favour of an ASEAN Free Trade Area, developed an **ASEAN University Network** (AUN). The general objective of AUN is to strengthen the existing network of cooperation among universities in ASEAN by promoting collaborative studies and research programs on the priorities identified by ASEAN. Specific objectives are to promote collaboration and solidarity among scientists and scholars in the member states, to develop academic and professional human resources in the region, and to produce and transmit scholarly knowledge and information to achieve ASEAN goals. In 2000, AUN began an initiative focussing on quality assurance as 'an instrument for maintaining, improving and enhancing teaching, research and overall institutional academic standards of higher education of AUN member universities while recognizing and respecting the differences among member universities in their institutions and environment' (quoted by Peace Lenn, p. 19). Three workshops have since developed common quality assurance policies and criteria, discussed benchmarking procedures and best practice in teaching and learning. According to Peace Lenn, each country's strongest universities are represented on the AUN, and a total of 17 universities are involved in this project (each country can send two universities). She believes that AUN, although an important initiative, is not yet broad-based enough to have an impact on neighbouring universities and influence national quality assurance systems.

The **South East Asian Ministers of Education Organization** (SEAMEO) based in Bangkok has included quality assurance as a topic in its meetings. At the end of 2002, it discussed a draft proposal on the develop-

---

46 Brunei Darussalam, Cambodia, Indonesia, Lao People's Democratic Republic, Malaysia, Myanmar, Philippines, Singapore, Thailand, Vietnam.

ment of a regional quality assurance framework from 12 participants, representing three countries: Indonesia (3), Thailand (7) and Vietnam (2). It includes a training program sponsored by the Dutch government and calls on the development of a single responsible body to strengthen and maintain quality assurance culture in the region (p. 20).

Within the wider *Asia Pacific Economic Cooperation* (APEC), 21 member states try to enhance economic cooperation with the goal of a free trade agreement in 2020[47]. **APEC Education Centres** have been established in designated universities in member states. An **APEC Education Foundation** was set up through the efforts of South Korea and the US. The activities are not binding, but there is an opportunity for formal deliberation on issues of common concern. Peace Lenn mentions mobility schemes for engineers and architects, promoted by Australia (p. 24).

The association **University Mobility in Asia and the Pacific** (UMAP) was already mentioned in §6.e. This voluntary association of government and non-government representatives in the region has the purpose of achieving enhanced international understanding through increased mobility of university students and staff. UMAP members and their universities are working toward standard arrangements for the recognition of study undertaken by UMAP students and have agreed to pilot a *UMAP Credit Transfer Scheme* (UCTS) in which university participation is voluntary. The objective is to increase student mobility by ensuring that credits are received by students for study undertaken when on exchange with other universities. The *UMAP International Secretariat* is located in Japan (Peace Lenn, p. 25).

Apart from the regional activities mentioned above, both the World Bank and UNESCO should be mentioned. UNESCO sponsored two regional conferences on quality assurance, one in Thailand in November 2000, and another in India in August 2002. And the World Bank began sponsoring projects to support the creation and enhancement of national accreditation bodies in Cambodia and Vietnam in 2002.

---

47 The members are Australia, Brunei Darussalam, Canada, Chile, China, Hong Kong (China), Indonesia, Japan, the Republic of Korea, Malaysia, Mexico, New Zealand, Papua New Guinea, Peru, the Philippines, the Russian Federation, Singapore, Taiwan (China), Thailand, United States, and Vietnam.

Part IV:
The Non-Governmental Organizations

11. The Non-Governmental Organizations

Various non-governmental organizations have played roles in the Bologna Process. Some NGOs anald interest groups deserve more attention.

a. The European University Association (EUA)

This organization has been closely involved in the Bologna Process from the beginning. The **European University Association** (EUA) is the result of a merger between two predecessor organizations, which represented both European universities (CRE: Association of European Universities) and EU national rectors' conferences (Confederation of European Union Rectors' Conferences). On 31 March 2001, the two organizations merged into the EUA, which in 2005 represents some 750 members from 45 countries: higher education institutions, national rectors' conferences, national associations of other higher education institutions, regional and international associations and interuniversity institutions. The EUA regards itself as the main voice of the higher education community in Europe. It upholds the values and principles enshrined in the 1988 *Magna Charta Universitatum* (see §2.a) and aims to promote and safeguard values and the case for university autonomy, to represent higher education and research in policy-making circles, to develop a European dimension in members' activities, to provide information and other relevant services to members, to promote partnerships in higher education and research both within Europe and between Europe and the rest of the world. Its endeavours are guided by the goal of building a common European area for higher education and research. The EUA has two offices, one in Geneva and one in Brussels.[48]

The ministers of education who started the Bologna Process explicitly invited the European universities to participate. The two predecessor organizations committed themselves and, as a result of the Bologna Process, became one larger organization. The EUA sees its role as ensuring the full involvement of the universities at each step in the Bologna Process as the

---

48 Information and documents can be found on its website www.eua.be.

only way of bringing about sustainable reforms and a lasting impact. It organized meetings during or before the ministerial meetings and provided essential information, in particular through the three *Trends* reports (Trends in Learning Structures in Higher Education), which proved to be a solid basis for ministerial discussions. The EUA was granted consultative status in the Bologna Follow-Up Group and has taken an active role in the work program of the Bologna Process. It promotes activities that relate to the Bologna objectives, such as quality assurance, degree structures, mobility, ECTS, recognition of degrees and joint programs.

The Salamanca and Graz Declarations of the EUA

Before the Prague meeting, the two predecessor organizations gathered in Salamanca (29–30 March 2001) in order to prepare their input to the ministerial meeting. The *Salamanca Convention* reaffirmed its support to the principles of the *Bologna Declaration* and its commitment to the creation of the European Higher Education Area by the end of the decade. The major principles mentioned in the message of the Salamanca Convention are autonomy with accountability, education as a public responsibility, research-based higher education and organizing diversity (in terms of languages, national systems, institutional types and profiles and curricular orientation).

In May 2003, the EUA convened in Graz in order to prepare its input to the Berlin ministerial meeting. The *Graz Declaration: 2003 Forward from Berlin: The Role of the Universities to 2010 and beyond* resulting from this meeting contains an agreement on the priorities for the next phase of the Bologna Process. This 28-point declaration seeks to provide a long-term vision for universities and to express their own priorities for the next phase of the Bologna Process. It emphasizes that its main challenge now is to transform the multitude of legislative changes, which have taken place across Europe in the last years, into meaningful academic aims and institutional realities. It goes beyond the specific Bologna Action Lines to look at the wider role of European universities in a global context, how they see themselves and what are their core values. Its components are: 1. maintaining universities as a public responsibility; 2. consolidating research as an integral part of higher education; 3. improving academic quality by building strong institutions; 4. furthering mobility and the social dimension; 5. supporting the development of a policy framework in Europe in quality assurance; and 6. pushing forward the Bologna Process.

The Graz Declaration is reproduced as Annex 18.

The EUA is preparing for the Bergen ministerial meeting in two ways. First, there will be a new *Trends* report (*Trends IV*), which will be a different kind of report from the earlier ones. The EUA believes that its task now is to go more deeply into universities and to find out what is really happening from the point of view of all the stakeholders and actors (students, academic and administrative staff, institutional leaders). While *Trends III* (2003) presented impressions of institutions, the EUA with *Trends IV* wants to test the reality of these reform processes on the ground. This new *Trends* will provide an in-depth look at Bologna reforms. Second, the EUA is meeting in Glasgow on 31 March – 2 April 2005, in order to prepare its *Glasgow Declaration*, which will be presented to the ministerial meeting in Bergen in May. The Glasgow Convention is structured around three axes: 1. the context in which universities function; 2. the multiple mission of the university; and 3. the preconditions that enable institutions to respond to their environment and fulfil their mission. The results of the discussions and the *Trends IV* report will also be fed into the work of the Bologna Follow-Up Group.

b. EURASHE and Professional Higher Education

In some countries, all higher education is provided by the universities in a unitary system. In many European countries, however, the structure of higher education is a binary system, with a university sector and a sector for professional higher education, which includes colleges, polytechnics and universities of professional higher education. **EURASHE (European Association of Institutions in Higher Education)** is an international educational association whose aims include the promotion of the interests of institutions in the sector of professional higher education. During the ministerial meeting in Prague (2001), EURASHE was one of the non-governmental organizations to be consulted in the follow-up work.

EURASHE was established in 1990. It was engaged in setting up a directory of professional higher education institutions and, in 1994, on behalf of the European Commission, it undertook projects on staff mobility, networking, and liaising between higher education and the socio-economic world. It supported the general thrust of the *Bologna Declaration* and *Prague Communiqué* to establish a European Area of Higher Education. It supports the two-cycle Bachelor–Master framework, provided it does not seek to impose a rigid uniform model that would exclude sub-degree studies which have long been recognised as higher education in many European countries. Courses of two-year duration or their part-time equivalents in ECTS credits are an integral part of existing higher education qualification systems and a key element in the enhancement of transfer possibilities towards further study within lifelong learning scenarios. Other issues stressed by EURASHE are employability, lifelong learning and 'diversity versus convergence'. Whereas the *Bologna Declaration* calls for greater convergence in European higher education, EURASHE maintains, with the OECD that learners should be provided with a diversity of learning structures, pathways and programs.[49]

In June 2003 two short policy statements were issued by EURASHE. In a supplementary text, the important characteristics of the sector of professional higher education were described. Central issues are: 1. widening participation, i.e. enlarging the number of students; 2. improving the area of applied research by improving the position of professional higher education in the development and practical application of knowledge in enterprises and public institutions; 3. increasing the international recognition of professional higher education; 4. increasing the funding of professional higher education; and 5. networking with universities. EURASHE argues that networking and partnerships between universities and the sector of professional higher education may lead to convenient transitional programs between the two sectors.[50]

The theme of its annual conference in late April 2005 focusses on EURASHE's present priority areas: university colleges in the Bologna Process: quality culture and applied research.

c. The ESIB National Unions of Students

In 1982 ESIB (**The National Unions of Students in Europe**) was founded as an umbrella organization to represent and promote the educational, social, economic and cultural interests of students at a European level towards all relevant bodies, in particular the European Community, the Council of Europe and UNESCO. In 2005, some 50 national unions from 37 countries are members, representing between 10 and 11 million students. At the UNESCO World Conference on Higher Education in Paris in October 1998, ESIB issued a statement on higher education towards the next century, in which it dealt with the issues of access to higher education, quality of education and students' participation in decision-making at all levels.[51]

In October 1999, ESIB established the **Committee on Prague 2001** (CoP2001) in order to get an overview on what was happening at the European level and to participate in the Bologna Process. The consultative group, created by the *Bologna Declaration,* accepted ESIB as an observer in November 1999. After Prague, where ESIB was invited to an observer in the follow-up process, the Committee on Prague 2001 was transformed into the **Bologna Process Committee** (BPC).

---

49 *EURASHE Policy Statement on the Bologna – Prague – Berlin Process,* May 2002, to be found at the website www.eurashe.be. For the OECD position on the Bologna Process, see §8.d of this book. EURASHE refers to the OECD Report, *Redefining Tertiary Education* (1998).
50 *EURASHE Working Agenda on the Bologna Process,* 23 February 2004.
51 Documents to be found at its website www.esib.org.

ESIB issued statements on practically all issues covered by the Bologna Process. It generally welcomes increasing cooperation in higher education in Europe and supports the idea of a European Higher Education Area. It regards core academic values as the proper basis for cooperation in Europe and as the main driving factors of the creation of the higher education market. The strong focus on the competitiveness of Europe in the world is seen as a double-edged sword. On the one hand, this competitiveness can lead to an increase in quality and transparency, but on the other hand it may further the privatization agenda and brain drain, trends that ESIB clearly and strongly opposes. ESIB therefore welcomed the inclusion of attractiveness and the shift towards a more cooperative approach in the *Prague Communiqué*. ESIB regards an unequivocal commitment to the objectives of the Bologna Process as essential for achieving its aims. The Bologna Process should not be misused to carry out other reforms, which are only on national agendas in the name of the Bologna Process. ESIB condemns the attempts by some governments to hijack the process in favour of these kinds of national reforms. Such hijacking jeopardizes the creation of the Higher Education Area, because stakeholders will oppose the process and the implementation will become difficult. ESIB was also positive about the inclusion of the social dimension and the reaffirmation of higher education as a public good in the *Prague Communiqué*, because these elements counterbalance the economic goals in the Bologna Process.

With regard to the WTO *General Agreement on Trade in Services,* ESIB argues that education is an essential public service benefiting the whole society, which should be provided as a public service free of tuition fees. ESIB rejects the notion of students as consumers. It prefers to regard them as partners in the process of higher education. Rather than paying customers, students should be seen as contributors to the creation of knowledge and as partners for institutions. ESIB opposes the further inclusion of education in the GATS negotiations, and calls upon the EU and governments around the world not to schedule education into the GATS any further, because education should not be covered by an agreement primarily concerned with promoting free trade. ESIB regards higher education as a human right rather than as a privilege.

In March 2005, ESIB issued its *Luxemburg Student Declaration.* It reminds the ministers of education that the Bologna Process measures make sense only if they are taken together. Reforms à *la carte* that would vary from country to country would be meaningless. Because a balance between diversity and common action must be kept, ESIB believes that 'some commitments of participating states have been overlooked so far and should gain more focus in the second part of the original period'. Furthermore, ESIB criticizes the strong focus on the competitiveness of the European Higher Education Area in the world, because that stimulates the commodification process and brain drain, trends that ESIB opposes. It prefers the attractiveness of the European Higher Education Area to be promoted through the principle of sustainable development and through cooperation with other regions of the world.

The document ESIB and the Bologna Process – creating a European Higher Education Area for and with Students (May 2003) is reproduced as Annex 19.

In February 2002, doctoral students founded the **European Council of Doctoral Candidates and Young Researchers** (EURODOC) as a federation of national associations of Ph.D. candidates and young researchers. Its objectives are to represent doctoral students at the European level, to advance the quality of doctoral programs and to promote the circulation of relevant information. EURODOC participated in the Bologna Seminar organized by the Austrian and German Ministries of Education and the EUA in February 2005 in Salzburg.[52]

d. The European Employers (UNICE) and Trade Unions (ETUCE)

European employers fully support the goals of the Bologna Process. The **Union of Industrial and Employers' Confederations of Europe** (UNICE), which regards itself as 'The Voice of Business in Europe', issued a position paper *The Bologna Process. UNICE's Position and Expectations* on 15 October 2004.[53] UNICE considers the goals of the Bologna Process, when implemented, to be a reliable framework for preparing students for professional activities. Transparency and compatibility are important in order to facilitate student mobility, the flexibility of study courses and permeability between the different branches of higher education.

To turn the Bologna Process into a real success, UNICE regards it as crucial that the Bologna objectives and priorities be realized through implementation of measures at both national and institutional levels. It also is indispensable that all stakeholders, including employers, are involved in the three fields of comparable quality requirements, employability of graduates, and high quality student and teacher mobility.

Employers regard the inclusion of business an important prerequisite for successful realization of the Bologna Process. With regard to the ministerial meeting in Bergen in May 2005, UNICE believes that a broad agreement should be achieved on the need to have functioning quality assurance systems in all signatory states, linked to a common framework at European level. It also believes in the need to develop a European qualification framework that

---

52 Its website is www.eurodoc.net.
53 To be found at www.unice.org.

takes into account existing national qualification frameworks, and in concrete measures to increase the international attractiveness of European higher education.

The **European Trade Union Committee for Education** (ETUCE) was established in 1975. It represents 118 teachers' unions in 28 Western European countries and 48 unions in Central and Eastern Europe. **Education International** (EI) represents over one million academic and research staff worldwide, of whom some 400,000 live and work in the member states of the Bologna Process. ETUCE provides a forum for their unions.

In 2003, Education International and ETUCE issued a statement for the Berlin meeting, in which they observed that teachers and research workers have mostly been left out of the Bologna Process. As the result of a conference in February 2005, Education International issued a *Policy Statement on the Bologna Process in the 'Bergen' Round*, in which it once again expressed great concern at the lack of direct representation of the voice of academic and research staff within the Bologna Process.[54] The higher education and research staff unions of Europe welcome and support the Bologna Process as a means of protecting and enhancing higher education and research across Europe, and increasing transparency and mobility. They believe that the Bologna Process acknowledges the place within the public domain, and welcome the emphasis on quality, but assert that this will require a greater public investment in the system and its staff if quality is to be sustained, let alone enhanced.

Education International attaches great importance to the issue of representation, because academic staff and researchers are essential to the higher education and research community, and must be involved in the Bologna Process through their representative organizations. It argues that their lack of representation stands in stark contrast to the involvement of students' organizations. This is not to begrudge the involvement of students, but to call for the involvement of staff and researchers as essential to the transitions called for by the Bologna Process. This means that they should be accorded at least equal treatment with the students.

e. The International Association of Universities (IAU)

Quality in higher education across borders is also discussed at the global level. The **International Association of Universities** (IAU), founded in 1950, is the UNESCO-based worldwide association of universities, which brings together institutions and organizations from 150 countries. In 2004, it issued *Sharing Quality Higher Education Across Borders: A Statement on*

---

54 Available at www.bologna-bergen2005.no.

Behalf of Higher Education Institutions Worldwide.[55] It discusses *two main trends*: 1. the growing imperative of higher education institutions to internationalize; and 2. the growth of market-driven activities. The second trend and the complex issues it raises provided the impetus for the statement. The statement is based on the belief that market forces alone are inadequate to ensure that cross-border education contributes to the public good. It set forth eight principles for cross-border higher education, as well as recommendations for higher education institutions and other providers, plus recommendations to governments.

Under the recommendations to governments, it is said that some governments seek to manage cross-border higher education through multilateral and regional trade regimes designed to facilitate the flow of private goods and services. According to the IAU, there are *three main limitations* to that approach. First, trade frameworks are not designed to deal with the academic, research, or broader social and cultural purposes of cross-border higher education. Second, trade policy and national education policy may conflict with each other and jeopardize higher education's capacity to carry out its social and cultural mission. Third, applying trade rules to complex national higher education systems designed to serve the public interest may have unintended consequences that can be harmful to this mission.

The IAU has also been engaged in efforts to discuss higher education from the perspective of 'sustainable development'. In 2001, various private organizations and UNESCO issued the *Lüneburg Declaration on Higher Education for Sustainable Development*. Referring to the Plan of Implementation of the Earth Summit in Johannesburg (2002) and the UN Decade on Education for Sustainable Development 2005–2014, the various organizations proposed three recommendations for a Sustainable Bologna. The first proposal is on implementation of the UN Decade in Europe by using public means in favour of a sustainable development. The second proposal is on renewing teaching and learning in accordance with sustainable curricula and training methods. And the final proposal refers to sustainable institutional management in higher education, which is economically most affordable because it contributes to efficient resource mobilization. Keyconcepts in this approach are environmental protection, sustainable consumption patterns, an ecological lifestyle and environmentally responsible behaviour.[56]

---

55 See www.unesco.org/iau/p_statements/index.html.
56 *Sustainable Bologna. Proposal for the Implementation of the Education for Sustainable Development in the frame of the Bologna-Process*, by Copernicus-Campus, GHESP and WWF, available through www.bologna-bergen2005.no.

12. European Political Science and Public Administration

This chapter discusses networks and organizations in the fields of political science, international relations and public administration, in particular their position in the Bologna Process. It provides experience from the perspective of an academic discipline.

a. The European Political Science Network (epsNet)

In 1996, a **Thematic Network in Political Science** (TNPS) was set up. The main reason for its creation was to define and develop a European dimension within the broad field of political science and international relations through cooperation between different university faculties and departments, and academic associations all over Europe. The first partners addressed were the ICPs (Interuniversity Cooperation Projects) created by the Erasmus program of the European Commission, which allowed the network to profit from their experience in transnational cooperation. A first aim of this new cooperation was the collection of different curricula in political science in order to get an overview, to identify examples of good practice and to establish criteria to assess and promote quality in teaching. A second aim was the promotion and harmonization of ECTS in the field, which was to result in mutual recognition of curricula and further transnational cooperation. The Thematic Network received financial support from the European Commission and the Fondation Nationale des Sciences Politiques in Paris for such projects as Teaching Political Science, Political Science in Central and Eastern Europe and Political Science PhDs in Europe.

The Thematic Network and the ECPR (**European Consortium for Political Research**)[57] set up a directory of political science in Western Europe and in 2000 the Thematic Network began a directory of political science in

---

57   The ECPR was set up in 1970 by political science departments, and became the leading European organization in political science, but restricts itself mostly to research by providing an infrastructure for scholars to discuss their research. Its Western European base is stronger than its Eastern one.

Central and Eastern Europe. Various plenary conferences brought political scientists from all over Europe together. The first conference took place in Paris, France in 1998, the second one in Leiden, The Netherlands in 1999 and the third in Hamburg, Germany in 2000. In Hamburg it was decided to further institutionalize the thematic network and to create a new permanent organization in Europe devoted to the teaching of political science and the development of the profession. This became the **European Political Science Network** (epsNet), which in its name still has the word 'network'. EpsNet continued the tradition of annual conferences (in 2002 in Krakow, Poland; in 2003 in Paris; in 2004 in Prague, Czech Republic; in 2005 in Paris) and created projects on themes such as professional development, graduate education and labour market, gender issues, quality of political science teaching, ICT in political science teaching, development of political science and teaching Europe. It set up a website, began to publish reports and to issue its electronic journal *Kiosk Plus, THE NET Journal of Political Science.*[58] In 2002, an Interim Committee was replaced by an elected Executive Council. Membership came from both Eastern and Western Europe. A new program with five projects was created and financially supported by the European Commission, EPISTEME: Enhancing Political Science Teaching Quality and Mobility in Europe.

Doctoral students hold a special position within epsNet, because they are considered essential for the future development of the profession. They elect two members of the Executive Council and have their own section on the website and in *Kiosk Plus*, called Nethesis. This allows them to develop their own issue-oriented networks and projects. Their publications in *Kiosk Plus* are blindly refereed in order to support their CVs. During plenary conferences doctoral students have the opportunity to visit special workshops to discuss their experiences of teaching and to learn from more experienced teachers. The results will be visible in a series 'Teaching Political Science'.

b. The European Conference of Chairs of National Associations of Political Science (ECNA)

In November 1999, during a joint conference of the ECPR, the Thematic Network and the chairs of national political science associations in Siena, the chairs decided to found the **European Conference of Chairs of National Associations of Political Science** (ECNA). Things being as they were, the chairs were not going to establish a European association of associations, but decided to have an informal coordination among the chairs, which they called ECNA. This conference will have a rotating coordinator and will take advantage of other meetings, such as those of the ECPR and epsNet. In their

---

58 An overview of publications can be found at the website www.epsnet.org.

meetings the elected chairs of the national associations of political science discuss aspects and problems of the profession, of research, teaching and of jobs including a watching brief on, and cooperation with, the ECPR and epsNet.

Suggestions in 2000 and 2001, regarding the establishment of a European Association of Political Science Associations (EPSA) never materialized, given that ECPR and epsNet functioned as complementary institutions with a division of labour for research and education and the lack of means to set up another institution. However, Central European political science associations in 2000 founded the **Central European Association of Political Science Associations** (CEPSA), following a seven-year tradition of annual conferences.

Implementing the Bologna Process

In March 2002, epsNet and ECPR were invited to attend a meeting of the European Conference of National Political Science Associations in Torino. The consequences of implementing the *Bologna Declaration* in European political science constituted the major item on the agenda. It was agreed that a short stimulus paper should be drafted to kick off a broader discussion at the ECPR 2003 Edinburgh meeting. In early 2003, former ECNA president Klaus Armingeon and epsNet president Hans-Dieter Klingemann suggested a text as a starting point. Their discussion paper *Implementing the Bologna Declaration* did not reflect any formal positions of ECNA or epsNet. The Executive Council of epsNet discussed the topic as well, and agreed on a statement called *The Bologna Declaration and Political Science Curriculum*. The result of the debates following these texts was an ECNA document sketching out the basic requirements of a Bachelor of Arts (BA) in Political Science in Europe. This document was supported by both ECPR and epsNet. The heart of this recommendation is that students studying for a degree in political science, e.g. a BA in political science of 180 ECTS credits, should follow courses in political science of at least 90 ECTS credits. These courses should be taken from a list of core subject areas, which are mentioned in the text. In September 2003 the acting secretary of ECNA sent the recommendations to the participants at the Berlin ministerial meeting in order to inform them about the feelings within the profession. The use of the text, however, is not only political, but also practical. Political science departments have used the recommendations as a European benchmark from within the discipline itself, when reporting to quality assurance or accreditation institutions.

The three documents (The Armingeon/Klingemann text, the epsNet Executive Council Statement and the ECNA Recommendations) are reproduced as Annexes 20-22.[59]

---

59 The first two documents were published in *epsNet Kiosk Plus, THE NET Journal of Political Science*, Vol. I, no. I, June 2003, pp. 54–58; the third one in Vol. I, no. 2, November 2003, pp. 55–56.

There are no relevant relations between epsnet or ECNA with organized students of political science. In 1998, political science students established the **International Association for Political Science Students** (IAPSS), which functions as an information network. It started as an association in Europe, but attracted additional associations from Africa, Central America, and later North and Latin America and Asia. Its orientation is worldwide rather than European. There is no engagement with the Bologna Process.[60]

c. Public Administration Networks and Accreditation

The aim of the **European Public Administration Network** (EPAN) is to stimulate and promote Europeanization in teaching Public Administration. EPAN itself was founded in 1997 to follow up the Interuniversity Cooperation Projects of the Erasmus Program. When the European Commission shifted from the multilateral Erasmus regime to the bilateral Socrates regime, EPAN nearly collapsed. Another thematic network, however, saved it. The **Thematic Network in Public Administration** (TN-PA), which to a large extent has the same participants as EPAN, was supported by the Socrates program and coordinated by the University of Limerick. This TN-PA started a comprehensive inventory of public administration programs, which pointed out the lack of response by public administration programs to the increasing Europeanization of their field of study. As a result, the network developed a strategy for the Europeanization of higher education programs. It started various working groups on teaching materials, ICT in teaching and accreditation. With regard to the last issue, the network forged links with an accreditation project at the University of Twente in the Netherlands to address the problems of accreditation and standardization and their impact on the prospects for the Europeanization of teaching programs in public administration.

During the years 1997—2000, the Thematic Network in Public Administration and the Thematic Network in Political Science were part of a *Joint Thematic Network in Political Science and Public Administration*. This reflected the preference of the European Commission, but when the Commission understood that the networks of political science and public administration had different purposes, it accepted the dissolution of the Joint Thematic Network.

The two networks of public administration continued to exist, but the best way to describe their symbiosis is that EPAN incorporated the TN-PA and has built on the results produced by the Thematic Network. EPAN provides public administration departments a platform for exchange of information and facilitates the development of the European dimension through interuni-

---

60 The website can be found at www.iapss.org.

versity cooperation. Its objectives are to develop and improve the European dimension in public administration curricula, to stimulate the exchange of students and teachers, to increase the transferability of credits, to promote better links with the profession and to assist teaching institutions in representing their interests before national and EU institutions.[61]

Accreditation of Public Administration Programs

The accreditation project at the University of Twente, linked with a working group of the TN-PA, resulted in the **European Association of Public Administration Accreditation** (EAPAA). EAPAA was founded in 1999. The accreditation criteria and procedures developed by the EAPAA were discussed, evaluated and disseminated within the TN-PA during its first phase. The first round of accreditation started in 2001 and was concluded in 2002. By now four master programs of public administration have been accredited by EAPAA (two in the Netherlands, one in Sweden and one in Ukraine).[62]

The Thematic Network continues to support EAPAA in addressing problems of accreditation and quality improvement, and in 2003 set up a working group to develop a methodology to understand curricula and to make them comparable by approaching generic competences, subject-specific competences, the role of ECTS, and the role of learning, teaching, assessment and performance in relation to quality assurance and evaluation.

---

61 EPAN's website is to be found at http://bl.ul.ie/epan/.
62 EAPAA's website is to be found at http://bbt.utwente.nl/eapaa/.

13. Conclusion

This book contains the main events and documents on the Bologna Process plus related developments in other international organizations. All of them are relevant, because together they will define the rules for the universities of the 21st century in Europe. Given the fact that higher education has become a worldwide issue, traded to a certain extent on an international market, European politics should not be regarded as just a regional phenomenon, but rather as part of a larger, global process.

a. The Changing Context: The Worldwide Education Market

The rise of the worldwide education market is an intriguing phenomenon, because education generally is seen as a *national* public good. However, since the end of the last century, a shift in higher education has taken place from the public to the private domain, parallel to an increase in international trade in education services such as increasing student and staff mobility, international marketing of curricula, entrepreneurship by universities and the use of modern means of communication. These developments enhance the significance of the education market as an international institution, but also contribute to changing the structure of that market. In doing so, an increase in worldwide competition is being revealed.

Since regulation of international markets is a matter for governments and intergovernmental organizations, we may expect that such changes and their consequences for existing regulations and systems are discussed in international arenas. The World Trade Organization (WTO) and – given the fact that education is a service – its Council for Trade in Services are good indicators for revealing changes that are taking place. The Organization for Economic Cooperation and Development (OECD), UNESCO, the specialized organization of the United Nations in the field of education, and the International Bank for Reconstruction and Development (World Bank) are other international arenas where such changes are being recognized, not in the least because of the capacity of these organizations to provide statistical and other data which are most relevant for policy analysis and decision-making. The regulations and standard-setting activities of these intergovernmental organi-zations are meant to facilitate cross-border activities in the fields of higher education.

Higher education has become more important than before because of what now is known as the 'knowledge society' or 'knowledge economy'. Knowledge about almost all natural, technical and social processes is more relevant than ever. Education, and in particular higher education, plays a cru-cial role in fostering economic growth. This means that we may expect governments to take initiatives aimed at promoting education in general and higher education and professional training in particular. At the end of the last century this happened in Asian countries, which began to make substantial provisions for higher education in their development plans. To a certain ex-tent this was done internally by widening and enhancing national education systems, but more often by sending students abroad, expecting that these stu-dents will return and contribute to the further development of the country (those who do not return contribute to the 'brain drain'). This is also true, be it to a lesser extent, of Latin America, the Arab world and Africa.

European countries such as France, Germany and the United Kingdom have been big players on the international education market, but only if the three are taken together, they are – in the early 1990s – as strong as the world leader, the United States of America (see Table 3.1). Their orientation to-wards Asia, which was becoming an interesting source of students, was weak in comparison to the US. In line with its policies to favour more free trade and less protectionism, the US began pushing for more competition on the international education market. During the mid-1990s this became a topic in the Uruguay Round of the GATT in the context of trade in services and in the newly founded WTO. During the WTO meeting in Seattle (late 1999), the US surprised the European Commission by arguing that Europe was too protec-tionist on the international higher education market.

b. The Bologna Process in Europe

These international trends must be taken into account when discussing the Bologna Process, initiated in 1998 by the ministers of education of France, Germany, Italy and the United Kingdom. It is difficult to tell whether domes-tic or international politics dominated their decision to fundamentally change the structure of higher education in Europe by introducing a policy of har-monization. But it must be noted that domestic problems with their existing higher education systems have indeed played a role in their initiative. Expan-sion of the numbers of students and the necessary adaptation of their institutions plus related financial costs are the essence of these domestic problems. Resistance to changes to educational systems also played a role, as in France, where the minister of education was the first to initiate an international approach. Seen from a global perspective, the changes in the international context at the time seem to have provided a window of opportunity for the creation of domestic changes.

That the four ministers of education tried to find an international, rather than a national, solution for their higher education problems, is obvious given the international character of the education market and the emerging knowledge society. Striking, however, is that these major powers of the European Union did not try to find a solution within the EU but a pan-European solution by also inviting non-EU members to Paris and Bologna. The main reason for this must be the EU's restricted authority in the field of education, but it also refers to a strategic vision if one opts for a pan-European solution. The pan-European option did not prevent the ministers of education from using EU experience in transnational cooperation in the fields of vocational training and higher education, resulting from such Community programs as Erasmus and Socrates. But the ministers explicitly did not restrict themselves to the EU, nor did they put the matter in the hands of the European Commission, which later became an additional member of the otherwise strictly intergovernmental Bologna Process.

The instrument chosen for finding, and later implementing, a common solution is another interesting aspect of the Bologna Process. The ministers opted for a traditionally 19th-century model of a multilateral conference aimed at a written international agreement and extended by follow-up conferences for further decision-making and monitoring the implementation of common decisions. After the original meeting in Bologna, prepared the year before at the Sorbonne in Paris, follow-up conferences took place in Prague, Berlin and Bergen. Just as the development of multilateral conferences in the 19th century showed, we may observe an evolutionary process (rounds of decision making, or incrementalism) and a process of institutionalization (which in the 19th century led to the rise of public international unions, the predecessors of the intergovernmental organizations of the 20th century). The Bologna Process shows *ad hoc* follow-up conferences, but these are taking place at more or less regular intervals. There is a process of codification, given the requirements and procedures for joining the Bologna Process by those few European countries which are not yet members (see *Annex 9*). A Secretariat was created by the Berlin meeting. Although this still is a secretariat provided by the country hosting the next ministerial meeting, it can be expected that a more permanent secretariat will be needed by the time the Bologna Process will be monitoring the implementation of its regulations more precisely and more regularly. And that time will come.

By the time the Secretariat becomes permanent, the Bologna Process will meet the three official criteria for an intergovernmental organization: three or more member states, a permanent secretariat and a formal instrument of agreement between the governments of the member states. The formal instrument of agreement in this case is the *Bologna Declaration* of 1999. Seen from a judicial perspective, the declaration is indeed an instrument of agreement, but compared to modern resolutions or international conventions, its form is rather poor. Yet, a poor judicial form does not prevent states from intergovernmental cooperation, as was the case at multilateral conferences in the 19th century.

c. NGOs in the Bologna Process

Being an intergovernmental process on a pan-European scale, with by now essential action lines (a total of ten), it must be noted that the ministers of education have engaged some non-governmental organizations in the Bologna Process. Organizations representing the universities, both academic and professional, and students, have been explicitly invited by the ministers of education. Later they were granted official observer status. Organizations of the academic staff, teachers and researchers, however, have not been engaged, as was expressed by the European trade unions (see §11.d).

The 19th-century model of a multilateral conference was indeed based on a relatively open conference with regard to influence by private or non-governmental organizations. This meant that NGOs took the liberty of lobbying intergovernmental conferences. Even if not invited, they arrived with the aim of influencing official decision-making, either indirectly through public opinion or more directly by presence, lobbying and circulating ideas and solutions. Their engagement often resulted in recognition and, later, a consultative status. The Bologna Process, however, seems to rely on the invitation of a restricted number of relevant groups by the ministers, rather than granting an official consultative or observer status to all interested and qualified NGOs, as is the case in the UN, the Council of Europe and also in interest representation in the EU. This does not mean that organizations of staff are not able to send in their comments or visions but they are not recognized as official observers.

d. The EU and the Bologna Process

The relationship between the intergovernmental and pan-European Bologna Process on the one hand and the European Union on the other is a remarkable one, because, by tradition, education in the EU has been a topic of subsidiarity rather than supranationalism. The EU, however, has contributed to the Bologna Process in a very practical way. This is understandable, because EU machinery functions in the field of education, in particular the European Commission and its Directorate General for Education and Culture (rather than the Directorate General for Research). The Commission has contributed to the Bologna Process both financially, for such practical matters as *Trends* reports and rapporteurs, and as an expert relying on its experience from multilateral and bilateral cooperation under programs such as Erasmus and Socrates.

The engagement in the Bologna Process in fact enlarged the EU commitment to the field of higher education, compared with the period of the 1980s and 1990s, when education to a large extent remained a national issue. Although the Bologna Process also increased the Commission's engagement, the direction of the Bologna Process as initiated by the four ministers of education and the main orientation of the EU in this field have remained intergovernmental by nature. EU policies on the knowledge society, plus the Lisbon and Barcelona ambitions, are not the products of the Commission but of the European Council.

e. Intergovernmental Organizations and Higher Education

Some major aspects of the Bologna Process are discussed in both the EU and other intergovernmental organizations. Quality assurance and accreditation are discussed by ENQA, the European Association for Quality Assurance in Higher Education, which was set up in 2000 by a Council decision, and by UNESCO and the OECD. Recognition of academic qualifications is on the agenda of the EU NARIC network, but this network cooperates closely with the ENIC network of the Council of Europe and UNESCO. In fact, the Council of Europe is the major player in the issue of recognition of qualifications, given the status of its 1997 Lisbon Recognition Convention. The Council of Europe has further contributed to the Bologna Process by being a bridge between member states and non-member states. UNESCO and the OECD are engaged in the discussion of quality provision in cross-border higher education. Their perspective in this respect does not originate from academic institutions but from consumers of higher education. The OECD does not agree with the Bologna Process's ambition to enhance convergence of programs and qualifications, but instead favours diversification and comparability of learning outcomes rather than input and process characteristics.

At the beginning of this century, the discussion in the WTO Council for Trade in Services marked time. The debate was hindered by the troubles the WTO experienced when, in 1999, anti-globalist demonstrators succeeded in disturbing the normal WTO proceedings, but also by the consequences of the events of 9/11. In 2003, the European Union, which in the WTO context is represented by the European Commission, announced that it is in favour of a further internationalization of trade in services, but not in the field of education. Given the present situation in the US, where restrictive immigration practices have complicated the exchange of students and staff, it can be expected that this stasis will continue for a while. In the long run, however, the GATS discussion will be resumed. If the Bologna Process and the EU achieve progress in their ambitions, they may place Europe in a stronger position on the worldwide market in relation to the United States.

f. Asian Consciousness of Higher Education Salience

If the Bologna Process is to be successful worldwide, given the global character of the education market, it seems relevant to take note of what is going on elsewhere, not only in Asia, but also in Central and Latin America and in Africa. This global orientation was recognized by the World Bank, which at first did not give policy priority to higher education in developing countries. During the late 1990s, however, the World Bank went through a learning process, and in 2002 reached the conclusion that in the context of the knowledge society, higher education is also essential for developing countries.

Of all regions outside Europe, Asian countries seem to be most aware of this. Comparing Asia and Europe shows that quality assurance, accreditation and a credit transfer system have also been issues for discussion by regional networks and organizations in Asia, where economic growth and ICT development are major issues in governmental strategy and decision-making. These developments are comparable to what takes place in North America and Europe.

g. Assessing the Bologna Process More Critically

Having mapped developments in higher education in this book, four critical questions may be raised with regard to the Bologna Process and its wider international context.

1. Starting with the Bologna Process itself and the creation of a European Higher Education Area, it may be asked *whether it is clear what this European Higher Education Area actually is and how effective it will be*. There are ten action lines (see Table 2.1), and for the Bergen ministerial meeting in May 2005, three priorities were set: quality assurance, a two-cycle degree system and recognition of degrees and periods of studies (see §5.b). We may observe activities in all fields and priorities. Restricting ourselves to the basic two-cycle degree system (a Bachelor's and a Master's), however, we observe a landscape with many differences, notwithstanding the common desire for comparability. It was agreed that all countries engaged in the Bologna Process were to have begun the implementation of this two-cycle degree system by 2005. This, however, is theory rather than practice. Implementation of the two-cycle degree system takes place at different speeds and in different ways. A few countries are far ahead (the Scandinavian ones), some are well on

schedule, but most countries remain (far) behind (e.g. France and Spain). In some countries, such as the Netherlands, the two-cycle degree system replaces the old system, whereas in other countries the two-cycle degree system is introduced as a supplementary system (for instance in Germany). With regard to the Master's cycle there is agreement about a Bachelor's degree as an entrance requirement. However, various countries introduced additional and specific entrance requirements on top of the Bachelor's degree. Some countries have Master's programs of two years, others of one year. Given the present divergences there are no obvious indications that the education systems in the European countries will be substantially more consistent by 2010.

What will be needed to understand the European Higher Education Area is an inventory of those aspects of higher education that are seriously affected by the Bologna Process, and to what extent, and of those aspects that remain unaffected, such as fees or entrance requirements for access to different kinds of educational institution. In a review Erkki Berndtson has criticized the Bologna Process for 'the cosmetic nature of the actual reforms' and for its 'one-sided approach' in the sense of neglecting many of the real problems in universities.[63]

2. Implementation being to a large extent a national affair raises the issue of the strength of the machinery or regime: *How strong is the Bologna Process in this respect?* European-level coordination of national policies may be effected by either binding measures ('hard' or regulatory coordination in the form of, for instance, EU directives) or by 'soft' law (also called 'persuasive' coordination). Persuasive coordination does not require national educational institutions to participate, but supports those that wish to participate by ensuring a certain amount of coordination and by providing financial support. The EU Erasmus and Socrates programs provide examples of such persuasive coordination.[64] The implementation of the European Higher Education Area and its elements, such as the two-cycle degree system, is also based on 'soft' rather than on 'hard' measures. It must be added that the institutional structure of the Bologna Process is still in it infancy. Besides, at the moment it is more focussed on the inclusion of all countries on the continent than on monitoring implementation in very different countries, although it is correct to note that all participating countries sent in their reports for the 'stocktaking' process at the ministerial meeting in Bergen in May 2005. However, this remains a first inventory. It also shows that progress is not consistent across all participating countries. It takes time to construct an authoritative monitoring system, which has the capacity to find out what is really happening in

---

63 Erkki Berndtson, 'The European Higher Education Area: To Change or not to Change?' in: *epsNet Kiosk Plus. THE NET Journal of Political Science*, 1/2, November 2003, p. 67.
64 See Tamara Harvey, *European Social Law and Policy*, London and New York: Longman, 1998, p. 38.

countries and to enhance both formal implementation and – far more difficult – compliance with the common standards the Bologna Process agreed on.

It must also be noted that the countries engaged in the Bologna Process are very different, if one only thinks about the economic differences between Western, Central and Eastern European countries or between university systems in North-Western European, Mediterranean and Eastern European countries, not to mention the national interests of such powers as France, Germany and the Russian Federation that are at stake. The present lack of commitment to, and trust in, the underlying EU Lisbon strategy, which provided a binding force as a challenge, is a further sign of the weakness of the present machinery of the Bologna Process. The official European rationale may be clearly present, due to weak coordination instruments the national perspectives are also present, and in many cases probably more obvious.

3. Going inside the 'black box' of the decision-making of the Bologna Process, it may be asked *what kind of role the non-state actors play in it.* An intergovernmental structure means that governments decide, or, in the terms used by Robert Cox and Harold Jacobson, it is the 'representative subsystem' of an international organization that determines the outcome. The question then arises to what extent the 'participant subsystem' composed of governments plus all other actors may affect the outcome. Signals and inputs by other actors may be relevant, because their contributions and roles, for instance, enhance soft coordination mechanisms.[65]

Other actors are the organization's bureaucracy and the representatives of other intergovernmental organizations and non-governmental organizations (NGOs). Given the weak organizational structure of the Bologna Process and the non-permanent status of its Secretariat, it cannot be expected that this bureaucracy is playing a strong independent role. Instead, it is more correct to assume that the Secretariat's role is executive rather than initiating.

The European Commission is an additional full member of the Bologna Process, but remains one among many (41) players, including the member states of the EU, even if the Commission has practical, institutional and financial support to offer as well as expertise in 'soft' regulation programs. As far as we can see the main EU policies with regard to the Bologna Process are set by the Council of Ministers and the European Council. Within the wider framework of the Bologna Process this leaves little room for manoeuvre for entrepreneurship or autonomous policy-making by the European Commission. An observer position has been granted to the Council of Europe. This means that the Council of Europe has a weaker position than the European Commission. It plays a complementary role, nonetheless, thanks to

---

65 R.W. Cox, H.K. Jacobson (eds), *The Anatomy of Influence. Decision Making in International Organization*, New Haven: Yale University Press, 1973; see Bob Reinalda and Bertjan Verbeek, *Decision Making Within International Organizations*, London and New York: Routledge, 2004, pp. 14-20.

its standard-setting machinery for academic recognition of degrees and its pan-European membership.

How important are the NGOs of universities and students which were granted an observer status within the Bologna Process and to what degree do they act as a counterbalance? The description of the Bologna Process and a comparison with NGOs in 19th-century multilateral conferences suggest that the NGOs in the Bologna Process have been engaged by the ministers of education for reasons of legitimacy, rather than the converse, in which NGOs present themselves as 'the conscience of the world' or as critical actors in comparison to governments. The explanation of the *Bologna Declaration* by the predecessors of the European University Association served the purposes of the ministers. It can be asked whether the EUA has developed a sufficiently independent attitude towards the plans of the ministers who concentrate on teaching and whether the EUA lives up to the principle from the *Magna Charta Universitatum*, which says that teaching and research in universities must be inseparable. Although the students' organization ESIB seems a bit more critical of the Bologna Process than the EUA, it may be asked whether the students are critical and strong enough to seriously affect intergovernmental decision-making. And finally, the question should be raised what it means when the university staff, who must implement the changes, have not been directly represented in the Bologna Process until the Bergen ministerial meeting in 2005.

The conclusion of this analysis of the Bologna Process's 'participant subsystem' is that its non-state actors are relatively weak 'counterweights' to the governments involved. This means that the 'representative subsystem' does determine the outcome of decision-making in the Bologna Process.

4. With regard to the global context, in particular the worldwide education market, it may be asked *whether, and to what extent, the Bologna Process provides an adequate answer to the global commercial development of trade in educational services?* Although the Bologna Process focusses on harmonizing Europe's higher education, the global perspective is a definite part of this European effort. The *Bologna Declaration* stresses the 'objective of increasing the international competitiveness of the European system of higher education' and argues: 'We need to ensure that the European higher education system acquires a worldwide degree of attraction equal to our extraordinary cultural and scientific traditions'. The *Prague Communiqué* mentions 'students from Europe and other parts of the world', speaks about the 'readability and comparability of European higher education degrees worldwide' and argues that 'the quality of higher education and research is and should be an important determinant of Europe's international attractiveness and competitiveness'. And the *Berlin Communiqué* takes into due consideration the conclusions of the European Councils in Lisbon and Barcelona aimed at making Europe the most competitive and dynamic knowledge-based economy in the world. It also welcomes the 'interest shown by other regions of the world in the development of

the European Higher Education Area' and welcomes a representative from Central and Latin America.

Given these international objectives, it must be noted that efforts by the Bologna Process to gain a more adequate market share in the worldwide education market have remained weak in comparison to its pretensions. There is no thorough analysis of the available global market, nor of the opportunities it may offer, nor of the impediments it may create for the prospects of mobility and harmonization based on the Bologna Process fundamentals. As far as a strategy regarding the United States is concerned, it must be noted that this is based on an EU intervention (the Lisbon and Barcelona ambitions) in the Bologna Process. This EU strategy may have had a binding effect within the Bologna Process, but it has also created dependence on the strength, or weakness, of this EU strategy. Within the GATS, the EU may have taken a firm stand against the inclusion of educational services in the GATS negotiations, but it is to be expected that this issue will reappear on the agenda, which means that both the EU and the Bologna Process have to reconsider the issue of worldwide trade in educational services.

With regard to other continents or regions in the world, only one contact has been mentioned, but no specific strategies have been developed. This seems to be a weakness, in particular with regard to Asia, which is the most promising continent, where issues such as quality assurance, accreditation and credit transfer systems are being discussed at the regional level. International competition in this region is also relevant, given the fact that the US is losing market share since 9/11, whereas Australia and New Zealand are gaining market shares.

The answer to the fourth question raised is that the international dimension of the Bologna Process remains rather weak. It is both dependent on EU strategies and shows a lack of elaboration with regard to Europe's opportunities on the worldwide education market.

We conclude by repeating that the Bologna Process and the development of comparability in Europe's higher education are most interesting phenomena because they are laying the foundations of European academia in the 21st century, and in this respect help to define Europe's position in the world. Although much has been undertaken, much remains to be done. It should be remembered that the Bologna Process is a relatively young phenomenon: it is scarcely out of the egg.

List of websites

AAHE: American Association for Higher Education — www.aahe.org
ACA: Academic Cooperation Association — www.aca-secretariat.be
www.study-in-europe/org
APEC: Asia Pacific Economic Cooperation — www.apec.org
AUN: ASEAN University Network — www.aun.chula.ac.th
Bologna Process — www.bologna-berlin2003.de
www.bologna-bergen2005.no
www.dfes.gov.uk/bologna/ (= London secretariat until 2007)
CHEPS: Center for Higher Education Policy Studies — www.utwente.nl/cheps
Council of Europe — www.coe.int/T/E/Cultural_Co-operation/education/Higher_education/
EADTU: European Association of Distance Teaching Universities — www.eadtu.nl
EAIE: European Association for International Education — www.eaie.nl
EAPAA: European Association of Public Administration Accreditation — http://bbt.utwente.nl/eapaa/
ECA: European Consortium for Accreditation — www.ecaconsortium.net
ECTS — http://europa.eu.int/comm/education/socrates/ectswww.html
Education International — www.ei-ie.org
ENIC and NARIC Networks — www.enic-naric.net
ENQA: European Association for Quality Assurance in Higher Education — www.enqa-net
EPAN: European Public Administration Network — http://bl.ul.ie/epan/
EPSNET: European Political Science Network — www.epsNet.org
ESIB: National Unions of Students in Europe — www.esib.org
ETUCE: European Trade Union Committee for Education — www.etuce.homestead.com
EUA: European University Association — www.eua.be
EURASHE: European Associations of Institutions in Higher Education — www.eurashe.be
EURODOC: European Council of Doctoral Candidates and Young Researchers — www.eurodoc.net
European Commission — http://europa.eu.int/comm/education.html
http://europa.eu.int/comm/research/area.html
http://europa.eu.int/comm/trade
EURYDICE: Information Network on Education in Europe — www.eurydice.org

GATE: Global Alliance for Transnational Education   www.edugate.org
GATS Watch   www.gatswatch.org
IAPSS: International Association for Political Science   www.iapss.org
Students
IAU: International Association of Universities   www.unesco.org/iau
IBRD: World Bank   www.worldbank.org
IIE: Institute of International Education   www.iie.org
IMHE: Institutional Management in Higher   www.oecd.org/edu/higher
Education
INQAAHE: International Network for Quality   www.inqaahe.org
Assurance Agencies in Higher Education
Joint Quality Initiative   www.jointquality.org
NAFSA: Association of International Educators   www.nafsa.org
OECD: Organization for Economic Cooperation and   www.oecd.org
Development
PLOTEUS: Portal on Learning Opportunities   www.ploteus.net
throughout the European Space
SRHE: Society for Research into Higher Education   www.srhe.ac.uk
TFHE: Task Force on Higher Education   www.tfhe.net
UMAP: University Mobility in Asia and the Pacific   www.umap.org
UNESCO CEPES: European Centre for Higher   www.cepes.ro
Education
UNESCO: United Nations Educational, Scientific and   www.unesco.org/education/
Cultural Organization
UNICE: The Voice of Business in Europe   www.unice.org
US Council for Higher Education Accreditation   www.chea.org
WTO: World Trade Organization   www.wto.org

Annexes

ANNEX 1

Magna Charta Universitatum, Bologna, 18 September 1988

Preamble

The undersigned Rectors of European Universities, gathered in Bologna for the ninth centenary of the oldest University in Europe, four years before the definitive abolition of boundaries between the countries of the European Community; looking forward to far-reaching cooperation between all European nations and believing that peoples and States should become more than ever aware of the part that universities will be called upon to play in a changing and increasingly international society, Consider:

1) that at the approaching end of this millenium the future of mankind depends, largely on cultural, scientific and technical development; and that this is built up in centres of culture, knowledge and research as represented by true universities;
2) that the universities' task of spreading knowledge among the younger generations implies that, in today's world, they must also serve society as a whole; and that the cultural, social and economic future of society requires, in particular, a considerable investment in continuing education;
3) that universities must give future generations education and training that will teach them, and through them others, to respect the great harmonies of their natural environment and of life itself.

The undersigned Rectors of European universities proclaim to all States and to the conscience of all nations the fundamental principles which must, now and always, support the vocation of universities.

Fundamental Principles

1. The university is an autonomous institution at the heart of societies differently organized because of geography and historical heritage; it produces, examines, appraises and hands down culture by research and teaching. To meet the needs of the world around it, its research and teaching must be morally and intellectually independent of all political authority and intellectually independent of all political authority and economic power.
2. Teaching and research in universities must be inseparable if their tuition is not to lag behind changing needs, the demands of society, and advances in scientific knowledge.
3. Freedom in research and training is the fundamental principle of university life, and governments and universities, each as far as in them lies, must ensure respect for this fundamental requirement.

Rejecting intolerance and always open to dialogue, the university is an ideal meeting-ground for teachers capable of imparting their knowledge and well equipped to develop it by research and innovation and students entitled, able and willing to enrich their minds with that knowledge.

4. A university is the trustee of the European humanist tradition; its constant care is to attain universal knowledge; to fulfil its vocation it transcends geographical and political frontiers, and affirms the vital need for different cultures to know and influence each other.

The Means

To attain these goals by following such principles calls for effective means, suitable to present conditions.

1. To preserve freedom in research and teaching, the instruments appropriate to realize that freedom must be made available to all members of the university community.

2. Recruitment of teachers, and regulation of their status, must obey the principle that research is inseparable from teaching.

3. Each university must – with due allowance for particular circumstances – ensure that its students' freedoms are safeguarded and that they enjoy conditions in which they can acquire the culture and training which it is their purpose to possess.

4. Universities – particularly in Europe – regard the mutual exchange of information and documentation, and frequent joint projects for the advancement of learning, as essential to the steady progress of knowledge. Therefore, as in the earliest years of their history, they encourage mobility among teachers and students; furthermore, they consider a general policy of equivalent status, titles, examinations (without prejudice to national diplomas) and award of scholarships essential to the fulfilment of their mission in the conditions prevailing today.

The undersigned Rectors, on behalf of their Universities, undertake to do everything in their power to encourage each State, as well as the supranational organizations concerned, to mould their policy sedulously on this Magna Charta, which expresses the universities' unanimous desire freely determined and declared.

ANNEX 2

Sorbonne Declaration: *Joint declaration on harmonisation of the architecture of the European higher education system by the four Ministers in charge for France, Germany, Italy and the United Kingdom. Paris, the Sorbonne, May 25 1998*

The European process has very recently moved some extremely important steps ahead. Relevant as they are, they should not make one forget that Europe is not only that of the Euro, of the banks and the economy: it must be a Europe of knowledge as well. We must strengthen and build upon the intellectual, cultural, social and technical dimensions of our continent. These have to a large extent been shaped by its universities, which continue to play a pivotal role for their development.

Universities were born in Europe, some three quarters of a millennium ago. Our four countries boast some of the oldest, which are celebrating important anniversaries around now, as the University of Paris is doing today. In those times, students and academics would freely circulate and rapidly disseminate knowledge throughout the continent. Nowadays, too many of our students still graduate without having had the benefit of a study period outside of national boundaries.

We are heading for a period of major change in education and working conditions, to a diversification of courses of professional careers, with education and training throughout life becoming a clear obligation. We owe our students, and our society at large, a higher education system in which they are given the best opportunities to seek and find their own area of excellence.

An open European area for higher learning carries a wealth of positive perspectives, of course respecting our diversities, but requires on the other hand continuous efforts to remove barriers and to develop a framework for teaching and learning, which would enhance mobility and an ever closer cooperation.

The international recognition and attractive potential of our systems are directly related to their external and internal readabilities. A system, in which two main cycles, undergraduate and graduate, should be recognized for international comparison and equivalence, seems to emerge.

Much of the originality and flexibility in this system will be achieved through the use of credits (such as in the ECTS scheme) and semesters. This will allow for validation of these acquired credits for those who choose initial or continued education in different European universities and wish to be able to acquire degrees in due time throughout life. Indeed, students should be able to enter the academic world at any time in their professional life and from diverse backgrounds.

Undergraduates should have access to a diversity of programmes, including opportunities for multidisciplinary studies, development of a proficiency in languages and the ability to use new information technologies.

International recognition of the first cycle degree as an appropriate level of qualification is important for the success of this endeavour, in which we wish to make our higher education schemes clear to all.

In the graduate cycle, there would be a choice between a shorter master's degree and a longer doctor's degree, with possibilities to transfer from one to the other. In both graduate degrees, appropriate emphasis would be placed on research and autonomous work.

At both undergraduate and graduate level, students would be encouraged to spend at least one semester in universities outside their own country. At the same time, more teaching and research staff should be working in European countries other than their own. The fast growing support of the European Union for the mobility of students and teachers should be employed to the full.

Most countries, not only within Europe, have become fully conscious of the need to foster such evolution. The conferences of European rectors, University presidents, and groups of experts and academics in our respective countries have engaged in widespread thinking along these lines.

A convention, recognising higher education qualifications in the academic field within Europe, was agreed on last year in Lisbon. The convention set a number of basic requirements and acknowledged that individual countries could engage in an even more constructive scheme. Standing by these conclusions, one can build on them and go further. There is already much common ground for the mutual recognition of higher education degrees for professional purposes through the respective directives of the European Union.

Our governments, nevertheless, continue to have a significant role to play to these ends, by encouraging ways in which acquired knowledge can be validated and respective degrees can be better recognised. We expect this to promote further inter-university agreements. Progressive harmonisation of the overall framework of our degrees and cycles can be achieved through strengthening of already existing experience, joint diplomas, pilot initiatives, and dialogue with all concerned.

We hereby commit ourselves to encouraging a common frame of reference, aimed at improving external recognition and facilitating student mobility as well as employability. The anniversary of the University of Paris, today here in the Sorbonne, offers us a solemn opportunity to engage in the endeavour to create a European area of higher education, where national identities and common interests can interact and strengthen each other for the benefit of Europe, of its students, and more generally of its citizens. We call on other Member States of the Union and other European countries to join us in this objective and on all European Universities to consolidate

Europe's standing in the world through continuously improved and updated education for its citizens.

Claude Allègre, Minister of National Education, Research and Technology (France)
Luigi Berlinguer, Minister of Public Education, Universities and Research (Italy)
Tessa Blackstone, Minister of Higher Education (United Kingdom)
Jürgen Rüttgers, Minister of Education, Science, Research and Technology (Germany)

ANNEX 3

Bologna Declaration: *The European Higher Education Area.*
Joint Declaration of the European Ministers of Education Convened
in Bologna on the 19th of June 1999

The European process, thanks to the extraordinary achievements of the last few years, has become an increasingly concrete and relevant reality for the Union and its citizens. Enlargement prospects together with deepening relations with other European countries provide even wider dimensions to that reality. Meanwhile, we are witnessing a growing awareness in large parts of the political and academic world and in public opinion of the need to establish a more complete and far-reaching Europe, in particular building upon and strengthening its intellectual, cultural, social and scientific and technological dimensions.

A Europe of Knowledge is now widely recognised as an irreplaceable factor for social and human growth and as an indispensable component to consolidate and enrich the European citizenship, capable of giving its citizens the necessary competencies to face the challenges of the new millennium, together with an awareness of shared values and belonging to a common social and cultural space.

The importance of education and educational co-operation in the development and strengthening of stable, peaceful and democratic societies is universally acknowledged as paramount, the more so in view of the situation in South East Europe.

The Sorbonne declaration of 25th of May 1998, which was underpinned by these considerations, stressed the Universities' central role in developing European cultural dimensions. It emphasised the creation of the European area of higher education as a key way to promote citizens' mobility and employability and the Continent's overall development.

Several European countries have accepted the invitation to commit themselves to achieving the objectives set out in the declaration, by signing it or expressing their agreement in principle. The direction taken by several higher education reforms launched in the meantime in Europe has proved many Governments' determination to act.

European higher education institutions, for their part, have accepted the challenge and taken up a main role in constructing the European area of higher education, also in the wake of the fundamental principles laid down in the Bologna Magna Charta Universitatum of 1988. This is of the highest importance, given that Universities' independence and autonomy ensure that higher education and research systems continuously adapt to changing needs, society's demands and advances in scientific knowledge.

The course has been set in the right direction and with meaningful purpose. The achievement of greater compatibility and comparability of the systems of higher education nevertheless requires continual momentum in order to be fully accomplished. We need to support it through promoting concrete measures to achieve tangible forward steps. The 18th June meeting saw participation by authoritative experts and scholars from all our countries and provides us with very useful suggestions on the initiatives to be taken.

We must in particular look at the objective of increasing the international competitiveness of the European system of higher education. The vitality and efficiency of any civilisation can be measured by the appeal that its culture has for other countries. We need to ensure that the European higher education system acquires a worldwide degree of attraction equal to our extraordinary cultural and scientific traditions.

While affirming our support to the general principles laid down in the Sorbonne declaration, we engage in co-ordinating our policies to reach in the short term, and in any case within the first decade of the third millennium, the following objectives, which we consider to be of primary relevance in order to establish the European area of higher education and to promote the European system of higher education world-wide:

– Adoption of a system of easily readable and comparable degrees, also through the implementation of the Diploma Supplement, in order to promote European citizens employability and the international competitiveness of the European higher education system

– Adoption of a system essentially based on two main cycles, undergraduate and graduate. Access to the second cycle shall require successful completion of first cycle studies, lasting a minimum of three years. The degree awarded after the first cycle shall also be relevant to the European labour market as an appropriate level of qualification. The second cycle should lead to the master and/or doctorate degree as in many European countries.

– Establishment of a system of credits – such as in the ECTS system – as a proper means of promoting the most widespread student mobility. Credits could also be acquired in non-higher education contexts, including life-long learning, provided they are recognised by receiving Universities concerned.

– Promotion of mobility by overcoming obstacles to the effective exercise of free movement with particular attention to:

  – for students, access to study and training opportunities and to related services

  – for teachers, researchers and administrative staff, recognition and valorisation of periods spent in a European context researching, teaching and training, without prejudicing their statutory rights.

  – Promotion of European co-operation in quality assurance with a view to developing comparable criteria and methodologies

  – Promotion of the necessary European dimensions in higher education, particularly with regards to curricular development, inter-institutional co-operation, mobility schemes and integrated programmes of study, training and research.

We hereby undertake to attain these objectives – within the framework of our institutional competencies and taking full respect of the diversity of cultures, languages, national education systems and of University autonomy – to consolidate the European area of higher education. To that end, we will pursue the ways of intergovernmental co-operation, together with those of non-governmental European organisations with competence on higher education. We expect Universities again to respond promptly and positively and to contribute actively to the success of our endeavour.

Convinced that the establishment of the European area of higher education requires constant support, supervision and adaptation to the continuously evolving needs, we decide to meet again within two years in order to assess the progress achieved and the new steps to be taken.

The Bologna Declaration was signed by 29 countries in Bologna:
Austria
Belgium (both French and Flemish community)
Bulgaria
The Czech Republic
Denmark
Estonia
Finland
France
Germany
Greece
Hungary
Iceland
Ireland
Italy
Latvia
Lithuania
Luxembourg
Malta
The Netherlands
Norway
Poland
Portugal
Romania
The Slovak Republic
Slovenia
Spain
Sweden

Swiss Confederation
The United Kingdom

They were followed by:

Prague (2001):
Croatia
Cyprus
Liechtenstein
Turkey

Berlin (2003):
Albania
Andorra
Bosnia and Herzegovina
The Holy See
The Russian Federation
Serbia and Montenegro
The Former Yugoslav Republic of Macedonia

Bergen (2005):
Armenia
Azerbaijan
Georgia
Moldova
Ukraine

ANNEX 4

Confederation of European Union Rectors' Conferences and the Association of European Universities, *The Bologna Declaration on the European space for higher education: an explanation,* **20 February 2000**

> The Bologna Declaration on the European space for higher education: an explanation

This document was prepared by the Confederation of EU Rectors' Conferences and the Association of European Universities (CRE). It includes:

- a comment on the meaning and significance of the Bologna Declaration and information on the follow-up process in progress;
- the text of the Declaration;
- a list of internet addresses from which more detailed information can be obtained.

The authors are grateful to the European Commission for its support and its willingness to disseminate this document.

> The Bologna Declaration: an explanation
> The Bologna Declaration is a pledge by 29 countries to reform the structures of their higher education systems in a convergent way

The Declaration is a **key document** which marks a **turning point** in the development of European higher education.

- It was signed by 29 countries which "undertake to attain the Declaration's objectives" and to that end "engage in coordinating [their] policies".
- It is **a commitment freely taken** by each signatory country to reform its own higher education system or systems in order to create overall convergence at European level. The Bologna Declaration is not a reform imposed upon national governments or higher education institutions. Any pressure individual countries and higher education institutions may feel from the Bologna process could only result from their ignoring increasingly common features or staying outside the mainstream of change.
- The Bologna process aims at creating convergence and, thus, is not a path towards the "standardisation" or "uniformisation" of European higher education. The fundamental principles of autonomy and diversity are respected.
- The Declaration reflects a **search for a common European answer to common European problems**. The process originates from the recognition that in spite of their valuable differences, European higher education

systems are facing common internal and external challenges related to the growth and diversification of higher education, the employability of graduates, the shortage of skills in key areas, the expansion of private and transnational education, etc. The Declaration recognises the value of co-ordinated reforms, compatible systems and common action.

> The Bologna Declaration is not just a political statement, but a binding commitment to an action programme

The **action programme** set out in the Declaration is based on a clearly defined common goal, a deadline and a set of specified objectives:

- a clearly defined common goal: to create a European space for higher education in order to enhance the employability and mobility of citizens and to increase the international competitiveness of European higher education:
- a deadline: the European space for higher education should be completed in 2010;
- a set of specified objectives:
  - the adoption of a common framework of readable and comparable degrees, "also through the implementation of the Diploma Supplement";
  - the introduction of undergraduate and postgraduate levels in all countries, with first degrees no shorter than 3 years and relevant to the labour market;
  - ECTS-compatible credit systems also covering lifelong learning activities;
  - a European dimension in quality assurance, with comparable criteria and methods;
  - the elimination of remaining obstacles to the free mobility of students (as well as trainees and graduates) and teacher's (as well as researchers and higher education administrators).

> The Bologna Declaration and global competitiveness of European higher education

- Next to the need to "achieve greater compatibility and comparability in the systems of higher education" (mainly an intra-European issue), the Declaration wants "in particular" to increase "the international competitiveness of the European system of higher education". It says that the "vitality and efficiency of any civilisation can be measured by the appeal its culture has for other countries". The signatory countries explicitly express their goal to "**ensure that the European higher education system acquires a worldwide degree of attractiveness** equal to [Europe's] extraordinary cultural and scientific traditions".

–   **On these "external" issues, the Bologna Declaration is genuinely opening up new avenues.** In stressing so explicitly the need for European higher
education as a (cohesive) system to become more attractive to students
from other world regions, it provides one more reason for moving in the direction of a coherent European system and implicitly invites European
institutions to compete more resolutely than in the past for students, influence, prestige and money in the worldwide competition of universities.

From Declaration to implementation an organised follow-up structure and process

–   The 29 signatory countries committed to attain the Declaration's objectives will **"pursue the ways of intergovernmental cooperation"**, in
collaboration with higher education institutions and associations.
–   **Ministers have agreed to meet again in Prague in May 2001**, together
with representatives from European higher education institutions and associations, in order to assess progress achieved and to agree on new steps
to be taken.
–   They have also established a specific **follow-up structure with a mandate** to prepare the Prague Conference and to facilitate and coordinate the
action needed to advance the goals of the Bologna Declaration. The follow-up structure is based on:
    –   a "consultative group" consisting of representatives of all signatory
    countries;
    –   a smaller "follow-up group" comprising the countries successively
    holding the EU Presidency in the 2 years from Bologna to Prague
    (Finland, Portugal, France, Sweden), the Czech Republic, the Euro-
    pean Commission, CRE and the Confederation;
    –   in addition, since new political decisions may need to be taken in the
    process towards Prague, the follow-up to the Bologna Declaration will
    be on the agenda of meetings of EU education ministers.

–   **Follow-up work is in progress at the European, national and institutional level**. The Declaration states that the process of establishing a
European space for higher education requires constant support, supervision and adaptation to continuously changing needs.
    –   A series of surveys and studies are in progress at the initiative of the
    group of national contact persons of the signatory countries, the EU
    Presidency, the European Commission and higher education associa-
    tions and networks. They deal with transnational education,
    accreditation, credit systems, quality assurance, etc., and serve as pre-
    paratory steps for the next stages in the process.
    –   Signatory countries are considering or planning legislative reforms
    and/or governmental action in relevant areas of their higher education
    systems; **convergent reforms** have already been introduced or are in

progress in several European countries. They signal a move towards shorter studies, 2-tier degree structures, credit systems, external evaluation, more autonomy coupled with more accountability. Another trend is towards the blurring of boundaries between the different constituent sub-sectors of higher education.

- Individual universities as well as higher education consortia, networks and associations are studying and discussing the implications of the Bologna process in their particular country, subject area, or type of institution.

> The Bologna Declaration invites the higher education community to contribute to the success of the process of reform and convergence

- The Declaration acknowledges the crucial role of the higher education community for the success of the Bologna process. It says that intergovernmental cooperation should be "together with non-governmental European organisations with competencies in higher education". Governments also "expect universities to again respond positively and to contribute actively to the success of (their) endeavour". It is therefore clear that higher education institutions have a unique opportunity to shape their own European future and to play a crucial role in the development and implementation of the Bologna process.
- The Declaration specifically recognises the fundamental values and the diversity of European higher education:

  - it clearly acknowledges the necessary independence and autonomy of universities;
  - it explicitly refers to the fundamental principles laid down in the *Magna Charta Universitatum* signed (also in Bologna) in 1988;
  - it stresses the need to achieve a common space for higher education within the framework of the diversity of cultures languages and educational systems.

- In order to respond to the invitation contained in the Bologna Declaration, the higher education community needs to be able to tell Ministers in a convincing way what kind of European space for higher education it wants and is willing to promote. **Universities and other institutions of higher education can choose to be actors, rather than objects, of this essential process of change**. They may in particular

- profile their own curricula, in accordance with the emerging post-Bologna environment, in particular through the introduction of bachelor courses in systems where they have not traditionally existed, and through the creation of master courses meeting the needs of mobile postgraduate students from around the world;

- activate their networks in key areas such as joint curriculum development, joint ventures overseas or worldwide mobility schemes;
- contribute individually and collectively to the next steps in the process.

- The Confederation of EU Rectors' Conferences and the Association of European Universities (CRE) plan to organise a **convention of European universities and other institutions of higher education a few weeks before the Prague meeting**. This convention should provide an opportunity for the higher education community to discuss the main issues at stake and to produce a communication to Ministers on what higher education expects from the Prague meeting.

29 February 2000

ANNEX 5

'Contents' and 'Executive Summary' of the 'Lourtie Report':
Furthering the Bologna Process. Report to the Ministers of Education of the signatory countries,
by General Rapporteur Pedro Lourtie, Prague, May 2001

Contents

II.2 The Bologna Process

ANNEXES – Reports and conclusions of the events

1. Seminar on Credit Accumulation and Transfer Systems
2. Conference on Bachelor-Level Degrees
3. Seminar on Transnational Education
4. Convention of European Higher Education Institutions
5. Student Convention

Executive Summary

The follow-up group of the Bologna Process commissioned the rapporteur to present this report as a contribution to the meeting in Prague, in May 2001, of the European Ministers in charge of Higher Education of the countries that signed the Bologna Declaration in June 1999. The report gives a short overview of the follow-up, reviews succinctly the developments since Bologna and dwells on scenarios for the future.

The organisation of the process was decided by the EU Ministers in September 1999 and a work programme was established by the follow-up group in November 1999. This work programme has included international seminars on three topics ("Credit Accumulation and Transfer Systems", "Bachelor-Level Degrees" and "Transnational Education") and the Convention of European Higher Education Institutions, all leading to the preparation of the Prague Conference. ESIB organised a Student Convention to create input to this meeting.

A move towards a "bachelor"/"master" structure is continuing, both in countries where it started earlier, but also in new ones, with examples in all disciplines. However, some professionally oriented degrees remain long and leading directly to a "master".

Mobility and the instruments of recognition and transparency of qualifications (ECTS, Diploma Supplement and Lisboa Recognition Convention) are receiving unanimous support. Awareness of the employability issue is raising and more degrees with a clear professional orientation are being implemented. Competitiveness is rated highly, but awareness of transnational education challenges still seems to be low and lifelong learning is a priority only in a limited number of countries.

The introduction of ECTS-compatible credit systems is spreading and the acceptance of ECTS units as a basis for a European credit system is increasing. A subject-related approach to identify common learning outcomes was identified as necessary to overcome difficulties concerning both credits and degree structures.

More countries are creating or willing to create quality assurance systems and accreditation is on national and international agendas, at least as a topic for discussion.

With the aim of building the European Higher Education Area, the Bologna Declaration indicates three main goals (international competitiveness, mobility and employability), and six instrumental objectives. However, higher education has broader aims of the social, cultural and human development and the European Higher Education Area will also be the result of shared values and a common social and cultural heritage.

A number of factors contributing towards the goals may be identified. Among these factors are the readability of degrees, acceptance and recognition of qualifications and periods of study, clear information on objectives and learning outcomes, as well as relevance of the programmes, quality assurance and accreditation, dissemination of European knowledge, friendly student services, visa policies and support for mobility.

The main goals and the specific objectives of the Bologna Declaration have received wide acceptance and reforms are under way, both at national and institutional level. However, some issues require clarification, others may be pushed forward and some just need monitoring. Social issues were raised, namely by students, and issues like lifelong learning and transnational education are gaining renewed or new visibility.

A question, which is becoming more apparent as the process progresses, is that of which values and concepts, concerning higher education, are common or to what extent are they shared among the signatory countries. A study on the values, concepts and terminology would facilitate discussions and communication in the future.

The development of a comprehensive credit system, allowing for accumulation, has proven difficult, although a consensus has grown around basing it on ECTS units. Generalising the use of ECTS units and adopting ECTS compatible national systems is a step forward. National degree structures are converging, but difficulties have been identified in some subject areas. Both difficulties, concerning credits and degree structures, suggest that further work by subject area at European level is required and could lead to identify relevant reference levels, expressed as learning outcomes (including knowledge, competencies and skills). Common reference levels will also facilitate the development of joint degrees, involving institutions from two or more signatory countries.

The development of national quality assurance systems, besides pursuing national objectives, should aim at building mutual trust in the European Higher Education Area and world-wide through European co-operation. The discussions on accreditation suffered from differences in concept and approach, requiring further clarification before any concrete agreement on future action may be reached.

Instruments for recognition, either academic or professional, and transparency, such as the Lisboa Recognition Convention and the Diploma Supplement already exist, just requiring being fully developed and/or generalised. Although recognition is essential for mobility, there are still other obstacles. The Mobility Action Plan endorsed by the European Council is a useful reference for future action.

Lifelong learning has been on the international agenda for some time and there are some experiences. The development of national policies could benefit from sharing experiences and good practices and, besides raising the levels of education and employability, may improve attractiveness of European higher education.

Transnational education is growing and challenging traditional education. Policies geared towards transparency and quality of qualifications should contemplate the transnational offer. On the other hand, the signatory countries may adopt a pro-active approach by offering programmes outside the European Higher Education Area and joint efforts to this effect could be promoted.

To establish the European Higher Education Area, easily accessible information on programmes and institutions, including the conditions offered to students, is essential and can be done using ICT. This information should be available in a form that is relevant for candidates and students, but also for employers and society at large.

Attractiveness of higher education institutions, besides ensuring quality and relevance, require that institutions are aware and respond to the diversity of needs of candidates and students. Such needs are different depending on the student being national or foreign, young or mature, graduate or postgraduate, etc.

To monitor the progress of the European Higher Education Area as a whole, as a basis for future decisions for the Bologna Process, data collected in the various signatory counties should be comparable. If the decision is taken to collect such comparable data, a technical study is required. Besides data, background studies will be needed to prepare future discussions and to support decisions.

The Bologna Process has been conducted on a rather informal basis. This has certain advantages but is also a fragile arrangement, with some risks to the memory of the process. The organisation and mandate of the follow-up structure for the future should, in consequence, be considered.

ANNEX 6

Towards the European Higher Education Area. Communiqué
of the meeting of European Ministers in charge of Higher Education
in Prague on May 19th 2001 (hereafter Prague Communiqué)

Two years after signing the Bologna Declaration and three years after the Sorbonne Declaration, European Ministers in charge of higher education, representing 32 signatories, met in Prague in order to review the progress achieved and to set directions and priorities for the coming years of the process. Ministers reaffirmed their commitment to the objective of establishing the European Higher Education Area by 2010. The choice of Prague to hold this meeting is a symbol of their will to involve the whole of Europe in the process in the light of enlargement of the European Union.

Ministers welcomed and reviewed the report "Furthering the Bologna Process" commissioned by the follow-up group and found that the goals laid down in the Bologna Declaration have been widely accepted and used as a base for the development of higher education by most signatories as well as by universities and other higher education institutions. Ministers reaffirmed that efforts to promote mobility must be continued to enable students, teachers, researchers and administrative staff to benefit from the richness of the European Higher Education Area including its democratic values, diversity of cultures and languages and the diversity of the higher education systems.

Ministers took note of the Convention of European higher education institutions held in Salamanca on 29-30 March and the recommendations of the Convention of European Students, held in Göteborg on 24-25 March, and appreciated the active involvement of the European University Association (EUA) and the National Unions of Students in Europe (ESIB) in the Bologna process. They further noted and appreciated the many other initiatives to take the process further. Ministers also took note of the constructive assistance of the European Commission.

Ministers observed that the activities recommended in the Declaration concerning degree structure have been intensely and widely dealt with in most countries. They especially appreciated how the work on quality assurance is moving forward. Ministers recognized the need to cooperate to address the challenges brought about by transnational education. They also recognized the need for a lifelong learning perspective on education.

Further actions following the six objectives of the Bologna process

As the Bologna Declaration sets out, Ministers asserted that building the European Higher Education Area is a condition for enhancing the attractiveness and competitiveness of higher education institutions in Europe. They supported the idea that higher education should be considered a public good and is and will remain a public responsibility (regulations etc.), and that students are full members of the higher education community. From this point of view Ministers commented on the further process as follows:

Adoption of a system of easily readable and comparable degrees
Ministers strongly encouraged universities and other higher education institutions to take full advantage of existing national legislation and European tools aimed at facilitating academic and professional recognition of course units, degrees and other awards, so that citizens can effectively use their qualifications, competencies and skills throughout the European Higher Education Area.

Ministers called upon existing organisations and networks such as NARIC and ENIC to promote, at institutional, national and European level, simple, efficient and fair recognition reflecting the underlying diversity of qualifications.

Adoption of a system essentially based on two main cycles
Ministers noted with satisfaction that the objective of a degree structure based on two main cycles, articulating higher education in undergraduate and graduate studies, has been tackled and discussed. Some countries have already adopted this structure and several others are considering it with great interest. It is important to note that in many countries bachelor's and master's degrees, or comparable two cycle degrees, can be obtained at universities as well as at other higher education institutions. Programmes leading to a degree may, and indeed should, have different orientations and various profiles in order to accommodate a diversity of individual, academic and labour market needs as concluded at the Helsinki seminar on bachelor level degrees (February 2001).

Establishment of a system of credits
Ministers emphasized that for greater flexibility in learning and qualification processes the adoption of common cornerstones of qualifications, supported by a credit system such as the ECTS or one that is ECTS-compatible, providing both transferability and accumulation functions, is necessary. Together with mutually recognized quality assurance systems such arrangements will facilitate students' access to the European labour market and enhance the compatibility, attractiveness and competitiveness of European higher education. The generalized use of such a credit system and of the Diploma Supplement will foster progress in this direction.

Promotion of mobility
Ministers reaffirmed that the objective of improving the mobility of students, teachers, researchers and administrative staff as set out in the Bologna Decla-

ration is of the utmost importance. Therefore, they confirmed their commitment to pursue the removal of all obstacles to the free movement of students, teachers, researchers and administrative staff and emphasized the social dimension of mobility. They took note of the possibilities for mobility offered by the European Community programmes and the progress achieved in this field, e.g. in launching the Mobility Action Plan endorsed by the European Council in Nice in 2000.

Promotion of European cooperation in quality assurance
Ministers recognized the vital role that quality assurance systems play in ensuring high quality standards and in facilitating the comparability of qualifications throughout Europe. They also encouraged closer cooperation between recognition and quality assurance networks. They emphasized the necessity of close European cooperation and mutual trust in and acceptance of national quality assurance systems. Further they encouraged universities and other higher education institutions to disseminate examples of best practice and to design scenarios for mutual acceptance of evaluation and accreditation/certification mechanisms. Ministers called upon the universities and other higher educations institutions, national agencies and the European Network of Quality Assurance in Higher Education (ENQA), in cooperation with corresponding bodies from countries which are not members of ENQA, to collaborate in establishing a common framework of reference and to disseminate best practice.

Promotion of the European dimensions in higher education
In order to further strengthen the important European dimensions of higher education and graduate employability Ministers called upon the higher education sector to increase the development of modules, courses and curricula at all levels with "European" content, orientation or organisation. This concerns particularly modules, courses and degree curricula offered in partnership by institutions from different countries and leading to a recognized joint degree.

Furthermore ministers emphasized the following points:

Lifelong learning
Lifelong learning is an essential element of the European Higher Education Area. In the future Europe, built upon a knowledge-based society and economy, lifelong learning strategies are necessary to face the challenges of competitiveness and the use of new technologies and to improve social cohesion, equal opportunities and the quality of life.

Higher education institutions and students

Ministers stressed that the involvement of universities and other higher education institutions and of students as competent, active and constructive partners in the establishment and shaping of a European Higher Education Area is needed and welcomed. The institutions have demonstrated the importance they attach to the creation of a compatible and efficient, yet diversified and adaptable European Higher Education Area. Ministers also pointed out that quality is the basic underlying condition for trust, relevance, mobility, compatibility and attractiveness in the European Higher Education Area. Ministers expressed their appreciation of the contributions toward developing study programmes combining academic quality with relevance to lasting employability and called for a continued proactive role of higher education institutions.

Ministers affirmed that students should participate in and influence the organisation and content of education at universities and other higher education institutions. Ministers also reaffirmed the need, recalled by students, to take account of the social dimension in the Bologna process.

Promoting the attractiveness of the European Higher Education Area

Ministers agreed on the importance of enhancing attractiveness of European higher education to students from Europe and other parts of the world. The readability and comparability of European higher education degrees worldwide should be enhanced by the development of a common framework of qualifications, as well as by coherent quality assurance and accreditation/certification mechanisms and by increased information efforts. Ministers particularly stressed that the quality of higher education and research is and should be an important determinant of Europe's international attractiveness and competitiveness.

Ministers agreed that more attention should be paid to the benefit of a European Higher Education Area with institutions and programmes with different profiles. They called for increased collaboration between the European countries concerning the possible implications and perspectives of transnational education.

Continued follow-up

Ministers committed themselves to continue their cooperation based on the objectives set out in the Bologna Declaration, building on the similarities and benefiting from the differences between cultures, languages and national systems, and drawing on all possibilities of intergovernmental cooperation and the ongoing dialogue with European universities and other higher education institutions and student organisations as well as the Community programmes.

Ministers welcomed new members to join the Bologna process after applications from Ministers representing countries for which the European

Community programmes Socrates and Leonardo da Vinci or Tempus-Cards are open. They accepted applications from Croatia, Cyprus and Turkey.

Ministers decided that a new follow-up meeting will take place in the second half of 2003 in Berlin to review progress and set directions and priorities for the next stages of the process towards the European Higher Education Area. They confirmed the need for a structure for the follow-up work, consisting of a follow-up group and a preparatory group. The follow-up group should be composed of representatives of all signatories, new participants and the European Commission, and should be chaired by the EU Presidency at the time. The preparatory group should be composed of representatives of the countries hosting the previous ministerial meetings and the next ministerial meeting, two EU member states and two non-EU member states; these latter four representatives will be elected by the follow-up group. The EU Presidency at the time and the European Commission will also be part of the preparatory group. The preparatory group will be chaired by the representative of the country hosting the next ministerial meeting.

The European University Association, the European Association of Institutions in Higher Education (EURASHE), the National Unions of Students in Europe and the Council of Europe should be consulted in the follow-up work.

In order to take the process further, Ministers encouraged the follow-up group to arrange seminars to explore the following areas: cooperation concerning accreditation and quality assurance, recognition issues and the use of credits in the Bologna process, the development of joint degrees, the social dimension, with specific attention to obstacles to mobility, and the enlargement of the Bologna process, lifelong learning and student involvement.

ANNEX 7

'Contents' and 'Executive Summary' of the 'Zgaga Report':
Bologna Process between Prague and Berlin. Report to the Ministers of Education of the signatory countries, by General Rapporteur Pavel Zgaga, Berlin, September 2003

4.2 Internet
4.2.1 Governmental and nongovernmental international
organizations
4.2.2 National and/or regional multilingual "Bologna Web Sites
4.2.3 Organizations, networks and projects with specific relevance
to "Bologna issues"
TRANSFINE -Transfer between formal, informal and non formal education
5. ABBREVIATIONS
6. ANNEXES
Recommendations from the official Follow-up Seminars
6.1. Quality Assurance and Accreditation
6.1.1. "Working on the European Dimension of Quality"
6.2. Recognition Issues and the Use of Credits
6.2.1. "Recognition issues in the Bologna Process"
Recommendations
6.2.2. "Credit Transfer and Accumulation – The Challenge for
Institutions and Students"
Conclusions and Recommendations for Action
6.3. Development of Joint Degrees
6.3.1. "Development of Joint Degrees"
6.3.2. "Integrated Curricula: Implications and Prospects"
6.4. Degree and Qualification Structures
6.4.1. "Master-Level Degrees"
6.4.2. "Qualification Structures in Higher Education in Europe"
6.5. Social Dimensions of the Bologna Process
6.5.1. "Exploring the Social Dimensions of the European
Higher Education Area"
6.5.2. "Student Participation in Governance in Higher Education'
6.6. Lifelong Learning
6.6.1. "Recognition and Credit Validation of Education Acquired
in Non-Higher Education Contexts,
Including Lifelong Learning, for Further Bachelor, Master and
Doctoral Studies"

Executive Summary

The Prague Summit (2001) clearly confirmed that the idea initiated in Bologna two years earlier had evolved into a unique international process of exceptional importance for the future of higher education in Europe. *In the successive period 2001 – 2003, awareness of the importance of the Bologna process and the real need for a common European Higher Education Area (EHEA) dramatically increased all around Europe,* not only at governmental level but also at the level of institutions. Some new European countries expressed readiness to join the Bologna process while it has also received growing interest from other parts of the world. *"Bologna" has become a new European higher education brand, today easily recognized in governmental policies, academic activities, international organizations, networks and media.* The Process now enters a demanding phase in which answers to particular problems detected in the last follow-up period should be found, and detailed strategies and "tuned" structural as well as social tools should be developed.

During the 2001-2003 period, several factors have been pushing the signatory partners of "Bologna" towards a more substantial commitment to the process. They have been preparing and implementing substantial reforms in their higher education systems. There is no country today which has not found it essential to search for complex answers for its future, also through the educational system; there is no country which has not put the reform of higher education high on its political agenda. Even if a country considered this need only for itself, it would be enormously important to study the practices of other countries and their educational systems. However, the Bologna process is much more than just an excellent set of good practices. Challenges to national higher education systems are interlinked with challenges brought about by growing European associating, (re)integrating and globalising processes. In that sense, the Process expresses a conviction of countries and institutions that under these new circumstances national higher education systems should become more comparable and compatible but also more attractive on a global scale.

The "Bologna Club" and the European Union are not of the same composition but most of these principles are applicable in both cases. "The Club" has not been founded on out-voting each other but on jointly exploring the most important issues and searching for consensus. There are *national* educational systems and curricula but there is also a firm understanding that *European cultural diversity* gives us great advantages and richness. Our advantages and richness can be mutually and fully enjoyed only if we create solid "common roads" among us. Richness is the end; "common roads" are the necessary means.

Although the Bologna process was initiated as mainly an intergovernmental process, there is an evident and *growing convergence with EU processes* aimed at strengthening European co-operation in higher education. Decisions of the Spring European Councils, in particular of Lisbon (2000), Stockholm (2001) and Barcelona (2002), as well as the consecutive EU Education Councils have gradually altered the status of the *Bologna Declaration* from a voluntary action to a set of commitments in the framework of the follow-up of the report of the concrete future objectives of education and training systems, endorsed in Stockholm in 2001. At least from this point on, the Process was no longer merely a voluntary action for the EU Member States, or for the candidate Member States either. Therefore, in the light of

EU enlargement, the growing convergence between the Bologna process and educational policy making on the EU level will soon become more and more visible. However, since its establishment the "Bologna Club" has been wider than the EU, and even after the forthcoming EU enlargement in 2004 it will remain wider. This can only give additional dynamism to the Process.

In the forefront of the follow-up process between Prague and Berlin was *a series of official follow-up seminars which aime*d to explore the areas pointed out in the *Prague Communiqué*. The list of official conferences between Prague and Berlin consists of ten seminars, spread over the period between March 2002 and June 2003, organized in six problem areas (quality assurance and accreditation; recognition issues and the use of credits; development of joint degrees; degree and qualification structure; social dimensions of the Bologna process; lifelong learning) and covering all key issues of the Bologna Process. Altogether, more than 1 000 participants – representatives from national ministries and international organizations, experts, academics, students, employers etc. – took part in all ten official Bologna follow-up seminars. The seminars have developed into a unique pan-European forum, which reflects the "snowball effect" of the Bologna process.

On the other hand, particular contributions by the EU Commission as well as by the Council of Europe, the European University Association (EUA), the European association of institutions in higher education (EURASHE) and National Unions of Students in Europe (ESIB) have to be mentioned separately.

The Bologna process fits closely into the broader agenda defined at a meeting of the European Council in Lisbon in March 2000, stressing the importance of "education and training for living and working in the knowledge society". In 2002 and 2003, the *D. G. of Education and Culture* released successive *Progress Reports* that offered a systemic review of its various and continuous activities and measures related to the Process. In most cases, the Commission is implementing measures in direct partnership with the higher education sector of the EU member and associate countries but also other countries. Today, the Community programme Socrates (and Erasmus within it) is a widely known promoter of the developmental projects and of the continuous increase of students' and teachers' mobility in European higher education. Socrates-Erasmus is also the main mechanism for the promotion of ECTS and the large-scale introduction of the Diploma Supplement. New exploratory projects have been launched in 2002, aimed at expanding the ECTS experience to lifelong learning. Measures to promote European co-operation in quality assurance are also high on their agenda.

The Council of Europe is another important contributor to the Bologna process. First and foremost, it has taken on the distinguished role of a bridge between those countries party to the Bologna process and the remaining European countries – signatories of the European Cultural Convention – that may benefit from the Process but that are not (yet) party to it. It is also an important actor in recognition issues. Traditionally, the Council has offered a platform for debate between Ministry and academic representatives, through the double composition of representatives in its *Steering Committee on Higher Education and Research* (CD-ESR). At the October 2002 plenary session of the CD-ESR a well-attended round table debate on the Bologna process was organized; it was one of those events of the period between Prague and Berlin with the highest representation (over 50 delegations). Finally, one particularly important contribution refers to a number of seminars on the Process in the countries that have not yet joined officially (South-Eastern Europe, the Russian Federation).

EUA in general, and various activities of individual *universities and higher education institutions* in particular, have also been very influential during the period 2001–2003. EUA's contributions during this period are numerous and wide-ranging: they arch from Council meetings and animation of internal discussions on main issues with members institutions, through active involvement in the work of the official follow up bodies (as an observer) as well as participation in the follow-up seminars, to launching pilot projects with help from EC Socrates Programme, coordinating ECTS and DS counsellors, etc. In this context, the *Trends III Report* is not to be missed. A special mention should be given to the EUA Convention on *Strengthening the Role of Institutions* in Graz (Austria) in May 2003, which formed the peak of activities for this period and was an important advance in the Bologna process. The Convention affirmed that its common vision is a Europe of knowledge based on strong research and research-based education in universities across the continent.

EURASHE represents *professional higher education institutions* which form an important part of tertiary education. Through its active contribution at follow-up events, it has presented specific aspects and concerns that are essential to a complete understanding of key issues. EURASHE's Annual Conference held in Gyöngyös (Hungary) in June 2003 confirmed again that institutions of professional higher education definitely belong to the emerging EHEA. These institutions also play a part in implementing the two-tier structure throughout Europe putting strong emphasis on social relevance and practical preparation of students for the reality of the world of work. EURASHE's particular contribution to the follow-up process between Prague and Berlin is the *Survey of Tertiary Short-Cycle Education in Europe*. It defines tertiary short-cycle education with regard to existing sub-degree education in European countries. A comprehensive, up-to-date presentation of this sector could well be used as the main reference in comparative discussions.

Student organizations have been particularly active partners in the Process during the follow-up period 2001–2003. There were no official Bologna follow-up seminars without student representatives, and they have always contributed competently and constructively to seminar results. Numerous activities have been well co-ordinated through ESIB as the students' representative at the European level. Today, there is no key theme within the Process that has not been discussed in the framework of European student organizations. As a result, ESIB produced a set of valuable policy documents. ESIB's *Brussels Student Declaration* (November 2001) states that creating a genuine European Higher Education Area requires more than educational, structural and institutional changes; what is really important is access to higher education on an equitable basis. The *Communiqué of* the 5th European student convention (Athens, February 2003) emphasizes the multiple benefits of study abroad but also deals with a number of factors that limit and hinder genuine student mobility and need to be progressively removed to achieve a higher participation rate in mobility schemes.

An important extension of the Bologna process in the period between the Prague and Berlin Summits are the "Bologna activities" at national and institutional levels. Any attempt to report on numerous activities at these levels would be doomed to remain incomplete. National reports (prepared in spring and summer 2003) offer an extremely useful insight into them. A high degree of correspondence between national higher education reforms and "Bologna" action lines is evident. Almost all countries report on establishing "Bologna co-ordination groups" and on organizing national "Bologna events".

Reports from most countries also contain information about *lively activities at the institutional level and in student organizations.* Partners in these activities are becoming aware that round tables, debates and communication on various "Bologna" issues are meaningful and productive in relation to their own national and local problems. In a growing number of cases, other stakeholders – employers and social partners in particular – take part in these discussions and communications.

Probably the clearest proof that the Process has now reached the concrete level of subject-specific study areas comes from the growing number of reports and communications from specialized organizations, academic and professional associations, networks, various initiative groups, etc. Here also, we witness an extremely wide spectrum of activities and initiatives. It is impossible to review them all here in the limited frame of this report; therefore, only a few specific cases – e.g. associations in engineering (CESAER and SEFI), in arts (ELIA and AEC), in law (ELFA), in education (TNTEE); co-operation projects as "Tuning", "Joint Masters' Project", Quality Culture Project, Joint Quality Initiative, ENQA, ECA, ICE-PLAR; contributions by ENIC and NARIC Networks, European Access Network, etc. – are given to illustrate their dimension, frequency, weight and importance while bibliographical and website sources are given for a more comprehensive picture.

Since the Prague Summit, a constant and growing interest for joining the Bologna process and/or for various modes of participating has been observed. Official follow-up bodies (BFUG and BPG) paid considerable attention to issues of further accessions to the Process and its "external dimension".

BFUG and BPG were in a permanent communication with countries which applied for joining at the Berlin Summit. On the other hand, *an internal discussion on further accessions* focused on the need to revise the eligibility criteria laid down in the *Prague Communiqué*, and to introduce into the *Berlin Communiqué* also a specific commitment of the signatory states to realize the Bologna objectives, notwithstanding national differences and particularities. While the origin of this debate is to be found in (a) possible applications for further accessions, it quickly became clear that this was only one of the issues in the further development of the Bologna process as a framework for the reform of higher education in Europe, and that the question of new accessions cannot be divorced from (b) considerations of the implementation of the Bologna process by its current members. *The closer we get to 2010, the more important it will be to assess whether policies have been implemented or are likely to be put in place in time for the EHEA to be established.*

The increasing relevance and attractiveness of the Bologna process in the global higher education arena also manifested itself in the 2001-2003 period. Partly, these issues have been linked to the UNESCO agenda and its various international fora; partly there have also been purely "regionally grounded" interests, for example from some Latin American or Caribbean countries where the Bologna process is being considered as a possible model of good practice for the further development of higher education. In discussions, it was pointed out that the Process has its own identity; but it is clear that ways need to be found to deal with the "external dimension" of the Process in future. It was agreed that UNESCO Headquarters might offer a great service, and in fact it has already expressed its interest in participating more actively in the Bologna process.

How the particular goals of both the Bologna Declaration and the Prague Communiqué are reflected in all these discussions, findings and documents of the follow-up period? As we saw, conclusions and recommendations from official follow up seminars are important but they are not the only reference points to answer this question; surveys and studies developed in parallel to the seminars, other discussions, various projects and events should be also taken into account. For that reason, the impact of various Bologna events of the period 2001-2003 is considered in two roughly-drawn clusters – structural and social dimensions of the Bologna process – at the end of the main chapter.

This is a report commissioned by the Follow-up Group of the Bologna process; therefore, at the end a notice on *the work of both follow-up bodies (BFUG and BPG)* as well as some *remarks on steering the Process* are also made. BFUG and BPG have been responsible for the successful implementation of decisions from Prague but they also had to take care of the steering process itself: to reflect on and evaluate their own work, advantages and deficiencies of structures, and methods developed since Bologna and Prague.

Thus, BFUG prepared a "Berlin" proposal for further "handling" of the Process aiming at even more efficient work of the next follow up period 2003 – 2005.

At the end, *Bibliography and Internet sources* are listed for everybody who would like to study results of the follow up period 2001 – 2003 in details, and *a list of abbreviations* is also added. In the *annexes,* recommendations from all ten official Bologna follow-up seminars are given.

ANNEX 8

"Realising the European Higher Education Area". Communiqué of the
Conference of Ministers responsible for Higher Education in Berlin
on 19 September 2003 (hereafter Berlin Communiqué)

Preamble

On 19 June 1999, one year after the Sorbonne Declaration, Ministers responsible for higher education from 29 European countries signed the Bologna
Declaration. They agreed on important joint objectives for the development
of a coherent and cohesive European Higher Education Area by 2010. In the
first follow-up conference held in Prague on 19 May 2001, they increased the
number of the objectives and reaffirmed their commitment to establish the
European Higher Education Area by 2010. On 19 September 2003, Ministers
responsible for higher education from 33 European countries met in Berlin in
order to review the progress achieved and to set priorities and new objectives
for the coming years, with a view to speeding up the realisation of the European Higher Education Area. They agreed on the following considerations,
principles and priorities:

Ministers reaffirm the importance of the social dimension of the Bologna
Process. The need to increase competitiveness must be balanced with the objective of improving the social characteristics of the European Higher
Education Area, aiming at strengthening social cohesion and reducing social
and gender inequalities both at national and at European level. In that context, Ministers reaffirm their position that higher education is a public good
and a public responsibility. They emphasise that in international academic
cooperation and exchanges, academic values should prevail.

Ministers take into due consideration the conclusions of the European
Councils in Lisbon (2000) and Barcelona (2002) aimed at making Europe
"the most competitive and dynamic knowledge-based economy in the world,
capable of sustainable economic growth with more and better jobs and
greater social cohesion" and calling for further action and closer co-operation
in the context of the Bologna Process.

Ministers take note of the Progress Report commissioned by the Follow-
up Group on the development of the Bologna Process between Prague and
Berlin. They also take note of the Trends-III Report prepared by the European University Association (EUA), as well as of the results of the seminars,
which were organised as part of the work programme between Prague and
Berlin by several member States and Higher Education Institutions, organisations and students. Ministers further note the National Reports, which are
evidence of the considerable progress being made in the application of the
principles of the Bologna Process. Finally, they take note of the messages

from the European Commission and the Council of Europe and acknowledge their support for the implementation of the Process.

Ministers agree that efforts shall be undertaken in order to secure closer links overall between the higher education and research systems in their respective countries. The emerging European Higher Education Area will benefit from synergies with the European Research Area, thus strengthening the basis of the Europe of Knowledge. The aim is to preserve Europe's cultural richness and linguistic diversity, based on its heritage of diversified traditions, and to foster its potential of innovation and social and economic development through enhanced co-operation among European Higher Education Institutions.

Ministers recognise the fundamental role in the development of the European Higher Education Area played by Higher Education Institutions and student organisations.

They take note of the message from the European University Association (EUA) arising from the Graz Convention of Higher Education Institutions, the contributions from the European Association of Institutions in Higher Education (EURASHE) and the communications from ESIB – The National Unions of Students in Europe.

Ministers welcome the interest shown by other regions of the world in the development of the European Higher Education Area, and welcome in particular the presence of representatives from European countries not yet party to the Bologna Process as well as from the Follow-up Committee of the European Union, Latin America and Caribbean (EULAC) Common Space for Higher Education as guests at this conference.

Progress

Ministers welcome the various initiatives undertaken since the Prague Higher Education Summit to move towards more comparability and compatibility, to make higher education systems more transparent and to enhance the quality of European higher education at institutional and national levels. They appreciate the co-operation and commitment of all partners – Higher Education Institutions, students and other stakeholders – to this effect.

Ministers emphasise the importance of all elements of the Bologna Process for establishing the European Higher Education Area and stress the need to intensify the efforts at institutional, national and European level. However, to give the Process further momentum, they commit themselves to intermediate priorities for the next two years. They will strengthen their efforts to promote effective quality assurance systems, to step up effective use of the system based on two cycles and to improve the recognition system of degrees and periods of studies.

Quality Assurance

The quality of higher education has proven to be at the heart of the setting up of a European Higher Education Area. Ministers commit themselves to supporting further development of quality assurance at institutional, national and European level. They stress the need to develop mutually shared criteria and methodologies on quality assurance.

They also stress that consistent with the principle of institutional autonomy, the primary responsibility for quality assurance in higher education lies with each institution itself and this provides the basis for real accountability of the academic system within the national quality framework.

Therefore, they agree that by 2005 national quality assurance systems should include:

- A definition of the responsibilities of the bodies and institutions involved.
- Evaluation of programmes or institutions, including internal assessment, external review, participation of students and the publication of results.
- A system of accreditation, certification or comparable procedures.
- International participation, co-operation and networking.

At the European level, Ministers call upon ENQA through its members, in co-operation with the EUA, EURASHE and ESIB, to develop an agreed set of standards, procedures and guidelines on quality assurance, to explore ways of ensuring an adequate peer review system for quality assurance and/or accreditation agencies or bodies, and to report back through the Follow-up Group to Ministers in 2005. Due account will be taken of the expertise of other quality assurance associations and networks.

Degree structure: Adoption of a system essentially based on two main cycles

Ministers are pleased to note that, following their commitment in the Bologna Declaration to the two-cycle system, a comprehensive restructuring of the European landscape of higher education is now under way. All Ministers commit themselves to having started the implementation of the two cycle system by 2005.

Ministers underline the importance of consolidating the progress made, and of improving understanding and acceptance of the new qualifications through reinforcing dialogue within institutions and between institutions and employers.

Ministers encourage the member States to elaborate a framework of comparable and compatible qualifications for their higher education systems, which should seek to describe qualifications in terms of workload, level, learning outcomes, competences and profile. They also undertake to elaborate an overarching framework of qualifications for the European Higher Education Area.

Within such frameworks, degrees should have different defined outcomes. First and second cycle degrees should have different orientations and various profiles in order to accommodate a diversity of individual, academic and labour market needs. First cycle degrees should give access, in the sense of the Lisbon Recognition Convention, to second cycle programmes. Second cycle degrees should give access to doctoral studies.

Ministers invite the Follow-up Group to explore whether and how shorter higher education may be linked to the first cycle of a qualifications framework for the European Higher Education Area.

Ministers stress their commitment to making higher education equally accessible to all, on the basis of capacity, by every appropriate means.

Promotion of mobility

Mobility of students and academic and administrative staff is the basis for establishing a European Higher Education Area. Ministers emphasise its importance for academic and cultural as well as political, social and economic spheres. They note with satisfaction that since their last meeting, mobility figures have increased, thanks also to the substantial support of the European Union programmes, and agree to undertake the necessary steps to improve the quality and coverage of statistical data on student mobility.

They reaffirm their intention to make every effort to remove all obstacles to mobility within the European Higher Education Area. With a view to promoting student mobility,

Ministers will take the necessary steps to enable the portability of national loans and grants.

Establishment of a system of credits

Ministers stress the important role played by the European Credit Transfer System (ECTS) in facilitating student mobility and international curriculum development. They note that ECTS is increasingly becoming a generalised basis for the national credit systems. They encourage further progress with the goal that the ECTS becomes not only a transfer but also an accumulation system, to be applied consistently as it develops within the emerging European Higher Education Area.

Recognition of degrees: Adoption of a system of easily readable and comparable degrees

Ministers underline the importance of the Lisbon Recognition Convention, which should be ratified by all countries participating in the Bologna Process, and call on the ENIC and NARIC networks along with the competent National Authorities to further the implementation of the Convention.

They set the objective that every student graduating as from 2005 should receive the Diploma Supplement automatically and free of charge. It should be issued in a widely spoken European language.

They appeal to institutions and employers to make full use of the Diploma Supplement, so as to take advantage of the improved transparency and flexibility of the higher education degree systems, for fostering employability and facilitating academic recognition for further studies.

Higher education institutions and students
Ministers welcome the commitment of Higher Education Institutions and students to the Bologna Process and recognise that it is ultimately the active participation of all partners in the Process that will ensure its long-term success.

Aware of the contribution strong institutions can make to economic and societal development, Ministers accept that institutions need to be empowered to take decisions on their internal organisation and administration. Ministers further call upon institutions to ensure that the reforms become fully integrated into core institutional functions and processes.

Ministers note the constructive participation of student organisations in the Bologna Process and underline the necessity to include the students continuously and at an early stage in further activities.

Students are full partners in higher education governance. Ministers note that national legal measures for ensuring student participation are largely in place throughout the European Higher Education Area. They also call on institutions and student organisations to identify ways of increasing actual student involvement in higher education governance.

Ministers stress the need for appropriate studying and living conditions for the students, so that they can successfully complete their studies within an appropriate period of time without obstacles related to their social and economic background. They also stress the need for more comparable data on the social and economic situation of students.

Promotion of the European dimension in higher education
Ministers note that, following their call in Prague, additional modules, courses and curricula with European content, orientation or organisation are being developed.

They note that initiatives have been taken by Higher Education Institutions in various European countries to pool their academic resources and cultural traditions in order to promote the development of integrated study programmes and joint degrees at first, second and third level.

Moreover, they stress the necessity of ensuring a substantial period of study abroad in joint degree programmes as well as proper provision for linguistic diversity and language learning, so that students may achieve their full potential for European identity, citizenship and employability.

Ministers agree to engage at the national level to remove legal obstacles to the establishment and recognition of such degrees and to actively support the development and adequate quality assurance of integrated curricula leading to joint degrees.

Promoting the attractiveness of the European Higher Education Area
Ministers agree that the attractiveness and openness of the European higher education should be reinforced. They confirm their readiness to further develop scholarship programmes for students from third countries.

Ministers declare that transnational exchanges in higher education should be governed on the basis of academic quality and academic values, and agree to work in all appropriate fora to that end. In all appropriate circumstances such fora should include the social and economic partners.

They encourage the co-operation with regions in other parts of the world by opening Bologna seminars and conferences to representatives of these regions.

Lifelong learning
Ministers underline the important contribution of higher education in making lifelong learning a reality. They are taking steps to align their national policies to realise this goal and urge Higher Education Institutions and all concerned to enhance the possibilities for lifelong learning at higher education level including the recognition of prior learning. They emphasise that such action must be an integral part of higher education activity.

Ministers furthermore call those working on qualifications frameworks for the European Higher Education Area to encompass the wide range of flexible learning paths, opportunities and techniques and to make appropriate use of the ECTS credits.

They stress the need to improve opportunities for all citizens, in accordance with their aspirations and abilities, to follow the lifelong learning paths into and within higher education.

Additional Actions

European Higher Education Area and European Research Area –
two pillars of the knowledge based society
Conscious of the need to promote closer links between the EHEA and the ERA in a Europe of Knowledge, and of the importance of research as an integral part of higher education across Europe, Ministers consider it necessary to go beyond the present focus on two main cycles of higher education to include the doctoral level as the third cycle in the Bologna Process. They emphasise the importance of research and research training and the promotion of interdisciplinarity in maintaining and improving the quality of higher education and in enhancing the competitiveness of European higher education more generally. Ministers call for increased mobility at the doctoral and post-doctoral levels and encourage the institutions concerned to increase their cooperation in doctoral studies and the training of young researchers.

Ministers will make the necessary effort to make European Higher Education Institutions an even more attractive and efficient partner. Therefore Ministers ask Higher Education Institutions to increase the role and relevance of research to technological, social and cultural evolution and to the needs of society.

Ministers understand that there are obstacles inhibiting the achievement of these goals and these cannot be resolved by Higher Education Institutions alone. It requires strong support, including financial, and appropriate decisions from national Governments and European Bodies.

Finally, Ministers state that networks at doctoral level should be given support to stimulate the development of excellence and to become one of the hallmarks of the European Higher Education Area.

Stocktaking

With a view to the goals set for 2010, it is expected that measures will be introduced to take stock of progress achieved in the Bologna Process. A mid-term stocktaking exercise would provide reliable information on how the Process is actually advancing and would offer the possibility to take corrective measures, if appropriate.

Ministers charge the Follow-up Group with organising a stocktaking process in time for their summit in 2005 and undertaking to prepare detailed reports on the progress and implementation of the intermediate priorities set for the next two years:

- quality assurance
- two-cycle system
- recognition of degrees and periods of studies

Participating countries will, furthermore, be prepared to allow access to the necessary information for research on higher education relating to the objectives of the Bologna Process. Access to data banks on ongoing research and research results shall be facilitated.

Further Follow-up

New members

Ministers consider it necessary to adapt the clause in the Prague Communiqué on applications for membership as follows:

Countries party to the European Cultural Convention shall be eligible for membership of the European Higher Education Area provided that they at the same time declare their willingness to pursue and implement the objectives of the Bologna Process in their own systems of higher education. Their applications should contain information on how they will implement the principles and objectives of the declaration.

Ministers decide to accept the requests for membership of Albania, Andorra, Bosnia and Herzegovina, Holy See, Russia, Serbia and Montenegro, "the Former Yugoslav Republic of Macedonia" and to welcome these states as new members thus expanding the process to 40 European Countries.

Ministers recognise that membership of the Bologna Process implies substantial change and reform for all signatory countries. They agree to support the new signatory countries in those changes and reforms, incorporating them within the mutual discussions and assistance, which the Bologna Process involves.

Follow-up structure
Ministers entrust the implementation of all the issues covered in the Communiqué, the overall steering of the Bologna Process and the preparation of the next ministerial meeting to a Follow-up Group, which shall be composed of the representatives of all members of the Bologna Process and the European Commission, with the Council of Europe, the EUA, EURASHE, ESIB and UNESCO/CEPES as consultative members. This group, which should be convened at least twice a year, shall be chaired by the EU Presidency, with the host country of the next Ministerial Conference as vice-chair.

A Board also chaired by the EU Presidency shall oversee the work between the meetings of the Follow-up Group. The Board will be composed of the chair, the next host country as vice-chair, the preceding and the following EU Presidencies, three participating countries elected by the Follow-up Group for one year, the European Commission and, as consultative members, the Council of Europe, the EUA, EURASHE and ESIB. The Follow-up Group as well as the Board may convene ad hoc working groups as they deem necessary.

The overall follow-up work will be supported by a Secretariat which the country hosting the next Ministerial Conference will provide.

In its first meeting after the Berlin Conference, the Follow-up Group is asked to further define the responsibilities of the Board and the tasks of the Secretariat.

Work programme 2003-2005
Ministers ask the Follow-up Group to co-ordinate activities for progress of the Bologna Process as indicated in the themes and actions covered by this Communiqué and report on them in time for the next ministerial meeting in 2005.

Next Conference
Ministers decide to hold the next conference in the city of Bergen (Norway) in May 2005.

ANNEX 9

Requirements and Procedures for Joining the Bologna Process, BFUG B3 7fin, 6 July 2004

The criteria for admission of new members to the Bologna Process at the Ministerial Conference in Bergen have been set by the Berlin Communiqué:

> *Countries party to the European Cultural Convention shall be eligible for membership of the European Higher Education Area provided that they at the same time declare their willingness to pursue and implement the objectives of the Bologna Process in their own systems of higher education. Their applications should contain information on how they will implement the principles and objectives of the declaration.*

Applicant countries have sought guidance on the procedures and requirements for membership of the Bologna Process. The purpose of this document is to meet this objective in a fair and transparent manner. It also consolidates both principles and action lines of the Bologna Process into a single document.

1. PRINCIPLES

While the 10 actions lines are the main focus of members, it is equally important to note the underlying principles of the Bologna Process. The realisation of the European Higher Education Area can only be achieved by incorporating their philosophy within the higher education system of each country. These principles, which all come from the Bologna Declaration and/or from the Prague and Berlin Communiqués, are elaborated below:

- International mobility of students and staff;
- Autonomous universities;
- Student participation in the governance of higher education;
- Public responsibility for higher education;
- The social dimension of the Bologna Process.

Applicant States are requested to confirm their adherence to these principles in their applications.

1.1. International mobility of students and staff

"Promotion of mobility by overcoming obstacles to the effective exercise of free movement" (Bologna declaration).

"Ministers reaffirmed that efforts to promote mobility must be continued to enable students, teachers, researchers and administrative staff to benefit

from the richness of the European Higher Education Area including its democratic values, diversity of cultures and languages and the diversity of the higher education systems." (Prague Communiqué)

1.2. Autonomous universities

"European higher education institutions, for their part, have accepted the challenge and taken up a main role in constructing the European area of higher education, also in the wake of the fundamental principles laid down in the Bologna Magna Charta Universitatum of 1988.[1] This is of the highest importance, given that Universities' independence and autonomy ensure that higher education and research systems continuously adapt to changing needs, society's demands and advances in scientific knowledge." (Bologna Declaration)

"Ministers accept that institutions need to be empowered to take decisions on their internal organisation and administration." (Berlin Communiqué)

1.3. Student participation in the governance of higher education

"Ministers affirmed that students should participate in and influence the organisation and content of education at universities and other higher education institutions." (Prague Communiqué)

"Ministers note the constructive participation of student organisations in the Bologna Process and underline the necessity to include the students continuously and at an early stage in further activities. Students are full partners in higher education governance. Ministers note that national legal measures for ensuring student participation are largely in place throughout the European Higher Education Area. They also call on institutions and student organisations to identify ways of increasing actual student involvement in higher education governance." (Berlin Communiqué)

1.4. Higher education as a public responsibility

"They [the Ministers] supported the idea that higher education should be considered a public good and is and will remain a public responsibility..." (Prague Communiqué)

1.5. The social dimension of the Bologna Process

"Ministers reaffirm the importance of the social dimension of the Bologna Process. The need to increase competitiveness must be balanced with the objective of improving the social characteristics of the European Higher Education Area, aiming at strengthening social cohesion and reducing social

---

1   "The university is an autonomous institution at the heart of societies differently organized because of geography and historical heritage; it produces, examines, appraises and hands down culture by research and teaching."

and gender inequalities both at national and at European level." (Berlin Communiqué)

2. OBJECTIVES

The objectives of the Bologna Process are summarised in its 10 action lines. In common with all members, applicants are equally obliged to reach the common goals by 2010 as defined in the Bologna Declaration supplemented by the Prague and Berlin Communiqués. Three intermediate goals for 2005 were defined in the Berlin Communiqué.

2.1. The Bologna Action Lines
Six action lines were introduced in the Bologna Declaration:
1. Adoption of a system of easily readable and comparable degrees;
2. Adoption of a system essentially based on two cycles;
3. Establishment of a system of credits;
4. Promotion of mobility;
5. Promotion of European co-operation in quality assurance;
6. Promotion of the European dimension in higher education.
Three more were introduced in the Prague Communiqué:
7. Lifelong learning;
8. Higher education institutions and students;
9. Promoting the attractiveness of the European Higher Education Area

(EHEA).
A tenth action line was introduced in the Berlin Communiqué:
10. Doctoral studies and the synergy between the EHEA and the ERA (European Research Area).
The various action lines of the Bologna Process are reflected in the BFUG Work Programme 2003-2005. The social dimension of the Bologna Process might be seen as an overarching or transversal action line.

3. REPORTS FROM POTENTIAL NEW MEMBERS

All members of the Bologna Process will be asked to produce a national report before the Bergen Ministerial Conference. Potential members will be asked to produce a report in a similar format.

In Berlin, Ministers defined three intermediate priorities: quality assurance, the two-cycle degree system and recognition of degrees and periods of studies. The achievement of these goals by the 40 members States will be the subject of a Stocktaking exercise, and while potential members will not be part of the stocktaking, they will be required to indicate the extent to which existing (or planned) reforms of their higher education systems meet the same goals. The specific targets are as follows:

3.1. Quality assurance
The primary responsibility for quality assurance should lie with the institutions.
The national quality assurance system should include:
- A definition of the responsibilities of the bodies and institutions involved;
- Evaluation of programmes or institutions, including internal assessment, external review, participation of students and the publication of results;
- A system of accreditation, certification or comparable procedures.

3.2. Two-cycle degree system
A national degree system for higher education based on two main cycles should have been introduced. Access to the second cycle shall require successful completion of first cycle studies lasting a minimum of three years. The degree awarded after the first cycle should also be relevant to the labour market. The second cycle should lead to the master's and/or doctoral degree.

Members of the Bologna Process are committed to having started the implementation of the two-cycle system by 2005.

3.3. Recognition of degrees and periods of studies
In terms of the adoption of a system of easily readable and comparable degrees, members are encouraged to ratify the Lisbon Recognition Convention. Allied to this, members are committed that every student graduating should receive the Diploma Supplement automatically and free of charge, in a widely spoken European language.

4. PROCEDURE FOR APPLICATION

The decision to accept new members to the Bologna Process will be taken by the next Ministerial Conference (Bergen, 19–20 May 2005). The role of the BFUG is to make a recommendation, having satisfied itself of the credentials and commitment of the applicants.

Potential members should send an application for membership to the Minister responsible for Higher Education in the Host Country of the next Ministerial Conference[2], with a copy to the BFUG Chair[3]. The application, which should be signed by the (national) Minister responsible for higher education, should declare their commitment to pursue and implement the principles and objectives of the Bologna Process in their own systems of

2 Minister Kristin Clemet, Norwegian Ministry of Education and Research, Postboks 8119 Dep, NO-0032 Oslo
3 m.e.leegwater@minocw.nl

higher education. The application should be complemented by a report, detailing the current higher education policies of the country in the light of the Bologna Process and outlining what reforms they plan to undertake to meet the goals of the Process. The attached template identifies headlines and key questions which should be addressed in the context of this report.

The report should be sent to the BFUG Chair and Secretariat[4], in English, before 31 December 2004. This is also the final deadline for applications.

When an application is received, the BFUG Chair and Secretariat will verify that it satisfies the prescribed procedures. A confirmation of receipt will be sent to the applicant country. At the same time, the BFUG will be informed of the application. The applicant country will then be invited to seminars and other events in the Bologna Process.

Further procedures regarding the processing and assessment of applications will be decided by the BFUG meeting on 12-13 October 2004.

Decisions regarding membership will be taken by the Ministerial Conference on 19-20 May 2005.

SUMMARY

- Applications for membership of the Bologna Process should be signed by the Minister responsible for higher education.
- They should be addressed to the Norwegian Minister of Education, as host of the next Ministerial Conference, with a copy to the Dutch Minister of Education as Chair of the Bologna Process in the autumn of 2004.
- Applications should be accompanied by – or followed by – a national report in English elaborated in accordance with the guidelines in the appendix.
- The deadline for submitting applications as well as national reports is **31 December 2004.**

The Bologna Secretariat may be contacted for further information.

All about the Bologna Process at: http://www.bologna-bergen2005.no/

---

4   bologna@ufd.dep.no

ANNEX 10a

The European Higher Education Area – Achieving the Goals.
Communiqué of the Conference of European Ministers Responsible
for Higher Education, Bergen, 19-20 May 2005
(hereafter Bergen Communiqué)

We, Ministers responsible for higher education in the participating countries of the Bologna Process, have met for a mid-term review and for
setting goals and priorities towards 2010. At this conference, we have welcomed Armenia, Azerbaijan, Georgia, Moldova and Ukraine as new
participating countries in the Bologna Process. We all share the common
understanding of the principles, objectives and commitments of the Process
as expressed in the Bologna Declaration and in the subsequent communiqués from the Ministerial Conferences in Prague and Berlin. We confirm
our commitment to coordinating our policies through the Bologna Process
to establish the European Higher Education Area (EHEA) by 2010, and we
commit ourselves to assisting the new participating countries to implement
the goals of the Process.

I. Partnership

We underline the central role of higher education institutions, their staff and
students as partners in the Bologna Process. Their role in the implementation
of the Process becomes all the more important now that the necessary legislative reforms are largely in place, and we encourage them to continue and
intensify their efforts to establish the EHEA. We welcome the clear commitment of higher education institutions across Europe to the Process, and we
recognise that time is needed to optimise the impact of structural change on
curricula and thus to ensure the introduction of the innovative teaching and
learning processes that Europe needs.

We welcome the support of organisations representing business and the
social partners and look forward to intensified cooperation in reaching the
goals of the Bologna Process. We further welcome the contributions of the
international institutions and organisations that are partners to the Process.

II. Taking stock

We take note of the significant progress made towards our goals, as set out in
the General Report 2003-2005 from the Follow-up Group, in EUA's *Trends
IV* report, and in ESIB's report *Bologna with Student Eyes.*

At our meeting in Berlin, we asked the Follow-up Group for a mid-term stocktaking, focusing on three priorities – the degree system, quality assurance and the recognition of degrees and periods of study. From the stocktaking report we note that substantial progress has been made in these three priority areas. It will be important to ensure that progress is consistent across all participating countries. We therefore see a need for greater sharing of expertise to build capacity at both institutional and governmental level.

The degree system

We note with satisfaction that the two-cycle degree system is being implemented on a large scale, with more than half of the students being enrolled in it in most countries. However, there are still some obstacles to access between cycles. Furthermore, there is a need for greater dialogue, involving Governments, institutions and social partners, to increase the employability of graduates with bachelor qualifications, including in appropriate posts within the public service.

We adopt the overarching framework for qualifications in the EHEA, comprising three cycles (including, within national contexts, the possibility of intermediate qualifications), generic descriptors for each cycle based on learning outcomes and competences, and credit ranges in the first and second cycles. We commit ourselves to elaborating national frameworks for qualifications compatible with the overarching framework for qualifications in the EHEA by 2010, and to having started work on this by 2007. We ask the Follow-up Group to report on the implementation and further development of the overarching framework.

We underline the importance of ensuring complementarity between the overarching framework for the EHEA and the proposed broader framework for qualifications for lifelong learning encompassing general education as well as vocational education and training as now being developed within the European Union as well as among participating countries. We ask the European Commission fully to consult all parties to the Bologna Process as work progresses.

Quality assurance

Almost all countries have made provision for a quality assurance system based on the criteria set out in the Berlin Communiqué and with a high degree of cooperation and networking. However, there is still progress to be made, in particular as regards student involvement and international cooperation. Furthermore, we urge higher education institutions to continue their efforts to enhance the quality of their activities through the systematic introduction of internal mechanisms and their direct correlation to external quality assurance.

We adopt the standards and guidelines for quality assurance in the European Higher Education Area as proposed by ENQA. We commit ourselves to
introducing the proposed model for peer review of quality assurance agencies
on a national basis, while respecting the commonly accepted guidelines and
criteria. We welcome the principle of a European register of quality assurance agencies based on national review. We ask that the practicalities of
implementation be further developed by ENQA in cooperation with EUA,
EURASHE and ESIB with a report back to us through the Follow-up Group.
We underline the importance of cooperation between nationally recognised
agencies with a view to enhancing the mutual recognition of accreditation or
quality assurance decisions.

Recognition of degrees and study periods

We note that 36 of the 45 participating countries have now ratified the Lisbon
Recognition Convention. We urge those that have not already done so to ratify the Convention without delay. We commit ourselves to ensuring the full
implementation of its principles, and to incorporating them in national legislation as appropriate. We call on all participating countries to address
recognition problems identified by the ENIC/NARIC networks. We will draw
up national action plans to improve the quality of the process associated with
the recognition of foreign qualifications. These plans will form part of each
country's national report for the next Ministerial Conference. We express
support for the subsidiary texts to the Lisbon Recognition Convention and
call upon all national authorities and other stakeholders to recognise joint
degrees awarded in two or more countries in the EHEA.
   We see the development of national and European frameworks for qualifications as an opportunity to further embed lifelong learning in higher
education. We will work with higher education institutions and others to improve recognition of prior learning including, where possible, non-formal and
informal learning for access to, and as elements in, higher education programmes.

III. Further challenges and priorities Higher education and research

We underline the importance of higher education in further enhancing research and the importance of research in underpinning higher education for
the economic and cultural development of our societies and for social cohesion. We note that the efforts to introduce structural change and improve the
quality of teaching should not detract from the effort to strengthen research
and innovation. We therefore emphasise the importance of research and research training in maintaining and improving the quality of and enhancing

the competitiveness and attractiveness of the EHEA. With a view to achieving better results we recognise the need to improve the synergy between the higher education sector and other research sectors throughout our respective countries and between the EHEA and the European Research Area.

To achieve these objectives, doctoral level qualifications need to be fully aligned with the EHEA overarching framework for qualifications using the outcomes-based approach. The core component of doctoral training is the advancement of knowledge through original research. Considering the need for structured doctoral programmes and the need for transparent supervision and assessment, we note that the normal workload of the third cycle in most countries would correspond to 3-4 years full time. We urge universities to ensure that their doctoral programmes promote interdisciplinary training and the development of transferable skills, thus meeting the needs of the wider employment market. We need to achieve an overall increase in the numbers of doctoral candidates taking up research careers within the EHEA. We consider participants in third cycle programmes both as students and as early stage researchers. We charge the Bologna Follow-up Group with inviting the European University Association, together with other interested partners, to prepare a report under the responsibility of the Follow-up Group on the further development of the basic principles for doctoral programmes, to be presented to Ministers in 2007. Overregulation of doctoral programmes must be avoided.

The social dimension

The social dimension of the Bologna Process is a constituent part of the EHEA and a necessary condition for the attractiveness and competitiveness of the EHEA. We therefore renew our commitment to making quality higher education equally accessible to all, and stress the need for appropriate conditions for students so that they can complete their studies without obstacles related to their social and economic background. The social dimension includes measures taken by governments to help students, especially from socially disadvantaged groups, in financial and economic aspects and to provide them with guidance and counselling services with a view to widening access.

Mobility

We recognise that mobility of students and staff among all participating countries remains one of the key objectives of the Bologna Process. Aware of the many remaining challenges to be overcome, we reconfirm our commitment to facilitate the portability of grants and loans where appropriate through joint action, with a view to making mobility within the EHEA a reality. We shall intensify our efforts to lift obstacles to mobility by facilitating the delivery of visa and work permits and by encouraging participation in mobility programmes. We urge institutions and students to make full use of mobility programmes, advocating full recognition of study periods abroad within such programmes.

The attractiveness of the EHEA and cooperation with other parts of the world

The European Higher Education Area must be open and should be attractive to other parts of the world. Our contribution to achieving education for all should be based on the principle of sustainable development and be in accordance with the ongoing international work on developing guidelines for quality provision of cross-border higher education. We reiterate that in international academic cooperation, academic values should prevail.

We see the European Higher Education Area as a partner of higher education systems in other regions of the world, stimulating balanced student and staff exchange and cooperation between higher education institutions. We underline the importance of intercultural understanding and respect. We look forward to enhancing the understanding of the Bologna Process in other continents by sharing our experiences of reform processes with neighbouring regions. We stress the need for dialogue on issues of mutual interest. We see the need to identify partner regions and intensify the exchange of ideas and experiences with those regions. We ask the Follow-up Group to elaborate and agree on a strategy for the external dimension.

IV. Taking stock on progress for 2007

We charge the Follow-up Group with continuing and widening the stocktaking process and reporting in time for the next Ministerial Conference. We expect stocktaking to be based on the appropriate methodology and to continue in the fields of the degree system, quality assurance and recognition of degrees and study periods, and by 2007 we will have largely completed the implementation of these three intermediate priorities.

In particular, we shall look for progress in:

- implementation of the standards and guidelines for quality assurance as proposed in the ENQA report;
- implementation of the national frameworks for qualifications;
- the awarding and recognition of joint degrees, including at the doctorate level;
- creating opportunities for flexible learning paths in higher education, including procedures for the recognition of prior learning.

We also charge the Follow-up Group with presenting comparable data on the mobility of staff and students as well as on the social and economic situation of students in participating countries as a basis for future stocktaking and reporting in time for the next Ministerial Conference. The future stocktaking will have to take into account the social dimension as defined above.

V. Preparing for 2010

Building on the achievements so far in the Bologna Process, we wish to establish a European Higher Education Area based on the principles of quality and transparency. We must cherish our rich heritage and cultural diversity in contributing to a knowledge-based society. We commit ourselves to upholding the principle of public responsibility for higher education in the context of complex modern societies. As higher education is situated at the crossroads of research, education and innovation, it is also the key to Europe's competitiveness. As we move closer to 2010, we undertake to ensure that higher education institutions enjoy the necessary autonomy to implement the agreed reforms, and we recognise the need for sustainable funding of institutions.

The European Higher Education Area is structured around three cycles, where each level has the function of preparing the student for the labour market, for further competence building and for active citizenship. The overarching framework for qualifications, the agreed set of European standards and guidelines for quality assurance and the recognition of degrees and periods of study are also key characteristics of the structure of the EHEA.

We endorse the follow-up structure set up in Berlin, with the inclusion of the Education International (EI) Pan-European Structure, the European Association for Quality Assurance in Higher Education (ENQA), and the Union of Industrial and Employers' Confederations of Europe (UNICE) as new consultative members of the Follow-up Group.

As the Bologna Process leads to the establishment of the EHEA, we have to consider the appropriate arrangements needed to support the continuing development beyond 2010, and we ask the Follow-up Group to explore these issues.

We will hold the next Ministerial Conference in London in 2007.

45 countries participate in the Bologna Process and are members of the Follow-up Group: Albania, Andorra, Armenia, Austria, Azerbaijan, Belgium (Flemish Community and French Community), Bosnia and Herzegovina, Bulgaria, Croatia, Cyprus, the Czech Republic, Denmark, Estonia, Finland, France, Georgia, Germany, Greece, the Holy See, Hungary, Iceland, Ireland, Italy, Latvia, Liechtenstein, Lithuania, Luxembourg, Malta, Moldova, the Netherlands, Norway, Poland, Portugal, Romania, the Russian Federation, Serbia and Montenegro, the Slovak Republic, Slovenia, Spain, Sweden, Switzerland, "the former Yugoslav Republic of Macedonia", Turkey, Ukraine and the United Kingdom. In addition, the European Commission is a voting member of the Follow-up Group.

The Council of Europe, the National Unions of Students in Europe (ESIB), the Education International (EI) Pan-European Structure, the European Association for Quality Assurance in Higher Education (ENQA), the European University Association (EUA), the European Association of Institutions in Higher Education (EURASHE), the European Centre for Higher Education (UNESCO-CEPES) and the Union of Industrial and Employers' Confederations of Europe (UNICE) are consultative members of the Follow-up Group.

Annex 10b

'Index' and 'Executive Summary' of the General Report
"From Berlin to Bergen" by the Bologna Follow-up Group to Conference
of Ministers Responsible for Higher Education, Bergen, 19-20 May 2005

Index

"From Berlin to Bergen"

Executive Summary of the General Report of the Bologna Follow-up Group to the Conference of Ministers Responsible for Higher Education, Bergen, 19-20 May 2005

Halfway towards 2010

Halfway in the Bologna Process towards 2010, we start to see the contours of the European Higher Education Area (EHEA). It is not a single, unified higher education system, but a group of more than forty national systems developing according to jointly agreed principles.

For many countries, "Bologna" is an inspiration and a recipe for highly needed reforms in their higher education systems. At the same time we are jointly building a common framework to turn into reality the idea that students and staff shall be able to move freely within the EHEA, having full recognition of their qualifications. Priority has been given to developing

- a three-cycle degree system in each participating country,
- national quality assurance systems cooperating in a Europe-wide network,
- mutual recognition between participating countries of degrees and study periods.

Each of these elements has a national dimension and a European Dimension. So has the concept of qualifications frameworks now introduced in the Bologna Process, with national frameworks fitting into an overarching framework for the EHEA. Agreed standards and guidelines introduce a European dimension also in quality assurance.

Developments

As the Bologna Process has been developing, its ten action lines have tended to overlap or merge and new concepts have been introduced. The action lines have been imperative for the dynamics of the Bologna Process, but they do not explicitly define the final goal.

Recommendations from the fourteen *Bologna Follow-up Seminars* included in the BFUG Work Programme have fed into the stocktaking project, into the development of the overarching framework for qualifications and into the joint efforts in quality assurance, and have also directly influenced the drafting of the Bergen Communiqué.

All participating countries have produced National Reports. These reports have given information on planned reforms as well as on what has already been accomplished.

An overarching framework of qualifications for the EHEA

The report from the Working Group established by the BFUG provides a series of recommendations, among them the following:

- the framework for qualifications in the EHEA should be an overarching framework with a high level of generality, consisting of three main cycles, with additional provision for a short cycle within the first cycle;
- the framework should include cycle descriptors in the form of generic qualification descriptors that can be used as reference points. It is proposed that the Dublin Descriptors are adopted as the cycle descriptors for the framework for qualifications of the European Higher Education Area;
- *guidelines* for the credit range typically associated with the completion of each cycle:

  - Short cycle (within the first cycle) qualifications: 120 ECTS credits;
  - First cycle qualifications: 180-240 ECTS credits;
  - Second cycle qualifications: 90-120 ECTS credits, with a minimum of 60 credits at the level of the 2nd cycle;
  - Third cycle qualifications do not necessarily have credits associated with them.

Considerations by the Bologna Follow-up Group
The Bologna Follow-up Group has advised Ministers that they may adopt the overarching framework for qualifications in the EHEA, comprising three cycles (including the possibility of shorter higher education linked to the first cycle), generic descriptors for each cycle based on learning outcomes and competences, and credit ranges for the first and second cycles.

The BFUG has also advised Ministers to commit themselves to elaborating national frameworks for qualifications compatible with the overarching framework for qualifications in the EHEA by 2010, and to having started work on this by 2007.

The BFUG has further advised Ministers to underline the importance of complementarity between the overarching framework for the EHEA and the broader European framework of qualifications for lifelong learning now being developed within the European Union.

European cooperation in quality assurance
In Berlin, Ministers called upon ENQA, in cooperation with the EUA, EURASHE and ESIB, to develop an agreed set of standards, procedures and guidelines on quality assurance and a peer review system for quality assurance bodies. The main results and recommendations are:

- There will be European standards for internal and external quality assurance, and for external quality assurance agencies.
- European quality assurance agencies will be expected to submit themselves to a cyclical review within five years.
- A European register of quality assurance agencies will be established.
- A European Register Committee will act as a gatekeeper for the register.

Considerations by the Bologna Follow-up Group
The BFUG has advised Ministers that the proposed standards and guidelines for quality assurance in the EHEA and the proposed model for peer review of quality assurance agencies may be introduced and tried out on a national basis in the participating countries.

The BFUG has welcomed the establishment of a European Register of quality assurance agencies and asked ENQA to develop rules and regulations for such a register. The BFUG has advised Ministers that the practicalities of implementation of the Register and the Register Committee may be further developed by ENQA in cooperation with EUA, EURASHE and ESIB.

Recognition of degrees and study periods
In June 2004, a Recommendation on the Recognition of Joint Degrees was adopted as a subsidiary text to the Lisbon Recognition Convention. Governments should review their legislation and introduce legal provisions that would facilitate recognition of joint degrees.

By April 2005, 31 of the 40 participating countries in the Bologna Process and all five applicant countries had ratified the Lisbon Recognition Convention.

Considerations by the Bologna Follow-up Group
The BFUG has advised Ministers to urge participating countries that have not already done so to ratify the Convention without delay. They should ensure the full implementation of its principles, and incorporate them in national legislation. Ministers may call on all participating countries to address recognition problems identified by the ENIC/NARIC networks. Ministers should express support for the subsidiary texts to the Lisbon Recognition Convention and call upon all national authorities and other stakeholders to recognise joint degrees awarded in two or more countries in the EHEA.

Higher education institutions and others should improve recognition of prior learning including non-formal and informal learning for access to and as elements in higher education programmes. The development of national and European frameworks for qualifications may be an opportunity to further embed lifelong learning in higher education.

Stocktaking
To conduct the stocktaking exercise asked for by Ministers in Berlin, a Working Group was established by the BFUG. At the request of the Working Group, the EURYDICE report *"Focus on the Structure of Higher Education in Europe"* extended its review beyond the 31 countries normally covered by its network in order to provide a uniform analysis of the 40 "Bologna" countries. Along with the material prepared by EURYDICE, the National Reports represented the main source of information.

Scorecards have been developed for each participating country as well as average scores for the forty countries. The analysis indicates that overall, participating countries have made good progress in the three priority action lines. However, the strength of the Bologna Process has been its voluntary and collaborative nature. The increased membership underlines the need to ensure consistency of progress, and participating countries should be prepared to take responsibility to assist each other as we all move towards 2010.

Considerations by the Bologna Follow-up Group

The BFUG has noted that substantial progress has been made in the three priority areas. It is important to ensure that progress is consistent across all participating countries, and the BFUG will advise Ministers that there is a need for greater sharing of expertise to build capacity at both institutional and government level.

The BFUG has noted that the two-cycle degree system is being implemented on a large scale, with more than half of the students being enrolled in it in most countries. However, there are still some obstacles to access between cycles. Ministers may see the need for greater dialogue, involving governments, institutions and social partners, to increase the employability of graduates with bachelor qualifications, including posts within the public service.

The BFUG has noted that almost all countries have made provision for a quality assurance system based on the criteria set out in the Berlin Communiqué and with a high degree of cooperation and networking. However, there is still progress to be made, in particular as regards student involvement and international cooperation.

With reference also to the follow-up of the Lisbon Recognition Convention mentioned above, Ministers are advised to draw up national action plans to improve the quality of the process associated with the recognition of foreign qualifications.

Five new participating countries

The criteria for admission of new participating countries (members) to the Bologna Process were set by the Berlin Communiqué, saying that

> *"countries party to the European Cultural Convention shall be eligible for membership of the European Higher Education Area provided that they at the same time declare their willingness to pursue and implement the objectives of the Bologna Process in their own systems of higher education.["]*

A document consolidating principles and action lines of the Bologna Process made it clear to potential newcomers that the EHEA can only be achieved by incorporating the "Bologna" principles in the higher education system of each country. Just as all participating countries were asked to produce a National Report, newcomers were asked to produce a report in a similar format, with a special focus on the three intermediate priorities.

By the deadline applications had been received from Armenia, Azerbaijan, Georgia, Kazakhstan, Moldova and Ukraine. Later, Kosovo also applied.

All applications were in accordance with the prescribed procedure; however, Kazakhstan and Kosovo are not signatories to the European Cultural Convention.

Considerations by the Bologna Follow-up Group
Based on the applications and reports received, the BFUG has advised Ministers to welcome Armenia, Azerbaijan, Georgia, Moldova and Ukraine as participating countries (members) in the Bologna Process at the Bergen conference.

2010 and beyond
The Bologna Process is a process of voluntary cooperation between different national systems overseen by the BFUG and associating the various partners. There are no legally binding provisions except for the Lisbon Recognition Convention; the cooperation is based on mutual trust. Participating countries have adapted their legislation to the principles and objectives of the Bologna Process, and higher education institutions are committed to implementing them.

The Follow-up Group has had preliminary discussions concerning 2010 and beyond, as the vision of the European Higher Education Area is gradually being translated into reality. Within the overarching framework for the EHEA, all participating countries should have developed by 2010 a national framework of qualifications based on three cycles in higher education, and national quality assurance arrangements implementing an agreed set of standards and guidelines. All higher education institutions in participating countries will recognise degrees and periods of studies according to the Lisbon Recognition Convention. The social dimension of the Bologna Process will be a constituent part of the EHEA: Higher education should be equally accessible to all and students should be able to complete their studies without obstacles related to their social and economic background. The EHEA will encompass the principles of public responsibility for higher education, institutional autonomy, and the participation of students in higher education governance.

Annex 10c

Bologna Follow-Up Group, *The European Higher Education Area Beyond 2010.* BFUGB8 5 final, 27 April 2005

BFUGB8 5 final
27 April 2005

THE EUROPEAN HIGHER EDUCATION AREA BEYOND 2010

As the Bologna Process leads to the establishment of the EHEA, we have to consider the appropriate arrangements needed to support the continuing development beyond 2010. At the Ministerial Conference in Bergen, time will be allotted for Ministers to have an open discussion on this issue. This paper may be helpful for setting the background.

1. The emerging European Higher Education Area

In order to establish the European Area of Higher Education, the Bologna process set itself a first set of objectives spelled out in the Bologna declaration:

– Adoption of a system of easily readable and comparable degrees;
– Adoption of a system essentially based on two cycles;
– Establishment of a system of credits;
– Promotion of mobility promotion of European co-operation in quality assurance;
– Promotion of the necessary European dimensions in higher education.

In subsequent ministerial conferences these objectives were further specified and at the Berlin Summit the third cycle was added to the two-cycle system.

Building on achievements so far in the Bologna Process, the European Higher Education Area will be founded on the following structural elements:

– Within the overarching framework for the EHEA, all participating countries will have a national framework of qualifications based on three cycles in higher education, where the levels have a double function: to prepare the student for the labour market and for further competence building. Each level builds on the preceding level, and the qualification obtained will give access to higher levels.
– All participating countries will have national quality assurance arrangements implementing an agreed set of standards and guidelines for the EHEA.
– All higher education institutions in participating countries will recognise degrees and periods of studies according to the Lisbon Recognition Convention.

As first laid down in the Bologna declaration, the rationale behind the Bologna process has been to promote European citizens' lasting employability and the international competitiveness of the European higher education system. The Prague Summit has added a further dimension by supporting the idea that higher education should be considered a public good and that it will remain a public responsibility.

The social dimension of the Bologna Process is a constituent part of the EHEA and a necessary condition for the attractiveness and competitiveness of the EHEA. Higher education should be equally accessible to all and students should be able to complete their studies without obstacles related to their social and economic background.

Built on these fundamental objectives the European Higher education Area will encompass the following principles:

- Public responsibility for higher education;
- Institutional autonomy;
- Participation of students in higher education governance;
- Cooperation and trust between the participating countries and organisations.

2. The Bologna process in the context of the European Union and beyond

From an EU perspective, the Bologna process fits into the broader agenda defined by the Lisbon agenda and by the Barcelona summit stating that the European education and training systems should become a "world quality reference". In areas like quality assurance, recognition of degrees and study periods abroad as well the establishment of a European Qualifications Framework the European Commission plays both a supportive and a complementary role. In other policy areas the two directives on the mobility of students and researchers promote mobility across European higher education.

However, the Bologna process has its own identity as can be seen from the perception of the process outside Europe. This also means that the Bologna process should be able and willing to share its findings and experiences with those countries in geographical proximity that are willing to engage in quality assurance, qualifications frameworks and descriptors, or curricula for a changed degree structure. In line with the organising principle of the Bologna process providing this type of assistance and in a more general way giving information is a communal effort made by all participants. In order to make European higher education attractive in other regions of the world it is important to support universities that encourage quality in Europe and the perception of that quality outside Europe.

3. The governance of the Bologna process

The Bologna process started off as inter-governmental cooperation, the Bologna Declaration having been signed by 29 ministers of education. However, from its very inception onwards the Bologna process has heavily relied on the participation of the academic community and of the student representatives. The Bologna process is thus based on cooperation and trust between the partners.

Moreover, the European Commission, the Council of Europe and UNESCO/CEPES have been associated in the shaping and in the implementation of the Process. The European Commission has increasingly contributed to organising and supporting various action lines and seminars through its programmes.

The Bologna process is thus a voluntary cooperation between different national systems overseen by the Bologna Follow-up Group and associating the various partners. There is no legally binding provision except for the Lisbon Recognition Convention, the arrangement being based on mutual trust.

Participating countries have adapted their legislation to the principles and objectives of the Bologna Process, and higher education institutions are committed to implementing them. The European Higher Education Area consists of 40/45 individual systems

However, developments in higher education will not stop in 2010. As the EHEA should be seen as a common framework for the time *after* 2010, Ministers should consider a continuing follow-up mechanism that may meet the challenges of a dynamic higher education sector.

4. Questions that may be asked

In Bologna, Ministers engaged in coordinating their policies to achieve the goals set forth in the Bologna declaration within the first decade of the third millennium. Halfway through the process it is not only time to take stock of the achievements so far, but also to start reflecting on the development of the European Higher Education Area after 2010.

The following questions may be used as a starting point for a discussion about the future development of the European Higher Education Area:

1. What should be included in an agreed description of the European Higher Education Area: principles, objectives, structures, a social dimension?
2. Is there a need to strengthen the organisation of the Bologna Process for the further development of the EHEA after 2010?
3. Can the European Higher Education Area be established as a sustainable structure without a formal / formally binding commitment from participating countries?

ANNEX 11

*Treaty establishing the European Economic
Community (Rome, 25 March 1957)
Articles 57, 118 and 125*

Article 57

1. In order to make it easier for persons to take up and pursue activities as self-employed persons, the Council shall, on a proposal from the Commission and after consulting the Assembly, acting unanimously during the first stage and by a qualified majority thereafter, issue directives for the mutual recognition of diplomas, certificates and other evidence of formal qualifications.

2. For the same purpose, the Council shall, before the end of the transitional period, acting on a proposal from the Commission and after consulting the Assembly, issue directives for the coordination of the provisions laid down by law, regulation or administrative action in Member States concerning the taking-up and pursuit of activities as self-employed persons.
    ...

3. In the case of the medical and allied, and pharmaceutical professions, the progressive abolition of restrictions shall be dependent upon coordination of the conditions for their exercise in the various Member States.

Article 118

Without prejudice to the other provisions of this Treaty and in conformity with its general objectives, the Commission shall have the task of promoting close cooperation between Member States in the social field, particularly in matters relating to:

- employment;
- labour law and working conditions'
- basic and advanced vocational training;
- social security;
- prevention of occupational accidents and diseases;
- occupational hygiene;
- the right of association, and collective bargaining between employers and workers.

To this end, the Commission shall act in close contact with the Member States by making studies, delivering opinions and arranging consultations both on problems arising at national level and on those of concern to international organisations.

Before delivering the opinions provided for in this Article, the Commission shall consult the Economic and Social Committee.

Article 125

1. On application by a Member State the Fund shall, within the framework of the rules provided for in Article 127, meet 50% of the expenditure incurred after the entry onto force of this Treaty by that State or by a body governed by public law for the purpose of:

(a) ensuring productive re-employment of workers by means of:
   - vocational retraining;
   - resettlement allowances;
(b) granting aid for the benefit of workers whose employment is reduced or temporarily suspended, in whole or in part, as a result of the conversion of an undertaking to other production, in order that they may retain the same wage level pending their full re-employment.

2. Assistance granted by the Fund towards the cost of vocational retraining shall be granted only if the unemployed workers could not be found employment except in a new occupation and only if they have been in productive employment for at least six months in the occupation for which they have been retrained.

   Assistance towards resettlement allowances shall be granted only if the unemployed workers have been caused to change their home within the Community and have been in productive employment for at least six months in their new place of residence.

   Assistance for workers in the case of the conversion of an undertaking shall be granted only if:

(a) the workers concerned have again been fully employed in that undertaking for at least six months;
(b) the government concerned has submitted a plan beforehand, drawn up by the undertaking in question, for that particular conversion and for financing it;
(c) the Commission has given its prior approval to the conversion plan.

ANNEX 12

Consolidated version of the Treaty establishing the European Community.
Article 47 and Articles 149 and 150 from: Title XI. Social policy, education, vocational training and youth. Chapter 3. Education, vocational training and youth.
The Articles 57, 126 and 127 of the Treaty on European Union (Maastricht, 7 February 1992) became Articles 47, 149 and 150 in the Treaty of Amsterdam (2 October 1997).

CHAPTER 2
RIGHT OF ESTABLISHMENT
...
Article 47

1. In order to make it easier for persons to take up and pursue activities as self-employed persons, the Council shall, acting in accordance with the procedure referred to in Article 251, issue directives for the mutual recognition of diplomas, certificates and other evidence of formal qualifications.

2. For the same purpose, the Council shall, acting in accordance with the procedure referred to in Article 251, issue directives for the coordination of the provisions laid down by law, regulation or administrative action in Member States concerning the taking-up and pursuit of activities as self-employed persons. ...

3. In the case of the medical and allied and pharmaceutical professions, the progressive abolition of restrictions shall be dependent upon coordination of the conditions for their exercise in the various Member States.

CHAPTER 3
EDUCATION, VOCATIONAL TRAINING AND YOUTH
Article 149

1. The Community shall contribute to the development of quality education by encouraging cooperation between Member States and, if necessary, by supporting and supplementing their action, while fully respecting the responsibility of the Member States for the content of teaching and the organisation of education systems and their cultural and linguistic diversity.

2. Community action shall be aimed at:

– developing the European dimension in education, particularly through the teaching and dissemination of the languages of the Member States,
– encouraging mobility of students and teachers, by encouraging inter alia, the academic recognition of diplomas and periods of study,
– promoting cooperation between educational establishments,

- developing exchanges of information and experience on issues common to the education systems of the Member States,
- encouraging the development of youth exchanges and of exchanges of socioeducational instructors,
- encouraging the development of distance education.

3. The Community and the Member States shall foster cooperation with third countries and the competent international organisations in the field of education, in particular the Council of Europe.

4. In order to contribute to the achievement of the objectives referred to in this Article, the Council:

- acting in accordance with the procedure referred to in Article 251, after consulting the Economic and Social Committee and the Committee of the Regions, shall adopt incentive measures, excluding any harmonisation of the laws and regulations of the Member States,
- acting by a qualified majority on a proposal from the Commission, shall adopt recommendations.

Article 150

1. The Community shall implement a vocational training policy which shall support and supplement the action of the Member States, while fully respecting the responsibility of the Member States for the content and organisation of vocational training.

2. Community action shall aim to:

- facilitate adaptation to industrial changes, in particular through vocational training and retraining,
- improve initial and continuing vocational training in order to facilitate vocational integration and reintegration into the labour market,
- facilitate access to vocational training and encourage mobility of instructors and trainees and particularly young people,
- stimulate cooperation on training between educational or training establishments and firms,
- develop exchanges of information and experience on issues common to the training systems of the Member States.

3. The Community and the Member States shall foster cooperation with third countries and the competent international organisations in the sphere of vocational training.

4. The Council, acting in accordance with the procedure referred to in Article 251 and after consulting the Economic and Social Committee and the Committee of the Regions, shall adopt measures to contribute to the achievement of the objectives referred to in this article, excluding any harmonisation of the laws and regulations of the Member States.

ANNEX 13

Indicative features of quality assurance.
Annex to Recommendation on European cooperation in quality assurance in higher education (98/561 EC)

The features referred to below are common to existing European quality assurance systems. The European pilot projects assessing the quality of higher education have demonstrated that all parties involved in this area can benefit from observing these features.

The autonomy and/or independence, in terms of the relevant structures in each Member State, of the body responsible for quality assurance (as regards procedures and methods) is likely to contribute to the effectiveness of quality assurance procedures and the acceptance of their results.

Quality assurance criteria are closely linked to the aims assigned to each institution in relation to the needs of society and of the labour market; the different quality assurance procedures must therefore include allowance for the specific nature of the institution. Knowledge of the institution's objectives, be it at the level of the whole institution, at the level of a department or at the level of a single unit, is essential in this respect.

Quality assurance procedures should generally consist of an internal, self-examination component and an external component based on appraisal by external experts.

The internal element of self-examination should aim to involve all the relevant players, especially teaching staff and, where appropriate, administrators in charge of academic and professional guidance, as well as students. The external element should be a process of cooperation, consultation and advice between independent experts from outside and players from within the institution.

In the light of the objectives and criteria used in the quality assurance procedure and with reference to the structures of higher education in the Member States, professional associations, social partners and alumni could be included in the expert groups.

The participation of foreign experts in the procedures would be desirable in order to encourage exchange of experience acquired in other countries.

Reports on quality assurance procedures and their outcome should be published in a form appropriate to each Member State and should provide a source of good reference material for partners and for the general public.

ANNEX 14

*Proposal for a Recommendation of the Council and of
the European Parliament on further European cooperation in quality
assurance in higher education (presented by the Commission)*
(COM(2004)642 final) of 12 October 2004

THE COUNCIL OF THE EUROPEAN UNION AND THE EUROPEAN
PARLIAMENT

Having regard to the Treaty establishing the European Community, and in
particular Articles 149(4) and 150(4) thereof,

Having regard to the proposal of the European Commission,[1]

Having regard to the opinion of the Economic and Social Committee[2],

Having regard to the opinion of the Committee of the Regions[3],

Acting in accordance with the procedure laid down in Article 251 of the
Treaty[4],

Whereas:

(1) although the implementation of the Council recommendation of 24 September 1998 on European cooperation in quality assurance in higher
education has been a marked success as demonstrated in the report of the
Commission of .... 2004, there is still a need to improve the performance of European higher education for it to become more transparent and
trustworthy for European citizens and for students and scholars from
other continents.

(2) the Council Recommendation called for support to and, where necessary,
the establishment of transparent quality assurance systems, and almost all
Member States have set up national assurance systems and have initiated
or enabled the establishment of one or more quality assurance or accreditation agencies.

(3) the Council Recommendation called for quality assurance systems to be
based on a series of essential features, including evaluation of programmes or institutions through internal assessment, external review, and
involving the participation of students, publication of results and international participation.

---

1   OJ C [...], [...], p. [...].
2   OJ C [...], [...], p. [...].
3   OJ C [...], [...], p. [...].
4   OJ C [...], [...], p. [...].

(4) these features have generally been implemented in all quality assurance systems and they have been affirmed by European Ministers of Education, gathered in Berlin, in September 2003, in the context of the Bologna Process, working towards the realisation of a European Higher Education Area.

(5) the European Network for Quality Assurance in Higher Education ENQA was established in 2000 and has a growing membership of quality assurance or accreditation agencies in all Member States.

(6) Ministers of education, gathered in Berlin, in September 2003, "called upon ENQA through its members, in co-operation with the EUA, EURASHE and ESIB, to develop an agreed set of standards, procedures and guidelines on quality assurances, to explore ways of ensuring an adequate peer review for quality assurance and/or accreditation agencies or bodies, and to report back through the Follow-up Group to Ministers in 2005".

(7) It is desirable to draw up a positive list or register of independent and trustworthy quality assurance agencies operating in Europe, be they regional or national, general or specialised, public or private, profit-making or not for profit, to support transparency in higher education and help the recognition of qualifications and periods of study abroad.

(8) In the context of the Lisbon Strategy, the European Council, in Barcelona in March 2002, expressed their conclusion that European education and training systems should become a *"world quality reference."*[5]

HEREBY RECOMMEND THAT MEMBER STATES:

A. require all higher education institutions active within their territory to introduce or develop rigorous internal quality assurance mechanisms.

B. require all quality assurance or accreditation agencies active within their territory to be independent in their assessments, to apply the features of quality assurance laid down in the Council Recommendation of September 1998 and to apply a common set of standards, procedures and guidelines, for assessment purposes.

C. encourage quality assurance and accreditation agencies, together with organisations representing higher education, to set up a "European Register of Quality Assurance and Accreditation Agencies", as described in the Annex, and to define the conditions for registration.

D. enable higher education institutions active within their territory to choose among quality assurance or accreditation agencies in the European Register, an agency which meets their needs and profile.

---

5   Barcelona European Council – Presidency Conclusions. http://ue.eu.int/ueDocs/cms_Data/ docs/ pressData/en/ec/71025.pdf

E. accept the assessments made by all quality assurance and accreditation agencies listed in the European Register as a basis for decisions on licensing or funding of higher education institutions, including as regards such matters as eligibility for student grants and loans.

II. INVITE THE COMMISSION:

A. to continue, in close cooperation with the Member States, its support for cooperation between higher education institutions, quality assurance and accreditation agencies, competent authorities and other bodies active in the field.

B. to present triennial reports to the European Parliament, the Council, the Economic and Social Committee and the Committee of the Regions on progress in the development of quality assurance systems in the various Member States and on cooperation activities at European level, including the progress achieved with respect to the objectives referred to above.

Done at Brussels,

For the Council   *For the Parliament*
The President   *The President*

ANNEX 15

Committee of the Lisbon Recognition Convention, *Code of Good Practice in the Provision of Transnational Education* **(Riga, 6 June 2001)**

PREAMBLE

The Parties to the Convention on the Recognition of Qualifications concerning Higher Education in the European Region (the Lisbon Recognition Convention),

Conscious of the rapid development of transnational education, characterised by those arrangements and partnerships between institutions and organisations in which the students are located in a different country to the one where the institution providing the education is based, and of its impact on higher education globally, but also specifically in the Europe Region;

Conscious in particular of the challenges posed by transnational education institutions and programmes operating outside of the framework of any national education system;

Being aware of the fact that transnational higher education is rapidly expanding, due mainly to the growing and seemingly limitless uses of the new information technologies in providing educational services in a world of borderless higher education;

Convinced that national systems of higher education are, and will continue to be, entrusted *inter alia* to preserve the cultural, social, philosophical, and religious diversity of the European Region while also being expected to promote various forms of international and global co-operation;

Attaching great importance to the academic quality of study programmes and degrees awarded by higher education institutions engaged in transnational education;

Considering that, regardless of the procedures adopted for establishing and providing educational services, higher education institutions should comply with those standards of performance in teaching and learning that are required by the present and future development of knowledge, technology and the labour market;

Acknowledging that facilitating the recognition of qualifications awarded through transnational arrangements will contribute to promoting both the mobility of students and that of study programmes between higher education institutions and systems;

Having regard to the Council of Europe/UNESCO Convention on the Recognition of Qualifications concerning Higher Education in the European Region that provides an overall normative framework for dealing with academic recognition matters;

Having regard also to the Codes of good practice developed and monitored by some of the major providers, such as:

- **Code of Ethical Practice in the Provision of Education to International Students by Australian Universities,** Australian Vice-Chancellors' Committee;
- **Quality Assurance Code of Practice: Collaborative Provision,** United Kingdom Quality Assurance Agency for Higher Education;
- **Principles of Good Practice for Educational Programs for Non-U.S. Nationals**;

Mindful that such Codes provide working frameworks from the perspective of the sending institutions/systems of higher education, and that they have to be complemented by the perspectives of the receiving institutions/systems;

Having regard also to the Diploma Supplement developed jointly by the European Commission, the Council of Europe and UNESCO and aiming to provide supplementary information facilitating the assessment of qualifications;

Confident that ethical principles and values should closely guide the international and global cooperation between higher education systems and institutions;

Conscious of the need to find commonly agreed solutions to practical recognition problems in the European Region, and between the States of this Region, and those of other regions of the world, in an ever more global space of higher education;

Conscious of the need to permanently update the implementation mechanisms of the principles and provisions of the **Lisbon Recognition Convention**, thus keeping up with the pace of new developments in higher education cooperation;

Have agreed on the need for:

- **A Code of Good Practice** in the provision of higher education study programmes and other educational services by means of transnational arrangements;
- **Recommendation on procedures and criteria for the assessment of foreign qualifications,** with a view to implementing the Code of Good Practice and to facilitating the recognition of qualifications awarded following completion of transnational study programmes/courses of study;

– and for these to be considered as fully complementary and mutually supportive documents.

SECTION I. TERMINOLOGY

Terms defined in the **Lisbon Recognition Convention** are not mentioned here again and shall, for the purposes of this Code of Good Practice, have the same meaning as in the Convention. The following terms, listed in alphabetical order, shall have the following meaning:

Agents

Third parties, such as brokers, facilitators, or recruiters, that act as intermediaries between awarding and providing institutions for establishing transnational educational arrangements. An agent is not usually involved in the provision of educational services.

Agreement

A document agreed formally by the partners that contains all collaborative arrangements made between the awarding and providing institutions.

Awarding institution

A higher education institution issuing degrees, diplomas, certificates or other qualifications.

Educational services

Any study programme, course of study or parts of a course of study that leads, after successful completion, to a qualification. This also includes services such as reparatory/introductory modules to facilitate access to a course of study, or training modules that lead to professional development.

Partners

The awarding and providing institutions involved in transnational arrangements.

Providing institution

An institution or organization which is delivering all or part of a study programme.

Transnational arrangements

An educational, legal, financial or other arrangement leading to the establishment of (a) collaborative arrangements, such as: franchising, twinning, joint degrees, whereby study programmes, or parts of a course of study, or other educational services of the awarding institution are provided by another partner institution; (b) non-collaborative arrangements, such as branch campuses, off-shore institutions, corporate or international institutions, whereby study programmes, or parts of a course of study, or other educational services are provided directly by an awarding institution.

Transnational education
All types of higher education study programmes, or sets of courses of study, or educational services(including those of distance education) in which the learners are located in a country different from the one where the awarding institution is based. Such programmes may belong to the education system of a State different from the State in which it operates, or may operate independently of any national education system.

SECTION II. PRINCIPLES

1. Transnational arrangements should be so elaborated, enforced and monitored as to widen the access to higher education studies, fully respond to the learners' educational demands, contribute to their cognitive, cultural, social, personal and professional development, and comply with the national legislation regarding higher education in both receiving and sending countries. In the case of collaborative arrangements there should be written and legally binding agreements or contracts setting out the rights and obligations of all partners.

2. Academic quality and standards of transnational education programmes should be at least comparable to those of the awarding institution as well as to those of the receiving country. Awarding institutions as well as the providing institutions are accountable and fully responsible for quality assurance and control. Procedures and decisions concerning the quality of educational services provided by transnational arrangements should be based on specific criteria, which are transparent, systematic and open to scrutiny.

3. The policy and the mission statement of institutions established through transnational arrangements, their management structures and educational facilities, as well as **the goals, objectives and contents** of specific programmes, sets of courses of study, and other educational services, should be published, and made available upon request to the authorities and beneficiaries from both the sending and receiving countries.

4. Information given by the awarding institution, providing organization, or agent to prospective students and to those registered on a study programme established through transnational arrangements should be appropriate, accurate, consistent and reliable. The information should include directions to students about the appropriate channels for particular concerns, complains and appeals. Where a programme is delivered through a collaborative arrangement, the nature of that arrangement and the responsibilities of the parties should be clearly outlined. The awarding institution is responsible for and should control and monitor information made public by agents operating on its behalf, including claims about the recognition of the qualifications in the sending country, and elsewhere.

5. Staff members of the institutions or those teaching on the programmes established through transnational arrangements should be proficient in terms of qualifications, teaching, research and other professional experience. The awarding institution should ensure that it has in place effective measures to review the proficiency of staff delivering programmes that lead to its qualifications.

6. Transnational education arrangements should encourage the awareness and knowledge of the **culture and customs** of both the awarding institutions and receiving country among the students and staff.

7. The awarding institution should be responsible for the **agents** it, or its partner institutions, appoint to act on its behalf. Institutions using agents should conclude written and legally binding agreements or contracts with these, clearly stipulating their roles, responsibilities, delegated powers of action as well as monitoring, arbitration and termination provisions. These agreements or contracts should further be established with a view to avoiding conflicts of interests as well as the rights of students with regard to their studies.

8. Awarding institutions should be responsible for issuing the qualifications resulting from their transnational study programmes. They should provide clear and transparent information on the qualifications, in particular through the use of the Diploma Supplement, facilitating the assessment of the qualifications by competent recognition bodies, the higher education institutions, employers and others. This information should include the nature, duration, workload, location and language(s) of the study programme leading to the qualifications.

9. The admission of students for a course of study, **the teaching/learning activities, the examination and assessment requirements** for educational services provided under transnational arrangements should be equivalent to those of the same or comparable programmes delivered by the awarding institution.

10. The academic work load in transnational study programmes, expressed in credits, units, duration of studies or otherwise, should be that of comparable programmes in the awarding institution, any difference in this respect requiring a clear statement on its rationale and its consequences for the recognition of qualifications.

11. Qualifications issued through transnational educational programmes, complying with the provisions of the present Code, should be assessed in accordance with the stipulations of the Lisbon Recognition Convention.

ANNEX 16

Guidelines[1] for Quality Provision in Cross-border Higher Education Jointly developed by UNESCO and OECD (2 December 2005)

I. Introduction

Purpose of the Guidelines
1. The Guidelines aim to support and encourage international cooperation and enhance the understanding of the importance of quality provision in cross-border higher education.[2] The purposes of the Guidelines are to protect students and other stakeholders from low-quality provision and disreputable providers[3] as well as to encourage the development of quality cross-border higher education that meets human, social, economic and cultural needs.

Rationale for the Guidelines
2. Since the 1980s, cross-border higher education through the mobility of students, academic staff, programmes/institutions and professionals has grown considerably. In parallel, new delivery modes and cross-border providers have appeared, such as campuses abroad, electronic delivery of higher education and for-profit providers. These new forms of cross-border higher education offer increased opportunities for improving the skills and competencies of individual students and the quality of national higher education systems, provided they aim at benefiting the human, social, economic and cultural development of the receiving country.

3. While in some countries the national frameworks for quality assurance, accreditation and the recognition of qualifications take into account cross-border higher education, in many countries they are still not geared to addressing the challenges of cross-border provision. Furthermore, the lack of comprehensive frameworks for co-ordinating various initiatives at the international level, together with the diversity and unevenness of the quality assurance and accreditation systems at the national level, create gaps in the quality assurance of cross-border higher education, leaving some crossborder higher education provision outside any framework of quality assurance and

---

1   These Guidelines are not legally binding and member countries are expected to implement the Guidelines as appropriate in their national context.
2   In these Guidelines, cross-border higher education includes higher education that takes place in situations where the teacher, student, programme, institution/provider or course materials cross national jurisdictional borders. Cross-border higher education may include higher education by public/private and not-for-profit/for-profit providers. It encompasses a wide range of modalities, in a continuum from face-to-face (taking various forms such as students travelling abroad and campuses abroad) to distance learning (using a range of technologies and including e-learning).
3   In this context "'disreputable providers'" refer to degree and accreditation mills.

accreditation. This makes students and other stakeholders more vulnerable to low-quality provision and disreputable providers[4] of cross-border higher education. The challenge faced by current quality assurance and accreditation systems is to develop appropriate procedures and systems to cover foreign providers and programmes (in addition to national providers and programmes) in order to maximise the benefits and limit the potential drawbacks of the internationalisation of higher education. At the same time, the increase in cross-border student, academic staff, researcher and professional mobility has put the issue of the recognition of academic and professional qualifications high on the international cooperation agenda.

4. There is therefore a need for additional national initiatives, strengthened international co-operation and networking, and more transparent information on procedures and systems of quality assurance, accreditation and recognition of qualifications. These efforts should have a global range and should emphasise supporting the needs of developing countries to establish robust higher education systems. Given that some countries lack comprehensive frameworks for quality assurance, accreditation and the recognition of qualifications, capacity building should form an important part of the overall strengthening and co-ordination of national and international initiatives. In this light, UNESCO Secretariat and the OECD have worked closely together in the development of these Guidelines for quality provision in cross-border higher education ("*Guidelines*"). The implementation of these Guidelines could serve as a first step in the capacity building process.

5. The quality of a country's higher education sector and its assessment and monitoring is not only key to its social and economic well-being, it is also a determining factor affecting the status of that higher education system at the international level. The establishment of quality assurance systems has become a necessity, not only for monitoring quality in higher education delivered within the country, but also for engaging in delivery of higher education internationally. As a consequence, there has been an impressive rise in the number of quality assurance and accreditation bodies for higher education in the past two decades. However, existing national quality assurance capacity often focuses exclusively on domestic delivery by domestic institutions.

6. The increased cross-border mobility of students, academic staff, professionals, programmes and providers presents challenges for existing national quality assurance and accreditation frameworks and bodies as well as for the systems for recognising foreign qualifications. Some of these challenges are described below:

---

4 See footnote 3.

a) National capacity for quality assurance and accreditation often does not cover cross-border higher education. This increases the risk of students falling victim to misleading guidance and information and disreputable providers, dubious quality assurance and accreditation bodies and low-quality provision, leading to qualifications of limited validity.

b) National systems and bodies for the recognition of qualifications may have limited knowledge and experience in dealing with cross-border higher education. In some cases, the challenge becomes more complicated as cross-border higher education providers may deliver qualifications that are not of comparable quality to those which they offer in their home country.

c) The increasing need to obtain national recognition of foreign qualifications has posed challenges to national recognition bodies. This in turn, at times, leads to administrative and legal problems for the individuals concerned.

d) The professions depend on trustworthy, high-quality qualifications. It is essential that users of professional services including employers have full confidence in the skills of qualified professionals. The increasing possibility of obtaining low-quality qualifications could harm the professions themselves, and might in the long run undermine confidence in professional qualifications.

Scope of the Guidelines

7. The Guidelines aim to provide an international framework for quality provision in cross-border higher education that responds to the abovementioned challenges.

8. The Guidelines are based on the principle of mutual trust and respect among countries and on the recognition of the importance of international collaboration in higher education. They also recognise the importance of national authority and the diversity of higher education systems. Countries attach a high importance to national sovereignty over higher education. Higher education is a vital means for expressing a country's linguistic and cultural diversity and also for nurturing its economic development and social cohesion. It is therefore recognised that policy-making in higher education reflects national priorities. At the same time, it is recognised that in some countries, there are several competent authorities in higher education.

9. The effectiveness of the Guidelines largely depends on the possibility of strengthening the capacity of national systems to assure the quality of higher education. The development and implementation of the UNESCO regional conventions and further support to the ongoing capacity building initiatives of UNESCO, other multilateral organisations and bilateral donors in this area

will sustain and be complementary to the Guidelines. These initiatives should be supported by strong regional and national partners.

10. The Guidelines acknowledge the important role of non-governmental organisations such as higher education associations, student bodies, academic staff associations, networks of quality assurance and accreditation bodies, recognition and credential evaluation bodies and professional bodies in strengthening international co-operation for quality provision in crossborder higher education. The Guidelines aim to encourage the strengthening and co-ordination of existing initiatives by enhancing dialogue and collaboration among various bodies.

11. Cross-border higher education encompasses a wide range of modalities that range from face-to-face (taking various forms such as students travelling abroad and campuses abroad) to distance learning (using a range of technologies and including e-learning). In implementing the Guidelines, consideration should be given to the variety of provision and its different demands for quality assurance.

II. Guidelines for Higher Education Stakeholders

12. With due regard to the specific division of responsibilities in each country, the Guidelines recommend actions to six stakeholders:[5] governments; higher education institutions/providers including academic staff; student bodies; quality assurance and accreditation bodies; academic recognition bodies;[6] and professional bodies.

Guidelines for governments

13. Governments can be influential, if not responsible, in promoting adequate quality assurance, accreditation and the recognition of qualifications. They undertake the role of policy coordination in most higher education systems. However, it is acknowledged throughout these Guidelines that in some countries, the authority for overseeing quality assurance lies with sub-national government bodies or with nongovernmental organisations.

14. In this context, it is recommended that governments:

a) Establish, or encourage the establishment of a comprehensive, fair and transparent system of registration or licensing for cross-border higher education providers wishing to operate in their territory.

---

5   In the Guidelines, the distinctions among these stakeholders are made based on the functions and it is recognised that the different functions do not necessarily belong to separate bodies.

6   Academic recognition bodies include qualification recognition bodies, credential evaluation bodies, and advisory/information centres.

b) Establish, or encourage the establishment of a comprehensive capacity for reliable quality assurance and accreditation of cross-border higher education provision, recognising that quality assurance and accreditation of cross-border higher education provision involves both sending and receiving countries.

c) Consult and coordinate amongst the various competent bodies for quality assurance and accreditation both nationally and internationally.

d) Provide accurate, reliable and easily accessible information on the criteria and standards for registration, licensure, quality assurance and accreditation of cross-border higher education, their consequences on the funding of students, institutions or programmes, where applicable and their voluntary or mandatory nature.

e) Consider becoming party to and contribute to the development and/or updating of the appropriate UNESCO regional conventions on recognition of qualifications and establish national information centres as stipulated by the conventions.

f) Where appropriate develop or encourage bilateral or multilateral recognition agreements, facilitating the recognition or equivalence of each country's qualifications based on the procedures and criteria included in mutual agreements.

g) Contribute to efforts to improve the accessibility at the international level of up-to-date, accurate and comprehensive information on recognised higher education institutions/providers.

Guidelines for higher education institutions/providers

15. Commitment to quality by all higher education institutions/providers is essential.[7] To this end, the active and constructive contributions of academic staff are indispensable. Higher education institutions are responsible for the quality as well as the social, cultural and linguistic relevance of education and the standards of qualifications provided in their name, no matter where or how it is delivered.

16. In this context, it is recommended that higher education institutions/providers delivering cross-border higher education:

a) Ensure that the programmes they deliver across borders and in their home country are of comparable quality and that they also take into account the cultural and linguistic sensitivities of the receiving country. It is desirable that a commitment to this effect should be made public.

---

7 An important and relevant initiative for this is the statement "Sharing Quality Higher Education across Borders" by the International Association of Universities, the Association of Universities and Colleges of Canada, the American Council on Education and the Council on Higher Education Accreditation on behalf of higher education institutions worldwide.

b) Recognise that quality teaching and research is made possible by the quality of faculty and the quality of their working conditions that foster independent and critical inquiry. The UNESCO Recommendation concerning the Status of Higher Education Teaching Personnel[8] and other relevant instruments need to be taken into account by all institutions and providers to support good working conditions and terms of service, collegial governance and academic freedom.

c) Develop, maintain or review current internal quality management systems so that they make full use of the competencies of stakeholders such as academic staff, administrators, students and graduates and take full responsibility for delivering higher education qualifications comparable in standard in their home country and across borders. Furthermore, when promoting their programmes to potential students through agents, they should take full responsibility to ensure that the information and guidance provided by their agents are accurate, reliable and easily accessible.

d) Consult competent quality assurance and accreditation bodies and respect the quality assurance and accreditation systems of the receiving country when delivering higher education across borders, including distance education.

e) Share good practices by participating in sector organisations and interinstitutional networks at national and international levels.

f) Develop and maintain networks and partnerships to facilitate the process of recognition by acknowledging each other's qualifications as equivalent or comparable.

g) Where relevant, use codes of good practice such as the UNESCO/ Council of Europe *Code of Good Practice in the Provision of Transnational Education*[9] and other relevant codes such as the Council of Europe/UNESCO *Recommendation on Criteria and Procedures for the Assessment of Foreign Qualifications.*[10]

h) Provide accurate, reliable and easily accessible information on the criteria and procedures of external and internal quality assurance and the academic and professional recognition of qualifications they deliver and provide complete descriptions of programmes and qualifications, preferably with descriptions of the knowledge, understanding and skills that a successful student should acquire. Higher education institutions/providers should collaborate especially with

---

8   Available at: http://portal.unesco.org/en/ev.php-URL_ID=13144&URL_DO= DO_TOPIC& URL_SECTION=201.htm
9   Available at: http://www.coe.int/T/DG4/HigherEducation/Recognition/Code%20of%20good %20practice_EN.asp#TopOfPage
10 Available at: http://www.coe.int/T/DG4/HigherEducation/Recognition/Criteria%20and%20 procedures_EN.asp#TopOfPage

quality assurance and accreditation bodies and with student bodies to facilitate the dissemination of this information.

i) Ensure the transparency of the financial status of the institution and/or educational programme offered.

Guidelines for student bodies

17. As representatives of the direct recipients of cross-border higher education and as part of the higher education community, student bodies bear the responsibility of helping students and potential students to carefully scrutinise the information available and giving sufficient consideration in their decision making process.

18. In this context, it is recommended that the emergence of autonomous local, national and international student bodies be encouraged and that the student bodies:

a) Be involved as active partners at international, national and institutional levels in the development, monitoring and maintenance of the quality provision of cross-border higher education and take the necessary steps to achieve this objective.

b) Take active part in promoting quality provision, by increasing the awareness of the students of the potential risks such as misleading guidance and information, low-quality provision leading to qualifications of limited validity, and disreputable providers. They should also guide them to accurate and reliable information sources on cross-border higher education. This could be done by increasing the awareness of the existence of these guidelines as well as taking an active part in their implementation.

c) Encourage students and potential students to ask appropriate questions when enrolling in cross-border higher education programmes. A list of relevant questions could be established by student bodies, including foreign students where possible, in collaboration with bodies such as higher education institutions, quality assurance and accreditation bodies and academic recognition bodies. Such a list should include the following questions: whether the foreign institution/provider is recognised or accredited by a trustworthy body and whether the qualifications delivered by the foreign institution/provider are recognised in the students' home country for academic and/or professional purposes.

Guidelines for quality assurance and accreditation bodies

19. In addition to internal quality management of institutions/providers, external quality assurance and accreditation systems have been adopted in more than 60 countries. Quality assurance and accreditation bodies are responsible for assessing the quality of higher education provision. The existing systems

of quality assurance and accreditation often vary from country to country and sometimes within the countries themselves. Some have governmental bodies for quality assurance and accreditation, and others have non-governmental bodies. Furthermore, some differences exist in the terminologies used, the definition of "quality", the purpose and function of the system including its link to the funding of students, institutions or programmes, the methodologies used in quality assurance and accreditation, the scope and function of the responsible body or unit, and the voluntary or compulsory nature of participation. While respecting this diversity, a co-ordinated effort among the bodies of both sending and receiving countries is needed at both the regional and global level, in order to tackle the challenges raised by the growth of cross-border provision of higher education, especially in its new forms.[11]

20. In this context, it is recommended that quality assurance and accreditation bodies:

a) Ensure that their quality assurance and accreditation arrangements include cross-border education provision in its various modes. This can mean giving attention to assessment guidelines, ensuring that standards and processes are transparent, consistent and appropriate to take account of the shape and scope of the national higher education system, and adaptability to changes and developments in cross-border provision.

b) Sustain and strengthen the existing regional and international networks or establish regional networks in regions that do not already have one. These networks can serve as platforms to exchange information and good practice, disseminate knowledge, increase the understanding of international developments and challenges as well as to improve the professional expertise of their staff and quality assessors. These networks could also be used to improve awareness of disreputable providers and dubious quality assurance and accreditation bodies, and to develop monitoring and reporting systems that can lead to their identification.

c) Establish links to strengthen the collaboration between the bodies of the sending country and the receiving country and enhance the mutual understanding of different systems of quality assurance and accreditation. This may facilitate the process of assuring the quality of programmes delivered across borders and institutions operating across borders while respecting the quality assurance and accreditation systems of the receiving countries.

d) Provide accurate and easily accessible information on the assessment standards, procedures, and effects of the quality assurance mechanisms on the funding of students, institutions or programmes where

---

11 See footnote 2.

applicable as well as the results of the assessment. Quality assurance and accreditation bodies should collaborate with other actors, especially higher education institutions/providers, academic staff, student bodies and academic recognition bodies to facilitate the dissemination of such information.

e) Apply the principles reflected in current international documents on cross-border higher education such as the UNESCO/Council of Europe *Code of Good Practice in the Provision of Transnational Education.*[12]

f) Reach mutual recognition agreements with other bodies on the basis of trust in and understanding of each other's professional practice, develop systems of internal quality assurance and regularly undergo external evaluations, making full use of the competencies of stakeholders. Where feasible, consider undertaking experiments in international evaluation or peer reviews.

g) Consider adoption of procedures for the international composition of peer review panels, international benchmarking of standards, criteria and assessment procedures and undertake joint assessment projects to increase the comparability of evaluation activities of different quality assurance and accreditation bodies.

Guidelines for academic recognition bodies

21. The UNESCO regional conventions on the recognition of qualifications are important instruments facilitating the fair recognition of higher education qualifications, including the assessment of foreign qualifications resulting from cross-border mobility of students, skilled professionals and cross-border provision of higher education.

22. There is a need to build on existing initiatives with additional international action to facilitate fair processes of recognition of academic qualifications by making systems more transparent and comparable.

23. In this context, it is recommended that academic recognition bodies:

a) Establish and maintain regional and international networks that can serve as platforms to exchange information and good practice, disseminate knowledge, increase the understanding of international developments and challenges and improve the professional expertise of their staff.

b) Strengthen their cooperation with quality assurance and accreditation bodies to facilitate the process of determining whether a qualification

---

12 Available at: http://www.coe.int/T/DG4/HigherEducation/Recognition/Code%20of%20good %20practice_EN.asp#TopOfPage

meets basic quality standards, as well as to engage in cross-border co-operation and networking with quality assurance and accreditation bodies. This cooperation should be pursued both at regional and cross-regional level.

c) Establish and maintain contacts with all stakeholders to share the information and improve the links between academic and professional qualification assessment methodologies.

d) Where appropriate, address the professional recognition of qualifications in the labour market and provide necessary information on professional recognition, both to those who have a foreign qualification and to employers. Given the increasing scope of the international labour markets and growing professional mobility, collaboration and co-ordination with professional associations are recommended for this purpose.

e) Use codes of practice such as the Council of Europe/UNESCO *Recommendation on Criteria and Procedures for the Assessment of Foreign Qualifications*[13] and other relevant codes of practice to increase the public's confidence in their recognition procedures, and to reassure stakeholders that the processing of requests is conducted in a fair and consistent manner.

f) Provide clear, accurate and accessible information on the criteria for the assessment of qualifications, including qualifications resulting from cross-border provision.

Guidelines for professional bodies[14]

24. Systems of professional recognition differ from country to country and from profession to profession. For example, in some cases, a recognised academic qualification could be sufficient for entry into professional practice, whereas in other cases, additional requirements are imposed on holders of academic qualifications in order to enter the profession. Given the increasing scope of international labour markets and growing professional mobility, the holders of academic qualifications, as well as employers and professional associations are facing many challenges. Increasing transparency – *i.e.*, improving the availability and the quality of the information – is critical for fair recognition processes.

25. In this context, it is recommended that professional bodies responsible for professional recognition:

---

[13]   Available at: http://www.coe.int/T/DG4/HigherEducation/Recognition/Criteria%20and%20 procedures_EN.asp#TopOfPage

[14]   This section refers to institutions with legal competence in the field of regulated professions and professional recognition. In some countries, these institutions are professional bodies; in other countries, this role is being performed by other competent authorities, such as governmental ministries.

a) Develop information channels that are accessible both to national and foreign holders of qualifications to assist them in gaining professional recognition of their qualifications, and to employers who need advice on the professional recognition of foreign qualifications. Information should also be easily accessible to current and potential students.

b) Establish and maintain contacts between the professional bodies of both sending and receiving countries, higher education institutions/ providers, quality assurance and accreditation bodies, as well as academic recognition bodies to improve qualification assessment methodologies.

c) Establish, develop and implement assessment criteria and procedures for comparing programmes and qualifications to facilitate the recognition of qualifications and to accommodate learning outcomes and competencies that are culturally appropriate in addition to input and process requirements.

d) Improve the accessibility at the international level of up-to-date, accurate and comprehensive information on mutual recognition agreements for the professions and encourage the development of new agreements.

ANNEX 17

Definition of Education Services. **Annex 1 of the WTO Council for Trade in Services Secretariat Background Note** *Education Services* **(23 September 1998 S/C/W/49, pp. 15-16 plus Table 9)**

DEFINITION OF EDUCATION SERVICES

International data collection efforts have generally shown that, although countries have similar denominations of industries, the content may differ. This might be particularly relevant in cases where Members have undertaken commitments with no clear indication of the activities referred to, for example, by inscribing only "Other Education Services". Commonly used industry classification systems might provide some clarification as to the range of activities considered as education services.

The Services Sectoral Classification List, Document MTN.GNS/W/120, was developed during the Uruguay Round for scheduling purposes under the GATS. It was based on the UN Provisional Central Product Classification (CPC) and the activities covered are defined through reference to CPC codes. Although WTO Members are not legally bound to determine the sectoral scope of their commitments according to this classification, a large majority has done so.

According to the MTN.GNS/W/120, Education Services include:

A. PRIMARY EDUCATION SERVICES (CPC 921), which comprises Pre-school Education Services (CPC 92110) and Other Primary Education Services (CPC 92190). These categories do not include child-care services (considered as social services in CPC 93321) and services related to literary programmes for adults, which are part of the sub-category Adult Education Services (CPC 92400).

B. SECONDARY EDUCATION SERVICES (CPC 922), which comprises General Secondary Education Services (CPC 92210), Higher Secondary Education Services (CPC 2220), Technical and Vocational Secondary Education Services (CPC 92230), and Technical and Vocational Secondary Education Services for handicapped students (CPC 92240).

C. HIGHER EDUCATION SERVICES (CPC 923) including Post-Secondary Technical and Vocational Education Services (CPC 92310) and Other Higher Education Services (CPC 92390). The former refers to sub-degree technical and vocational education, while the latter refers to education leading to a university degree or equivalent.

D. ADULT EDUCATION (CPC 924) covering education for adults outside the regular education system.

E. OTHER EDUCATION SERVICES (CPC 929), covering all other education services not elsewhere classified, and excluding education services regarding recreation matters, for example, those provided by sport and game schools, which fall under sporting and other recreation services (CPC 964). For complete definitions see (Table 9).

The Central Product Classification Version 1.0 (CPC Rev.1), approved by the UN Statistical Commission in February 1997, maintains a full correspondence with Provisional CPC except in two instances. First, in the relevant correspondence tables, Technical and Vocational Secondary Education (CPC Rev.1 9223) is now defined to include Technical and Vocational Secondary Education for handicapped students (CPC 224); and second, group Adult Education Services n.e.c (CPC 924) and group Other Education Services (CPC 929) have been merged into "Other Education and Training Services" (CPC Rev.1 929). The definitions contained in CPC Rev.1 do not differ substantially from those contained in CPC. For example, no explicit reference to handicapped students is made in CPC Rev.1 9223; and no explicit reference is made to the inclusion of education services through radio or television broadcasting or by correspondence in the case of CPC Rev.1 924. Additionally, the definition of the latter has been made more descriptive through the listing of some included activities, such as Education Services for Professional Sports Instructors and Computer Training Services. In the International Standard Industrial Classification (ISIC), as well as in the General Industrial Classification of Economic activity within the European Communities (NACE), the education services sector is structured along the lines of UN CPC. Thus, part of the industry is clearly identified by levels of education within the regular school and university system, while the other part consists of education outside of the regular system. In the North American Industry Classification System (NAICS), the Education Services sector is structured according to level and type of educational services. Part of the industry groups corresponds to a recognized series of formal levels of education designated by diplomas and degrees. These groups would be the equivalent to those in the "regular school and university system" categories in UNCPC. The remaining groups are based on the type of instruction or training offered and the levels are not formally defined, explicitly including "non-instructional services" that support educational processes or systems. Examples of these activities are: the offering of apprenticeship training programmes, foreign language instruction; training for career development (provided either directly to individuals or through employers' training programmes); exam preparation tutoring; and educational support services – educational consultants, education guidance counselling, educational testing services, student exchange programmes, among others. Presumably these activities would be the equivalent to "Adult and Other Education Services" in the context of ISIC, NACE and UNCPC. While the definition of "Adult and Other Education Services" adopted by these classifications is far-reaching (i.e. education for adults outside of the regular school and education system, all other education services not definable by level, and education in specific subject matters not elsewhere classified), it does not specify the nature of those activities or what is meant by "education". It is unclear, for instance, whether this residual category covers only "educational services" defined as instructional activities, in turn creating uncertainty as to the coverage of the so-called "educational support services".

Table 9: Education Services in the GATS Scheduling Guidelines and CPC

Sectoral Classification List	Relevant CPC No.	Definition/coverage in provisional CPC
5. EDUCATIONAL SERVICES A. Primary education services	921	Preschool education services: Pre-primary school education services. Such education services are usually provided by nursery schools, kindergartens, or special sections attached to primary schools, and aim primarily to introduce very young children to anticipated school-type environment. Exclusion: Child day-care services are classified in subclass 93321.
		Other primary education services: Other primary school education services at the first level. Such education services are intended to give the students a basic education in diverse subjects, and are characterized by a relatively low specialization level. Exclusion: Services related to the provision of literacy programs for adults are classified in subclass 92400 (Adult education services n.e.c.).
B. Secondary education services	922	General secondary education services: General school education services at the second level, first stage. Such education services consist of education that continues the basic programs taught at the primary education level, but usually on a more subject-oriented pattern and with some beginning specialization.
		Higher secondary education services: General school education services at the second level, second stage. Such education services consist of general education programs covering a wide variety of subjects involving more specialization than at the first stage. The programs intend to qualify students either for technical or vocational education or for university entrance without any special subject prerequisite.
		Technical and vocational secondary education services: Technical and vocational education services below the university level. Such education services consist of programs emphasizing subject-matter specialization and instruction in both theoretical and practical skills. They usually apply to specific professions.
		Technical and vocational secondary school-type education services for handicapped students: Technical and vocational secondary school-type education services specially designed to meet the possibilities and needs of handicapped students below the university level.

Sectoral Classification List	Relevant CPC No.	Definition/coverage in provisional CPC
C. Higher education services	923	Post-secondary, technical and vocational education services: Post-secondary, sub-degree technical and vocational education services. Such education services consist of a great variety of subject-matter programs. They emphasize teaching of practical skills, but also involve substantial theoretical background instruction.
		Other higher education services: Education services leading to a university degree or equivalent. Such education services are provided by universities or specialized professional schools. The programs not only emphasize theoretical instruction, but also research training aiming to prepare students for participation in original work.
D. Adult education	924	Adult education services n.e.c: Education services for adults who are not in the regular school and university stem. Such education services may be provided in day or evening classes by schools or by special institutions for adult education. Included are education services through radio or television broadcasting or by correspondence. The programs may cover both general and vocational subjects. Services related to literacy programs for adults are also included. Exclusion: Higher education services provided within the regular education system are classified in subclass 92310 (Post-secondary technical and vocational education services) or 92390 (Other higher education services).
E. Other education services	929	Other education services: Education services at the first and second levels in specific subject matters not elsewhere classified, and all other education services that are not definable by level. Exclusions: Education services primarily concerned with recreational matters are classified in class 9641 (Sporting services). Education services provided by governess or tutors employed by private households are classified in subclass 98000 (Private households with employed persons).

Source: UN, Provisional Central Product Classification, 1991.

ANNEX 18

European University Association, *Forward from Berlin: the Role of the Universities to 2010 and beyond* (Graz Declaration 2003)

1. *Universities* are central to the development of European society. They create, safeguard and transmit knowledge vital for social and economic welfare, locally, regionally and globally. They cultivate European values and culture.
2. *Universities* advocate a Europe of knowledge, based on a strong research capacity and researchbased education in universities – singly and in partnership – across the continent. Cultural and linguistic diversity enhances teaching and research.
3. The development of European universities is based on a set of core values: equity and access; research and scholarship in all disciplines as an integral part of higher education; high academic quality; cultural and linguistic diversity.
4. *Students* are key partners within the academic community. The Bologna reforms will: facilitate the introduction of flexible and individualised learning paths for all students; improve the employability of graduates and make our institutions attractive to students from Europe and from other continents.
5. *European universities* are active on a global scale, contributing to innovation and sustainable economic development. Competitiveness and excellence must be balanced with social cohesion and access. The Bologna reforms will only be successful if universities address both the challenge of global competition and the importance of fostering a stronger civic society across Europe.
6. *Universities* must continue to foster the highest level of quality, governance and leadership.

UNIVERSITIES AS A PUBLIC RESPONSIBILITY
7. *Governments, universities and their students* must all be committed to the long-term vision of a Europe of knowledge. Universities should be encouraged to develop in different forms and to generate funds from a variety of sources. However, higher education remains first and foremost a public responsibility so as to maintain core academic and civic values, stimulate overall excellence and enable universities to play their role as essential partners in advancing social, economic and cultural development.
8. *Governments* must therefore empower institutions and strengthen their essential autonomy by providing stable legal and funding environments. Universities accept accountability and will assume the responsibility of implementing reform in close cooperation with students and stakeholders, improving institutional quality and strategic management capacity.

RESEARCH AS AN INTEGRAL PART OF HIGHER EDUCATION

9. The integral link between higher education and research is central to European higher education and a defining feature of Europe's universities. *Governments* need to be aware of this interaction and to promote closer links between the European Higher Education and Research Areas as a means of strengthening Europe's research capacity, and improving the quality and attractiveness of European higher education. They should therefore fully recognise the doctoral level as the third "cycle" in the Bologna Process. *Universities* need to keep pressing the case for research-led teaching and learning in Europe's universities. Graduates at all levels must have been exposed to a research environment and to research-based training in order to meet the needs of Europe as a knowledge society.

10. The diversity of universities across Europe provides great potential for fruitful collaboration based upon different interests, missions and strengths. Enhancing European collaboration and increasing mobility at the doctoral and post-doctoral levels are essential, for example through the promotion of joint doctoral programmes, as a further means of linking the European Higher Education and Research Areas.

IMPROVING ACADEMIC QUALITY BY BUILDING STRONG INSTITUTIONS

11. Successful implementation of reforms requires leadership, quality and strategic management within each institution. *Governments* must create the conditions enabling universities to take long-term decisions regarding their internal organisation and administration, e.g. the structure and internal balance between institutional level and faculties and the management of staff. *Governments and universities* should enter negotiated contracts of sufficient duration to allow and support innovation.

12. *Universities* for their part must foster leadership and create a structure of governance that will allow the institution as a whole to create rigorous internal quality assurance, accountability and transparency. Students should play their part by serving on relevant committees. External stakeholders should serve on governing or advisory boards.

PUSHING FORWARD THE BOLOGNA PROCESS

13. The Bologna Process must avoid over-regulation and instead develop reference points and common level and course descriptors.

14. Implementing a system of three levels (the doctoral level being the third) requires further change.

Universities see the priorities for action as:
  - Consolidating ECTS as a means to restructure and develop curricula with the aim of creating student-centred and flexible learning paths including lifelong learning;

- Discussing and developing common definitions of qualification frameworks and learning outcomes at the European level while safeguarding the benefits of diversity and institutional autonomy in relation to curricula;
- Involving academics, students, professional organisations and employers in redesigning the curricula in order to give bachelor and master degrees meaning in their own right;
- Continuing to define and promote employability skills in a broad sense in the curriculum and ensuring that first-cycle programmes offer the option of entering the labour market;
- Introducing the Diploma Supplement more widely, and in major languages, as a means to enhance employability, making it widely known among employers and professional organisations.

MOBILITY AND THE SOCIAL DIMENSION

15. Student mobility in itself promotes academic quality. It enables diversity to be an asset, enhancing the quality of teaching and research through comparative and distinctive approaches to learning. It increases the employability of individuals. Staff mobility has similar benefits.

16. If the EHEA is to become a reality *governments* must: tackle the current obstacles to mobility, amend legislation on student support, e.g. to make study grants and loans portable and improve regulations on health care, social services and work permits.

17. *Governments and institutions* together must give incentives to mobility by improving student support (including social support, housing and opportunities for part-time work) academic and professional counselling, language learning and the recognition of qualifications. Institutions must ensure that full use is made of tools which promote mobility, in particular ECTS and the Diploma Supplement. Possibilities also need to be increased for short-term mobility, and mobility of part-time, distance and mature students.

18. Career paths for young researchers and teachers, including measures to encourage young PhDs to continue working in/return to Europe, must be improved. Gender perspectives require special measures for dual career families. Restrictions on transfer of pension rights must be removed through portable pensions and other forms of social support.

19. Increasing the participation of women in research and teaching is essential in a competitive Europe. Gender equality promotes academic quality and *universities* must promote it through their human resource management policies.

20. The Trends 2003 report demonstrates that the information base, in particular in relation to mobility issues, is inadequate. National governments should cooperate to improve statistical data and work with the European Commission to review existing monitoring mechanisms. There should be more research on issues related to the development of the EHEA.

21. Joint programmes and degrees based on integrated curricula are excellent means for strengthening European cooperation. *Governments* must remove legal obstacles to the awarding and recognition of joint degrees and also consider the specific financial requirements of such collaboration.

22. *Institutions* should identify the need for and then develop joint programmes, promoting the exchange of best practice from current pilot projects and ensuring high quality by encouraging the definition of learning outcomes and competences and the widespread use of ECTS credits.

QUALITY ASSURANCE: A POLICY FRAMEWORK FOR EUROPE

23. Quality assurance is a major issue in the Bologna process, and its importance is increasing. The EUA proposes a coherent QA policy for Europe, based on the belief: that institutional autonomy creates and requires responsibility, that *universities* are responsible for developing internal quality cultures and that progress at European level involving all stakeholders is a necessary next step.

24. An internal quality culture and effective procedures foster vibrant intellectual and educational attainment. Effective leadership, management and governance also do this. With the active contribution of students, *universities* must monitor and evaluate all their activities, including study programmes and service departments. External quality assurance procedures should focus on checking through institutional audit that internal monitoring has been effectively done.

25. The purpose of a European dimension to quality assurance is to promote mutual trust and improve transparency while respecting the diversity of national contexts and subject areas.

26. QA procedures for Europe must: promote academic and organisational quality, respect institutional autonomy, develop internal quality cultures, be cost effective, include evaluation of the QA agencies, minimise bureaucracy and cost, and avoid over regulation.

27. EUA therefore proposes that stakeholders, and in particular universities, should collaborate to establish a provisional "Higher Education Quality Committee for Europe". This should be independent, respect the responsibility of institutions for quality and demonstrate responsiveness to public concerns. It would provide a forum for discussion and, through the appointment of a small board, monitor the application of a proposed code of principles, developing a true European dimension in quality assurance.

UNIVERSITIES AT THE CENTRE OF REFORM

28. The Bologna Process was initially politically driven. But it is now gaining momentum because of the active and voluntary participation of all interested partners: higher education institutions, governments, students and other stakeholders. Top down reforms are not sufficient to reach the ambitious goals set for 2010. The main challenge is now to ensure that the reforms are

fully integrated into core institutional functions and development processes, to make them self-sustaining. Universities must have time to transform legislative changes into meaningful academic aims and institutional realities.

29. Governments and other stakeholders need to acknowledge the extent of institutional innovation, and the crucial contribution universities do and must make to the European Research Area and the longerterm development of the European knowledge society as outlined in the Lisbon declaration of the European Union. By united action, European higher education – which now touches the lives of more than half of the population of Europe – can improve the entire continent.

Leuven, 4 July 2003

ANNEX 19

ESIB and the Bologna Process – creating a European Higher Education
Area for and with Students (May 2003)

Preamble

ESIB – the National Unions of Students has existed since 1982 and seeks to promote the social, cultural, political and economic interests of students in Europe towards decision makers and partners at national, European and international level. ESIB currently has 50 members from 37 countries and thus represents more than 11 million students in Europe.

Introduction

Beginning with the Sorbonne Declaration in June 1998, a discussion has been emerging about the setting up of a European Higher Education Area on the continent. In 1999 the group of countries signing the Bologna Declaration had already further increased from the four that signed the Sorbonne Declaration to 29 countries, and at the first follow up meeting in 2001 in Prague the group increased to 31 countries. While students had to invite themselves to the Bologna conference, they were included in Prague and ESIB has been actively and constructively participating in the follow-up to this process and has adopted a large number of policies on various aspects of the Bologna objectives. At this point, where almost half of the time dedicated towards reaching the goals of Bologna has passed, ESIB aims at providing an overall position on the various aspects of the process, also evaluating the reforms that have already taken place in the Bologna signatory countries.

This paper should be seen in the context of existing ESIB policy papers.

The international trends surrounding Bologna

In recent years, the world has seen an overall trend of privatisation and deregulation of higher education systems throughout the world. The massification of education has not been met by a sufficient increase of public funding. Rather, HEIs have been pressured to engage in commercial activities, selling research and education products to customers and thus generating an increasing proportion of their income through these activities. This trend involves the establishment of governance structures that abolish collegial bodies in favour of streamlined corporate governance models, where the power is located in the hands of a few managers rather than all students, staff and researchers in HEIs.

The introduction of various forms of fees for studying is another trend that is to be observed in Europe throughout the last years. ESIB considers education a human right and calls upon governments to meet their obligations under the International Covenant on Economic, Social and Cultural rights,

Article 13, which calls for a progressive introduction of free education rather than an introduction of fees.

On a global level, trade in education becomes more and more relevant and generates an increasing profit. The ongoing negotiations about the General Agreement on Trade in Services (GATS) in the World Trade Organisation (WTO) about liberalising trade in education services are a further step along the privatisation agenda. However, increasing public pressure and protests have resulted in a growing interest of governments and reluctance to go any further in this trade. ESIB has clearly stated its objection to trade in education services on several occasions and pointed out clearly that education is not a commodity from our point of view.

UNESCO and other UN agencies have been increasing their work in recent years to safeguard education as a public good and have called upon governments to ensure that trade in education does not jeopardise existing commitments of governments under international human rights legislation. UNESCO has furthermore developed frameworks for recognition of qualifications and codes of good practices for transnational education.

Lastly, the European Union has set the goal of becoming the most competitive knowledge-based economy by 2010 in the Lisbon Summit in 2000 and has since been working on the future objectives of the education and training systems in Europe in a number of working groups, which involve national goverments and NGOs representatives.

On the other hand, a number of reforms have been implemented in European countries and have led to big changes in the systems of higher education. The mobility programmes of the EU have been successful in significantly increasing the number of mobile students. Curricular reforms as well as more flexible programmes have allowed for a larger number of students from non-traditional backgrounds to enter HE. Lastly, by implementing ICT in the universities and other HEIs and implementing pedagogical reforms, more learner and thus student centered patterns of learning and teaching have evolved.

All these European and global trends form the context in which the Bologna process has started and is continuing in Europe and these trends have to be taken into account when evaluating the outcomes and objectives of Bologna and forming a student opinion.

The Bologna Process and ESIB's positions towards the objectives

ESIB generally welcomes the increasing co-operation in Higher Education in Europe and supports the idea of establishing a European Higher Education Area. When it comes to the general rationale behind the process, ESIB would like to stress that we see co-operation in Europe and beyond, based on core academic values as the main driving factors of the creation of the EHEA and its relation to other regions of the world. The strong focus on the competitiveness of Europe in the world is a twoedged sword. It can on the one hand lead to an increase in quality and transparency, can on the other hand further the privatisation agenda and brain drain, which are trends which ESIB clearly and heavily opposes. Therefore, the inclusion of attractiveness in the Prague communiqué and the shift towards this more co-operative approach is very much welcomed by ESIB. ESIB would also like to stress that a clear pursuit of the objectives of the Bologna process is essential for reaching its aims and that the Bologna process must not be abused to carry out other reforms which are only on the national agenda in the name of the Bologna process. A number of countries seem to be abusing the Bologna Process for these kinds of reforms and ESIB strongly condemns these attempts of governments to hijack the process. Such hijacking jeopardises the creation of the European Higher Education Area, because stakeholders will oppose the process and the implementation will become increasingly difficult.

The strong focus on economic goals in the Bologna process has been counterbalanced by the inclusion of the social dimension and the reaffirming of HE as a public good in the Prague communiqué. However, more work will need to be done to ensure that these objectives do not remain empty formulas but are met to ensure social inclusion and equity in the EHEA.

However, ESIB strongly believes in the potential for positive change in the Bologna Process and welcomes the process as an opportunity to reform the higher education systems as to make them more responsive to students and society, including the labour market.

When it comes to the concrete objectives, ESIB stresses the following:

1. Quality Assurance

ESIB welcomes the increasing European co-operation in quality assurance between countries and in the framework of ENQA. However, existing problems should not be overlooked. The lack of a common definition of accreditation, its aims and procedures, for example make it difficult to work on this issue into a clear direction. In accreditation diversification rather than a convergence seems to be the trend in Europe. A common European accreditation does not seem feasible and realistic from our opinion and the process should rather be steered into a mutual recognition of national systems.

ESIB also stresses that accreditation has to be accompanied by a continuous process of quality assurance and quality improvement through evaluation and that the set up of such systems where they do not yet exist is essential to guarantee not only the keeping of minimum criteria at a given point in time but a continuous assurance and enhancement of the quality of higher education. Quality assurance with a focus on formative improvement of the quality of courses and institutions should be properly implemented in all signatory countries and should focus on courses, programmes and institutions as such, assessing the quality culture of HEIs and how they work with quality internally at different levels.

National guidelines and bodies should be developed for both quality assurance and accreditation, which clearly state the responsibilities of different actors and must involve students, teachers, employers and other societal actors to make sure that the education system meets their expectations and demands. Transparency of quality assurance and accreditation must be ensured, particularly by widely disseminating the proceeding of such activities. Students, as the biggest stakeholder group in education, must always be included in both quality assurance and accreditation and this inclusion should be legally guaranteed.

2. Degree Structures: Adoption of a system of two main cycles

ESIB observes with great interest the adoption of the new degree structures. While it seems to be fairly easy and well done in a lot of eastern European countries and the Scandinavian countries, a lot of western and southern countries seem to have more problems in adopting this system.

For the first-cycle degree, ESIB stresses that the first cycle degree such as a Bachelor should allow for different profiles (i.e. practical vs. scientific profile), even though the inclusion of a certain number of both practical and scientific aspects of a subject has to be ensured. The employability of the graduates holding such degrees as well as societal gains should be more clearly defined than stating that first-cycle degrees shall be employable. Also, a focus should be placed on transferable skills that are gained in certain subjects. This will make qualifications not directly relevant to the labour market more easily relatable to the question of what a person with a certain degree can actually do in practice. Governments need to ensure that the labour market and employers recognise these degrees more easily as the reform of increasingly introducing those degrees will otherwise fail and face serious problems, a trend already apparent in a number of countries.

The successful completion of the first cycle must allow for entry into the second degree. ESIB opposes any additional selection mechanism, be it special entry exams or numerus clausus. The second cycle programme also must be provided free of tuition fees. Both first cycle and second cycle degree haver their own specific value, as they provide answers to different and sometimes complementary needs. There is no "normal" degree. Instead both should be equally valorised abnd students must be free to choose if they want to continue or stop after the first cycle.

ESIB recognises that issues of progression rates between first and second cycle vary widely forsocially disadvantaged and discriminated minority and indeed majority groups. Further to its commitment to access and prgression at all levels ESIB calls for research to establish which barriers exist for these students. In this process students from the disadvantaged groups and student unions should be consulted and instruments have to be developed to remove these barriers.

The aim of the reforms to degree structures should be more flexibility also in the light of lifelong learning and not to get the largest number of students out of the universities and polytechnics as quickly as possible. ESIB calls upon governments to ensure free access to the second cycle and also engage into a clearer definition of employability to ensure the success such reform. If these objectives are met, the reforms could decrease drop out rates as well as create the above mentioned flexibility which will allow a bigger and more diverse number of students to successfully reach different levels of higher education.

Lastly, ESIB would like to stress that a reform of the structures necessarily should involve a reform of the content of programmes rather than pressing old contents into a new form and then believing that all problems of these degrees will be solved. A thorough assessment and reform of the curricula is essential to ensure the success of the BA/MA structures.

3. Promotion of Mobility

While a lot of progress has been achieved with the new generation of Socrates programmes and an increasing number of students are mobile in Europe, there are a lot of issues still to be resolved.

The proper implementation of credit systems is essential to foster mobility and guarantee recognition of the gained qualifications.

Also, reforms of national student support schemes to make grants and other state funded financial support approved by students fully portable are necessary to make it easier for students to be mobile. Additionally, European mechanisms have to be developed to counterbalance the enormous differences between countries in the Bologna Process.

Also, to foster mobility, it is necessary to change and relax foreigner laws and further simplify the granting of visas and working permits both for the period of study and after graduation.

Furthermore, it has to be properly assessed in how far mobility affects brain drain within Europe and beyond and proper mechanisms addressing both the needs of individuals and the needs of countries have to be devised to balance these trends.

As an additional concern, ESIB would like to stress the need of continuous and tuition-free language courses of the language of the country of destination for studies to enhance the integration of the mobile students into the local communities and make mobility not only an academically but also a culturally challenging experience, contributing to more understanding, respect and tolerance for the diverse cultural differences in Europe.

Lastly, HEIs and student unions have to devise proper counselling mechanisms for foreign students to ensure their integration into the academic community and the social well-being of students from other countries.

4. Establishment of a system of credits

The introduction of a system of credits both for transfer and accumulation seems essential for a large number of aspects related to the creation of a EHEA. ESIB believes that it is essential that compatible and comparable credit systems be developed in all European countries.

When it comes to measuring workload, ESIB believes that students must be involved in this process.

The ECTS is a useful tool for credit transfer within the realm of mobility for the moment. However, more work is needed to develop it into a proper accumulation system. ESIB also stresses that governments should not be forced to introduce ECTS as a generalised credit system but that other compatible systems should coexist.

5. Recognition of Degrees: Adoption of a system of easily readable and comparable degrees

ESIB welcomes the efforts to facilitate the recognition of degrees and qualifications to stimulate mobility on the European labour market.

A proper implementation of the use of the Diploma Supplement is a means of easily facilitating this process. The Diploma Supplement should be issued automatically without students having to request it and free of charge. It should at least be issued in the language of the institution and another widely spoken European language.

For intermediate recognition, compatible credit accumulation systems should be used, which make it easier for students to get parts of their studies recognised when they change the country and/or city of studies.

A ratification of the Lisbon Recognition Convention by all signatory countries of the Bologna Process is urgently needed, especially if that is to be made a prerequisite of joining the process. ESIB believes that it is not possible to demand something from someone else, which one has not achieved oneself before. Therefore, we call upon all signatory countries to eliminate existing legal barriers and sign and ratify the Lisbon Convention. Furthermore, the Lisbon Convention should be made more legally binding, e.g. by making it part of their national higher education legislation. This legislation should also contain a more general paragraph on recognition issues to foster pre-degree recognition by credit accumulation. Lastly, the labour legislations of signatory countries need to be adjusted to facilitate recognition of qualifications in vocational higher education for labour market purposes. An observation of the discussions in the Bruges/Copenhagen process on these issues could help to solve the questions linked to professional recognition in government regulated portions of the labour market. In the light of these challenges, the mandate of the ENIC/NARIC network should be expanded to deal with all these recognition issues in different departments but in one main organisation responsible for assisting with the process.

It is also in this context, ESIB would like to highlight the issue of national and international qualification frameworks. ESIB calls for further research in this area in order to help and further policy development of all stakeholders.

6. Higher Education institutions and st udents

The inclusion of higher education institutions and students is essential for the success of any real student oriented reform. ESIB therefore calls upon all governments to include students into the national Bologna Follow-Up structures and all other reform bodies.

Furthermore, reforms of higher education governance structures must not lead to a process of abolishing democracy in higher education institutions. Efficiency in governance structures might be a useful goal, but efficiency must never mean that students, teachers and staff are being excluded in favour of corporate steering models for universities and polytechnics.

Furthermore, the autonomy of institutions should be designed in a way that gives a collective responsibility to all stakeholders of the higher education community, not by transferring all decision-making powers to the university leadership.

Lastly, ESIB considers it of importance to deepen the dialogue also with the teachers and researchers who have to implement the Bologna reforms in the faculties and departments. Leaving them out of the process will in the medium term have negative effects on the proper implementation of reforms and on the re-design of curricula and structures of studies.

7. Promotion of the European dimension in higher education

ESIB welcomes the design of new degrees with a specific European content. We believe that to create a European identity, European educational programmes are essential. This can be best achieved through joint bachelor and master programmes. For a joint degree, a stay abroad should be the norm. However, the needs of students with disabilities and parents have to be taken into account and means will have to be developed to allow for their access into these programmes as well.

Also, it seems essential that all degrees contain European aspects. This "Euromainstreaming" could be achieved by comparative analysis in social sciences for example. It has to be ensured, that these European aspects of programmes lad to a better understanding of similarities and differences between people on the continent and also critically reflect upon the concept of Europe. Furthermore, it is essential that these contents respect the huge cultural diversity on the continent and promote understanding, co-operation and tolerance between Europe and other regions of the world. It must never lead to the evolvement of a European nationalism which outs Europe above other regions of the world. Also, the autonomy of HEIs has to be respected in curricular matters.

8. Promoting the Attractiveness of the European Higher Education Area

ESIB believes that the shift of focus towards attractiveness is a positive development, as the term competitiveness can have a very negative meaning,
especially when it comes to competing at all costs, which undermines academic values such as co-operation.

ESIB further believes that attractiveness can best be reached by a high
quality of education and research and by a good international network of cooperation with various partner institutions around the globe.

When discussing the attractiveness of the EHEA, the problems of brain
drain need to be tackled and resolved. Although ESIB believes in the freedom of each student, reseracher and member of teaching staff to hoose their
place of study, work and life, special attention must be paid to the following
points. Making Europe one of the most attractive higher education areas,
countries have to act responsibly in relation to the problem of brain drain,
both between Bologna signatory countries and outside. Since a lot of talented
students, researchers and teaching staff in developing countries and countries
in transotion are emigrating, the creation of a cohesive higher education area
is endangered, as is the economic and social development of the countries
encountering brain drain. Signotory countries should respond to the fact that
the process of brain darin also has higly negative implications for the development and quality of higher education and research.. Guaranteeing safe
employment and working conditions for students, staff and reserachers in the
qualification phase can reduce the problem of brain drain and enhance the
attractiveness of the EHEA. This also means that PhD candidates should be
employed by the universities, and enough full time jobs have to be provided
for young researchers to make the academic workplace an attractive option
for them.

With regards to the GATS, ESIB reaffirms its strong opposition against
making any further commitments in education. ESIB calls upon governments
to not make further commitments in education while at the same time re-
viewing existing commitments and legally assessing their impact on the
public system. ESIB further calls upon governments to engage in a constructive dialogue with teachers, students and universities about the issues
surrounding trade in education services, as the existing trade in the framework of TNE arrangements has to be steered to make it beneficial. Generally,
ESIB reaffirms its commitment to education as a public good not a tradable
commodity.

9. Lifelong Learning

ESIB welcomes the steps towards implementing lifelong learning in Europe.
However, we feel that it is important to stress that lifelong learning should
not only mean to upgrade professional skills but also to realise the right to
education in an overall lifelong perspective.

ESIB believes that the flexibility that can be reached through a proper implementation of the Bologna objectives can have a positive effect on the role of higher education in the lifelong learning framework. Lifelong learning however must not mean that people's knowledge is automatically considered outdated or expired after a certain time period and everyone is obliged to up-date their skills.

Goverments, HEIs, teachers and students have to continue their work to accommodate the needs and expectations of these new and non-traditional students in the lifelong learning framework, which has to provide multiple entry and exit points to HE.

10. The social dimension
ESIB believes that the social dimension should be at the heart of the Bologna Process. This involves questions linked to equity in access as well as equal chances of completion of studies. Furthermore, the national support schemes for students need to be sufficient to cover the living costs of students. While ESIB acknowledges potential benefits from students working during their studies, ESIB stresses that this employment should primarily be linked to the study subject and students should not be forced to work in order to pay sub-sistence costs.

Additionally, ESIB stresses that grants are preferable to other financial support systems. Loan-based systems can seriously damage the financial situation of students with a weaker socio-economic background. Further-more, study financing systems should be portable, to enhance mobility, and independent of parental income.

Lastly, ESIB stresses that a social support system for students, which covers housing, health care, food and other counselling and social services should be properly implemented and enhanced to guarantee the social well-being of students. In the design and steering of these systems, students should form an integral part since they know student needs best.

The road ahead – opportunities and threats
ESIB believes that a proper implementation of the Bologna process can lead to the biggest changes in the landscape of Higher education in Europe since the early 1970's in Western and the early 1990's in Central and Eastern Europe.

ESIB considers that it is of utmost importance that the students' voice is being herad in the process. If students' concerns are not met this will provoke dissatisfaction and protests among students wheras is students concerns are met, the Bologna process and its implementation will have a beneficial effect for students, as well as teachers and universities.

However, a few shortcomings of the process have to be mentioned: The strong focus on the economic role of education and the strong focus on competition and competitiveness can foster market driven reforms and increase the trend of privatisation and deregulation of public education systems. One of the main dangers is that the structural reforms towards greater transparency of European higher education make this education tradable on a global market. Therefore, ESIB believes that a renewed commitment to education as a public good and a public responsibility is necessary within the Bologna Process. Furthermore, ESIB believes that it is essential that governments ensure sufficient funding of education, so that HEIs are not forced to engage in commercial activities. Only if this objective is met, the Bologna Process will be a European model that counterbalances the global developments as exemplified by the GATS negotiations. In this light, ESIB also feels that it is necessary within the Bologna Process to develop alternative frameworks to the GATS, for example within the UNESCO framework and to enhance existing UNESCO and Council of Europe regulatory structures.

As an additional point, ESIB considers it to be of great importance that the research dimension is included in the Bologna Process, because a true European Higher Education Area does not merely consist of study structures and recognition of degrees but has to encompass the research dimension of Higher Education as well.

Lastly, ESIB reaffirms that addressing the social dimension of mobility, as well as the general question of study financing systems, have to be addressed to guarantee free and equal access for all students in the EHEA.

ESIB also believes that cultural diversity in Europe is an asset worth protecting. While adjusting the structures of higher education, the cultural and linguistic diversity of the continent should be respected and reaffirmed.

Notwithstanding the above-mentioned criticism and weak points of the process, ESIB reaffirms its commitment to engaging in a constructive work within the Bologna process to ensure that the student voice is heard and that the objectives of setting up a European Higher Education Area for and with students are met by 2010.

ANNEX 20

Klaus Armingeon and Hans-Dieter Klingemann, *Implementing the Bologna Declaration. A discussion paper.* **Presented at the meeting of the European Conference of National Political Science Associations, Edinburgh, March 30, 2003**

The European Conference of National Political Science Associations and the European Political Science Network establish these recommendations and minimum requirements for a BA/MA in political science as major.
(Remark by authors: Given the differences in teaching between various scientific communities, it makes sense to limit these recommendations to minimum requirements.)

(1) BA
Given the limited resources of many political science departments BA studies should be designed in such a way that they lead to a BA in Social Sciences (Major: political science). Creating such a comprehensive BA, political science departments are put in a position to be able to co-operate with departments of sociology, departments of mass communication (Media), departments of economics etc.

(Remark by authors: Due to the small size of the median political science department in Europe, it makes sense to co-operate with other disciplines in order to provide high quality teaching. In addition, labor market perspectives of graduates may be better, if they have a broad background.)

(2) Students obtaining a BA in Social Sciences (Major: Political Science) have to take the following courses/seminars with the minimum of these ECTS:
 – Political theory/History of Political Ideas 6 ECTS
 – Political Economy and Sociology/Political Behavior 12 ECTS
 – Political Systems
   – Political system of ones own country 6 ECTS
   – Political system of the European Union 6 ECTS
 – Comparative Politics 6 ECTS
 – Policy Analysis 6 ECTS
 – International Relations 6 ECTS
 – Quantitative and qualitative methods in the social sciences 10 ECTS
 – Statistics 4 ECTS
(Remarks by authors: These are minimum requirements and it is up to the local political science communities to define additional requirements. How-

ever if these 62 ECTS are agreed upon as the 'base line' a precondition is created to enable greater mobility between universities.)

(3) Departments of Political Science should design Master and PhD programs (graduate courses) taking into account their own resources. However, at least one of the following main fields have to be offered:
  – Political Theory/History of Political Ideas
  – National and supra-national political system(s)
  – Political Economy and Sociology/Political Behavior
  – Policy Analysis
  – Comparative Politics
  – International Relations
(Remarks by authors: We should establish some 'core' fields in order to avoid a multitude of graduate programs.)

(4) Departments of Political Science are encouraged to develop international graduate and PhD programs as well as Summer Universities
(Remarks by authors: We should draw attention to this possibility by mentioning it. In the long run we have to compete with US universities and we have to compete for the best students. Setting up international programs could overcome some of the problems caused by the limited resources of most departments.)

(5) Departments of Political Sciences are encouraged to require that
  (a) there is stage practical work of at least 6 weeks before entering a graduate program
  (b) BA students should spend at least one semester at a university abroad where the teaching language is different than at the respective home university.
  (c) MA or PhD students have to spend at least one semester at a university abroad where teaching is offered in a language other than at the respective home university.
(Remarks by the authors: Both practical work and language skills of students improve their labor market chances. In addition, practical work helps to create motivation by demonstrating the problem-solving power of scientific analysis. The enforcement of mobility between language communities increases the likelihood that there is more co-operation between European universities, both on the level of teaching as on the level of learning.)

ANNEX 21

Epsnet Executive Council, *The Bologna Declaration and Political Science Curriculum*. Agreed by the Executive Council of epsNet at its meeting on 1 March 2003

The Bologna Declaration has changed the European Higher Education Area already more than one thought in 1999. Demands for 1) the adoption of a system of easily readable and comparable degrees, 2) the adoption of a system based on two cycles, 3) the establishment of a common system of credits, 4) increasing student and teacher mobility, 5) quality assurance and 6) the European dimension in teaching, affect also political science teaching.

Comparable degrees and a common system of credits with increasing student mobility require systems of quality assurance. How should political science as a discipline approach these issues?

The starting point must be an understanding of the present state of the discipline. There are at least three factors which make the situation in political science complex. First, political science has always been moulded by its political and social context. Whilst we believe there would be general agreement on the criteria as to what constitutes good political science, the discipline is bound to stress different aspects of politics depending on existing political structures and cultures.

Secondly, arising from the first condition, the history and status of the discipline has been and is different in different countries. In some countries modern political science traces its origins from the beginning of the last century, but in most West European countries the discipline did not develop until after the Second World War. On the other hand, modern political science in Central and Eastern Europe did not exist before the 1990s.

These two factors have led to a third feature of the discipline. Its organisational structures vary from one country to another. Increasingly political science has its own departments, but there are still many other organisational arrangements, for instance, general social science departments, where the study of politics is only a part of the work of the department. Sometimes the study of politics is also linked with the study of history, sometimes with business/management studies, economics or with law. In many cases political science and international politics (or relations) form a joint department, but in many cases they also have their own teaching units. The latter is also increasingly the case with public administration and with European studies.

These factors have led to the situation in which:

- political science has become seriously fragmented because of breakaway tendencies (above all, public administration and international politics);

- there are different kinds of political science degrees in Europe. There are degrees which consist mainly of studies in political science (in Britain and the Netherlands, for instance). On the other hand, there are social science degrees which have one social science as major, but the degree is broadly based in the sense that students are required to take courses in other social sciences as well (e.g, in Britain there are Joint honours degrees, in Sweden a BA in political science consists of 90 ECTS credits, while the other half is for minor subjects, in Finland a share of political science is usually only about 72 ECTS credits);
- there are departments which are joint departments of political science and some other discipline (e.g. Political Science and History, Politics and Sociology, Political Science and Journalism), whilst in some countries political science is still understood as political sciences. In France, for example, there are independent political science departments, but much political science in French universities is taught in law faculties. And the nine IEPs in France (which are the key political science institutions) organise studies somewhat differently from the approach an "ordinary" political science department might adopt. In Italy, on the other hand, it is mainly Faculties that organise teaching and in many universities departments are organisationally weak.

What should one do with this situation? We strongly believe that the fragmentation of the discipline has been harmful for the study of politics. On the other hand, we acknowledge that it is the right of different political science departments to plan their own programs, taking into account local higher education structures and indigenous needs of the discipline. But we strongly believe that there should be minimum requirements for the study of political science We cannot talk about political science as a discipline if those who call themselves political scientists and pretend to teach it are unable to agree on its basic substance and methodology. In this vein, we also argue that there is a need to re-integrate the various sub-fields of political science.

To achieve the goals of the Bologna Declaration in political science we should start to discuss about some minimum requirements in teaching of political science. We see the following core areas to be taught:

- History of Political Ideas
- Political System of one's own country
- Political System of the European Union
- Comparative Politics
- Public Administration (Political Institutions)
- International Politics.

At the same time every effort should be made to:

- link these core areas to political economy and/or to political sociology, either arranging courses in political economy and/or political sociology or highlighting economic and sociological aspects throughout the political science programme.

Furthermore, we believe that every political scientist should be well trained in scientific methodology, with a basic knowledge of statistics as well as qualitative and quantitative methods in the social sciences.

By proposing these minimum requirements in political science at the same time we recognise that departments must have flexibility in organising their studies. I t may not be necessary for all students to take all of the recommended courses. Specialisation is often the case already at the BA-level, reflecting not only the view of departments as to what should and can be taught but also the expectation students have concerning choice within their curriculum, as well as the desire of national authorities to see universities organise their teaching in such a way that students have a chance to decide for themselves what they study (even within a discipline). Departments may also want to organise political science courses in a way which combines different themes whilst in many departments there are highly sophisticated courses combining lectures, group work and independent research. Such freedoms should continue to be protected. Our recommendation is, however, that the core requirements in political science should be integrated in the teaching programme of political science departments in Europe in such a way that minimum requirements are met.

Achieving the minimum requirements would help to achieve a system of easily readable and comparable degrees and would help to define the European dimension in teaching. It would also help in transferring credits from one university to another due to increasing student mobility. By moving in these directions, political science will be positioning itself to implement not only the spirit of the Bologna declaration but the likely practical forms it is likely to take.

ANNEX 22

Political Science Response to the Bologna Process. *The Bologna Declaration and the Basic Requirements of a Bachelor of Arts (BA) in Political Science in Europe. Recommendations from the European Conference of National Political Science Associations*, July 2003

POLITICAL SCIENCE RESPONSE TO THE BOLOGNA PROCESS

To: all participants at the Berlin conference
From: the Acting Secretary, the European Conference of National Political Science Associations

1 September 2003

Dear Participant,

Attached is a document agreed by the European Conference of National Political Science Associations. It is a proposed common core syllabus, prepared as part of our response to the gathering momentum of the Bologna process. We submit it to you in the hope that we can contribute to the further development of the European Higher Education Area, both generally and with particular regard to teaching and research in Political Science in higher education across Europe.

The European Conference of National Political Science Associations is an informal grouping, established in 2001 with the purpose of providing a forum for collaboration in the development of European Political Science in the European Higher Education Area. All heads of national Political Science Associations in Europe are invited to its meetings. A full list of countries represented at our four meetings so far is appended. The Conference has close links with the other pan-European associations in Political Science, especially with the European Political Science Network (epsNET). epsNET undertook much of the original drafting of this note, and it was subsequently re-drafted after a meeting of national associations hosted by epsNET in Paris. The European Consortium for Political Research (ECPR), based in Essex, has also provided support.

The proposed syllabus is an authoritative statement by professional Political Scientists working in European Higher Education. It is the result of intensive and unprecedented discussion among senior representatives of widely differing Higher Education systems, and has been circulated widely among Heads of University Departments of Political Science across Europe. We are aware of the limitations of our proposals and of the work which remains to be done.

Nevertheless, our experience in meeting as a European Conference has been positive and worthwhile, and one we intend to continue. We think the document represents a valuable and significant first step in ensuring that the objectives of the Bologna process can be implemented in our discipline. What we propose should be understood as minimum requirement for the content and structure of a common Political Science syllabus appropriate to the convergence of frameworks for degrees in Europe envisaged by the Bologna process.

We look forward to the results of your meeting in Berlin and we hope our document contributes to your work. We wish you every success in your deliberations,

Yours sincerely,

Professor Paul Furlong
Head of School of European Studies, Cardiff University
Cardiff CF10 3YQ, Wales UK

Countries represented at the meetings of the European Conference of National Political Science Associations: Austria, Belgium, Finland, France, Germany, Holland, Hungary, Ireland, Italy, Latvia, Norway, Romania, Slovakia, Slovenia, Switzerland, United Kingdom

The Bologna Declaration and the basic requirements of a Bachelor of Arts (BA) in Political Science in Europe

Recommendations from the European Conference of National Political Science Associations

The Bologna Declaration has changed the European Higher Education Area. Demands for 1) the adoption of a system of easily readable and comparable degrees, 2) the adoption of a system based on two cycles, 3) the establishment of a common system of credits, 4) increasing student and teacher mobility, 5) quality assurance and 6) the European dimension in teaching, affect and challenge political science teaching.

To achieve the goals of the Bologna Declaration in political science, we recommend there should be some minimum requirements in the teaching of political science. At present we focus on the minimum requirements of a BA that comprises 180 ECTS usually taught over three years.

For a degree in political science (e.g. BA in Political Science) or with a major in political science, (e.g. within the framework of a BA in Social Sciences) that would be necessary for someone wishing to proceed in political science at the master's or subsequent plus 2 year level, we recommend the following:

Students follow courses in political science with a value of at least **90 ECTS** credits. Such credits are achieved by taking the following core subject areas:

- Political Theory/History of Political Ideas
- Methodology (including statistics)
- Political System of one's own country and of the European Union
- Comparative Politics
- International Relations
- Public Administration and Policy Analysis
- Political Economy/Political Sociology

By following other courses in minor subjects or through further specialisation in political science, students would be able to build on the core areas to complete their programme (180 ECTS).

These minimum requirements in political science would continue to give departments flexibility in organising their studies. Specialisation is often the case already at the BA-level, reflecting not only the view of departments as to what should and can be taught but also the expectation students have concerning choice within their curriculum, as well as the desire of national authorities to see universities organise their teaching in such a way that students have a chance to decide for themselves what they study (even within a discipline). Departments may also want to organise political science courses in a way that combines different themes whilst in many departments there are highly sophisticated courses combining lectures, group work and independent research. Such freedoms should continue to be protected. Our recommendation is, however, that the core requirements in political science should be integrated in the teaching programme of political science departments in Europe in such a way that minimum requirements are met.

Achieving the minimum requirements would help to achieve a system of easily readable and comparable degrees and would help to define the European dimension in teaching. It would also help in transferring credits from one university to another due to increasing student mobility. However, we consider that whilst in principle students should undertake study abroad for at least one semester, in practice this is difficult to organise and manage within the three years cycle. But within the 3+2 system, students should be required to have spent at least one semester abroad.

On similar organisational grounds, we recommend that a stage/work placement should be undertaken during the five years of study without making any recommendation whether this has to take place in the first three years or the ensuing two years of studies.

July 2003

Index

Notes

The World of Political Science –
The Development of the Discipline Book Series
Edited by Michael Stein and John Trent

The book series aims at going beyond the traditional "state-of-the-art review" and wants to make a major contribution not just to the description of the state of the discipline, but also to an explanation of its development and content.

Linda Shepherd (ed.)
Political Psychology
2006. 168 pp. Pb.
19.90 €/ US$ 23.95
ISBN 3-86649-027-5

The book provides detailed information about the development of the field of political psychology, a subfield of both political science and psychology. It describes the evolution of concepts and theories within political psychology, international influences in the field, current concepts and methodology, and trends that augur for the future of the enterprise.

R.B. Jain (ed.)
Governing development
across cultures
Challenges and dilemmas of an emerging
sub-discipline in political science
2006. Approx. 200 pp. Pb
Approx. 19.90 €/ US$ 23.95
ISBN 3-96649-029-1

The book is a critical examination and appraisal of the status, methodology and likely future of the emerging sub-discipline of "Governing Development" within the broader discipline of political science.

David Coen & Wyn Grant (eds.)
Business and Government
Methods and Practice
2006. 127 pp. Pb. 16.90 €/ US$ 19.90
ISBN 3-86649-033-X

This volume reviews current debates on the role of business in politics and it assesses emerging methodological approaches to its study.

 Verlag **Barbara Budrich**
Barbara Budrich Publishers

Head-office: Stauffenbergstr. 7 • D-51379 Leverkusen Opladen • Germany
Tel +49 (0)2171.344.594 • Fax +49 (0)2171.344.693 • info@budrich-verlag.de
US-office: 28347 Ridgebrook • Farmington Hills, MI 48334 • USA • info@barbara-budrich.net
Northamerican distribution: International Specialized Book Services
920 NE 58th Ave., suite 300 • Portland, OR 97213-3786 • USA
phone toll-free within North America 1-800-944-6190, fax 1-503-280-8832 •orders@isbs.com

www.budrich-verlag.de • www.barbara-budrich.net

Politics

Hans-Dieter Klingemann (ed.)
The State of Political Science in Western Europe
2006. c.360 pp.
Hc c.59.00 €/ US$ 69.00
ISBN 3-86649-045-3

Ralf Puchert
Marc Gärtner
Stephan Höyng (eds.)
Work Changes Gender
Men and Equality in the Transition of Labour Forms. 2005. 202 pp.
Pb 19.90 €/ US$ 23.90
ISBN 3-938094-13-3
Hc 39.90 €/ US$ 48.00
ISBN 3-938094-14-1

John E. Trent
Modernizing the United Nations System
From International Relations to Global Governance
2006. Approx. 250 pp. Pb.
Approx. 24.90 €/ US$ 28.90
ISBN 3-86649-003-8

Ursula J. van Beek (ed.)
Democracy under Construction:
Patterns from Four Continents
2005. 500 pp. Pb 49.00 €/ US$59.90
ISBN 3-938094-23-0
Hc 79,– €/ US$ 94.90
ISBN 3-938094-24-9

 Verlag **Barbara Budrich**
Barbara Budrich Publishers

Head-office: Stauffenbergstr. 7 • D-51379 Leverkusen Opladen • Germany
Tel +49 (0)2171.344.594 • Fax +49 (0)2171.344.693 • info@budrich-verlag.de
US-office: 28347 Ridgebrook • Farmington Hills, MI 48334 • USA • info@barbara-budrich.net
Northamerican distribution: International Specialized Book Services
920 NE 58th Ave., suite 300 • Portland, OR 97213-3786 • USA
toll-free within North America ph 1-800-944-6190, fax 1-503-280-8832 • orders@isbs.com

www.budrich-verlag.de • www.barbara-budrich.net